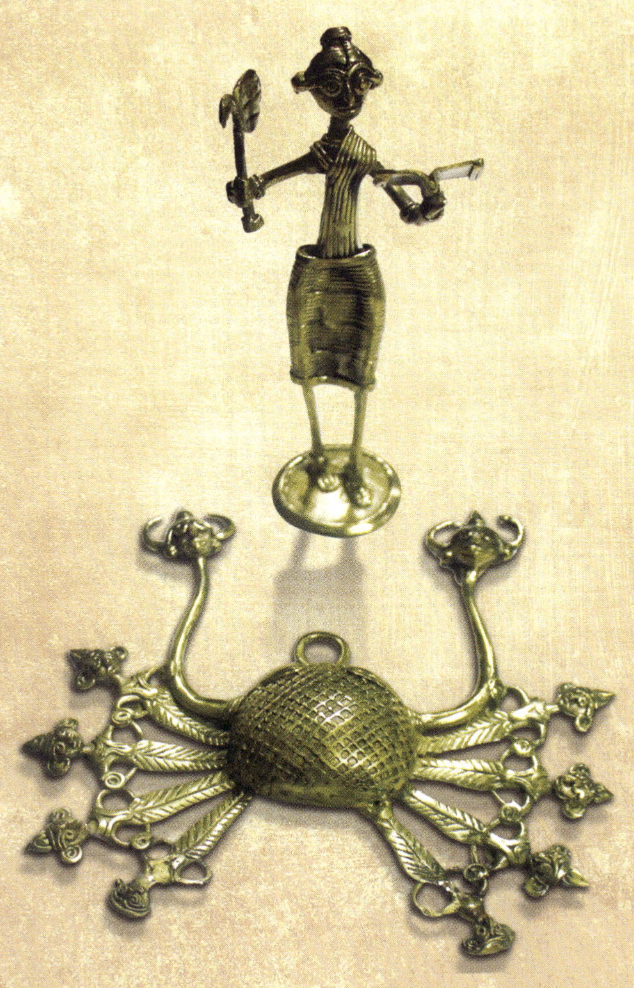

LIFE AMONG THE SCORPIONS

LIFE AMONG THE SCORPIONS

MEMOIRS OF A WOMAN IN INDIAN POLITICS

JAYA JAITLY

RUPA

Published by
Rupa Publications India Pvt. Ltd 2017
7/16, Ansari Road, Daryaganj
New Delhi 110002

Sales Centres:
Allahabad Bengaluru Chennai
Hyderabad Jaipur Kathmandu
Kolkata Mumbai

All photographs in the book are courtesy the author, unless otherwise mentioned.

Photograph on the back cover: Jaya Jaitly, George Fernandes and Nitish Kumar at a peace march in Patna, Bihar, 2000. Courtesy: AFP/Getty Images.

ISBN: 978-81-291-4909-1

First impression 2017

10 9 8 7 6 5 4 3 2 1

Printed by Replika Press Pvt. Ltd, India

For my children Akshay and Aditi, although they say they do not require a formal dedication from me.

To my craftspeople, my larger family, who have unknowingly given me solace when I needed it the most, but are not likely to read this book.

CONTENTS

PROLOGUE

Once, not too long ago in 2001, a twenty-four-year-old woman in Kota Baru, Malaysia, emerged from a two-by-six metre glass cage after living with 2,700 poisonous scorpions for thirty days. According to news reports that went around the world, she left the enclosure, which was positioned in the local museum, for just fifteen minutes every day to use the bathroom. She survived seven stings, two of them serious. Although she received a certificate from the museum's chairman, acknowledging her as the 'scorpion queen', she said that one of her best rewards was making some new clawed friends. 'I am particularly fond of two scorpions, and I named one of them Bob,' she said.

It would be difficult for me to understand why she performed the stunt.

When I read this story, I felt I was like the woman in that glass cage, her every move being watched by everyone outside. There was nothing one could hide. There was nowhere to escape. It was a public act for some intangible reason that was hard to define. Like her, I too made a couple of good friends. One of them could be called George Fernandes. He was not really one of the scorpions but, being among them, he taught me to survive them.

My storytelling does not lead to the conclusion that politics for a woman is a hellish choice and should be avoided. Quite to the contrary, it is cathartic, and teaches more about life in all its ramifications than anything else can. As in every other path one chooses to take in life, it is how we deal with what comes our way that forges the steel in us. It is best not to expect success or happiness in public life. At different times, survival itself is success enough, and happiness can be just the experience itself—at times tragic, and others, sublime.

My story is therefore not about me, but just an example of what a woman in India amid politics and public life, and its many-facedness, experiences in trying to keep her integrity and humanity intact.

A life is never a linear journey with a clear beginning and a perceptible end, unless you count the moments of birth and death. There is never total recall. When remembering what matters, one counts those incidents that left an impression on one's mind for some inexplicable reason. We also recall an experience as meaningful only if it carries a thread into a later context. This happens when some situations repeat themselves in different forms, and, within it, ironies reinforce earlier incidents. Our mind absorbs and records everything but we often remember only parts as worthy of our attention. This interplay and replay of incidents and experiences cannot be kept smoothly chronological if one really wants to draw meaning out of them. Consequently, my book follows the same pattern-less pattern, going back and forth in time, and sometimes proceeding along a straight line.

Memoirs are usually written when a feeling of retirement sets in. However, when there is no pause in the many aspects of one's work that covers decades, and when some battles are yet to be fought and won, a memoir becomes just another layer of activism in the palimpsest of life.

1

MY BEGINNINGS
Amidst Matriarchy and Bureaucracy

IT WAS A TIME OF transitions. Great Britain was preoccupied with the war against Hitler. Indians were in the throes of the last years of colonial rule. Mahatma Gandhi's voice had captured the hearts and minds of millions. And yet, the British in India continued moving the entire trappings of the governing bureaucracy from the colonial seat of Delhi up the hills to Simla to enjoy its cooler weather for six months of the year. My father, oddly named Krishna Krishna Chettur—one Krishna after his father and one for himself—was a part of that bureaucracy. That's how we came to be in Simla in the summer months of 1942, and I, a girl of South Indian parents, came to be born in the northern part of India. I was born ten years late and a month too early when my mother, Meenakshi Chettur, went into labour following a fall down a slope. One wonders why she would have chosen to wear fashionable high heels to go for a walk along a hilly path while heavily pregnant. But there it was. The result: a fall, and the birth of a premature daughter.

Our family belonged to the famous matrilineal society of Kerala which rejoiced when a girl was born. No frowns and tears or worrisome thoughts about dowries. No oppressive patriarchy silencing the woman's voice. Social scientists unequivocally state about the Nairs of Kerala that in even as late as into the nineteenth century, 'the absence of daughters meant a crisis'. The *New York Times* of 29 January 1988 described Kerala as a place 'Where the Births Are Kept Down and Women Aren't'.*

At that time, the position of women in the Nair community was far

*See http://www.nytimes.com/1988/01/29/world/trivandrum-journal-where-births-are-kept-down-and-women-aren-t.html

ahead of that in other parts of the country. Even while the entire social structure was segmented into various groups and castes, Nair women were accorded access to personal choices, the right to property, respect, and a freedom that extended to even selecting one's sexual partners. While the Brahmin Namboodris were the undisputed elite, the Nairs, who were initially Sudras, called themselves Kshatriyas; the Nairs were allowed a high caste status by the Namboodris who kept them as their warriors and retainers. Contrarily, the 'untouchable' lower castes were expected to cross over to the other side of the road if a Brahmin was walking along it. Even during the innocence of early childhood, I was aware of the derogatory tone in which some of the family elders referred to these castes. It was their way of feeling 'Brahmin', at the top of the caste ladder, when, in reality, they were not.

Marumakkatayam, as matriliny is known in Malayalam, is believed to have begun in the eleventh century during, and as a result, of the hundred-year war between the Chola and Chera kingdoms. Since men were needed in the battlefield, the management of the household and family properties was exercised through the continuing presence of women in the house of their nativity. Inheritance passed through the women's line, and their children remained the wards of their mothers, since their fathers often established new alliances with other Nair women available nearer the battlefields. The maternal uncles of these children became the heads of the household. The elderly males usually made decisions regarding war, trade or religious ceremonies, but women and men had equal freedom to acquire and discard as many partners as they wished during their lifetime. My mother once let slip that my great-grandmother, her father's mother, who ruled the household like a true matriarchal tyrant, actually went through five husbands. The last was the cook with whom she chose to hold hands while taking a holy dip in the Ganga. Pati, as everyone called her, of course, made sure that all the men in her life were Brahmins, including the last one. However, since I was the grandchild of her son and not her daughter, I was not a Brahmin, and hence no meals at the high table.

It is also believed by some that matriliny was devised by the Namboodris to enable them to have free access to Nair women while ensuring that their eldest sons alone married Namboodri women. This kept their lands and properties intact. The practice was first confined to the higher and land-controlling castes but was soon imitated by the Ezhavas who were part of the lower castes. In any event, this pattern of social functioning was well established when the Europeans arrived in the sixteenth century.

Women had a unique and confident place in the society of earlier Kerala which continues even today in the forms of high literacy rates and social recognition in the region. Into the twentieth century, women were able to continue their control of domestic management, take to careers, particularly in teaching and medicine, and even marry late. They always had an inalienable right to property. In fact, studies reveal how the position of women significantly contributed to the much touted 'Kerala model of development'. However, this portrayal of the emancipated woman still seemed to always stop short of true equality with men. Examine the fate of Akkamma Cheriyan, who lived for the most part of the twentieth century. She led the biggest political demonstration ever seen in Kerala. However, soon after Independence, she was forced out of the Congress party because not only was there objection to her participation in electoral politics but there were some who felt threatened by her chances of winning. K.R. Gouri, although prominent in Kerala's communist politics since 1947, was prevented from ever attaining the well-deserved position of chief minister of the state. She was repeatedly ridiculed by her male-dominated party and made to sit on the sidelines while men like E.K. Nayanar, known for his ribald public jokes about women, ruled the state in the name of communism and socialism.

In 1934, the All India Women's Conference held its tenth annual meeting in Kerala where topics such as family planning and birth control were avidly discussed. A resolution was moved by Anna Chandy, Kerala's first woman advocate. She was supported by Lakshmi N. Menon, who happened to be my only college-going aunt's professor. The Kerala Catholics condemned the very concept of an educated woman as sinister, anti-Christian, and an enemy of the home, but the resolution set the trend among women in the state to plan the size of their families. Lakshmi N. Menon, who was a highly popular, intelligent and respected woman, was appointed to be the Deputy Minister for External Affairs for a very short period in Jawaharlal Nehru's cabinet. She described the experience to me once when I was a teenager, while on a visit to my aunt's for lunch. 'A woman is put into the council of ministers like a curry leaf used to flavour a glass of *sambaram*. It is the last ingredient to be put in and the first to be taken out before it is consumed,' she had said. An elegant woman who stood tall and had a soft, pleasing face, she didn't shed her signature smile and twinkle in her eye as she gave me my first lesson about women in politics. I still remember the exact gesture of her hand as she enacted taking out an imaginary leaf from an imaginary glass of Kerala-style buttermilk and flicking it casually aside.

The decline of matriliny in the nineteenth century, and the rise of nationalist politics and the communist movement in Kerala went hand in hand. European missionaries had been calling the practice of matriliny abhorrent, one that also devalued the sanctity of marriage. The Hindus in other parts of India described it as looseness of morals and thought that the state was all but indulging in disreputable activity. However, prominent ladies from the matrilineal families of the ruling elite in territories like Travancore, Cochin and Malabar went about freely in public, even impressing some missionaries who described them as educated, refined and pleasant in their ways.

By the end of the Second World War, matrilineal *taravad*s, as the joint family households of the Nairs are known, had considerably reduced in number. Several women followed their husbands into unitary family establishments. My aunts and uncles divided themselves up into both categories. The aunts followed their husbands if they were part of the established gentry of lawyers or public officials, and stayed home to conduct the affairs of the *taravad* as if their husbands were socially expendable.

∽

My mother's father was among the nobility recognized by the British. They gave him the title of Rajah Sir Vasudeva Rajah of Kollengode (see photograph). Kollengode, 24 kilometres south of Palghat (locally called Palakkad), was administered by the Vengunad Nambidis, who claim descent from the ancient Kshatriya chief Vira Ravi Varma. It is said to have got its name from Kallakudil, meaning 'blacksmith's hut', where the founder of the line was said to have had his early childhood. A Kollan is an ironsmith in Malayalam and confirms the connection with the trade of blacksmiths. My grandfather was a member of the Legislative Council in Delhi, and like many heads of small and big chiefdoms in Kerala, was keen on progress. Among other things, he established the Rajah's High School in

Kollengode and brought a railway station to nearby Shoranur. He had three sons and three daughters from his wife, Thottekat Jayalakshmi Amma, whose mother was the first female Sanskrit poet of Kerala.

After my grandmother died during the birth of her seventh child, my mother, barely a year-and-a-half-old at the time, my grandfather married a woman who gave him another daughter; the second wife would die of tuberculosis soon after. My grandfather adored his brood of children but could not cope with their care. In fact, he did not really need to as they grew up under the watchful eye of Pati, with maidservants as wet nurses. A school area was set up in one of the wings of the large palace for the girls' education. The boys went to a proper school. Everything was done for them collectively. All the children would go on outings in bullock carts and celebrate religious festivals together. Amidst it all, the servants, who had a million tasks to perform, would be at the mercy of their mischievous pranks.

The programmes organized for ceremonial visitors from the British establishment were of particular interest since the students of Rajah's High School were made to compose songs, often lacking in rhyme and melody to greet them. My mother particularly remembered the song they sang to welcome a certain Baron Pentland, which went, 'Hail most noble BA (very loud)...(long pause)... ARON (softer) Penlen (as they pronounced it), hail to thee, all hail to thee!' The greeting sounded like a cross between a hymn and a sergeant major's order. We used to laugh every time my mother related this story, with mimicry and all thrown in.

Every child in the family received only four sets of *pavada*s (ankle-length skirts), blouses or shirts and shorts to wear each year at Onam. Everyone had to learn to play the veena or sing, study Sanskrit, recite verses from religious texts and eat and sleep with almost military-like discipline. The Rajah was there only occasionally. Maids mostly brought up the motherless children of the royal household. Aunts looked after their own progeny. My mother occasionally snuggled up to her father in his large four-poster teakwood bed when he was at home. On other days, for comfort, she used to play with the large exposed breasts of the elderly maid who would lie beside her till she went to sleep. All the children slept beside each other on handwoven grass mats laid out on smooth red-oxide floors that shone from daily caring.

While other communities could adapt to changing economic

circumstances, the Nairs could not. That was because laws prevented their family assets from being used for individual enterprises. Many men within these families became layabouts, spending their time doing nothing except conversing with the managerial staff, dabbling in petty business ideas, visiting the lands under cultivation and reading the Gita or the *Reader's Digest*. Some occasionally eyed the buxom maidservants with a touch of lust in their eyes. Some spent hours in their prayer rooms, reciting endless shlokas from the Gita to pass their time. Extreme religiosity absolved them of the responsibility to bother with much else.

Despite the Hindu Succession Act of 1956 and the Joint Hindu Family System (Abolition) Act which finally ended the legal entities of the matrilineal system in 1976, many families in Kerala still give the name of the mother's *taravad* to the child in the form of the initial before the given name. Named after my maternal grandmother, as per practice, I could choose to call myself T. (for Thottekat) Jayalakshmi, or Jayalakshmi (Jaya for short) Chettur, after my father, according to Western or north Indian practice. In the midst of these typically Malayali matrilineal confusions in nomenclature, an English nanny employed by my parents to look after me in New Delhi found it impossible to grapple with my real name. Nanny Gwynne thus decided to call me June after the month in which I was born. While she left when the British officially quit India, she left me with the name, in quite the same manner as India was left with Bombay, Calcutta, Madras, Cawnpore[*] and the rest, for quite some time. My mother didn't mind because the slight colonial warp still functioned in her psyche. Alongside high-heeled shoes and tennis at the Gymkhana Club, she rather liked an English name for me, and made me wear a fringed, short-cut hairstyle and learn to play the piano. I hated all of it but dared not rebel. As an only child, one had no instigators or a reliable support system that siblings usually provide.

Those who were in school and college still ask, 'Aren't you June?' In college in the USA it was June Jayalakshmi Chettur. It was only when I was about to be married to Ashok Jaitly that I decided that if I was

*The names of these cities have now changed to Mumbai, Kolkata, Chennai and Kanpur respectively.

changing one name, I might as well change the other. Thus, Jaya Jaitly finally emerged.

The transforming process of the matrilineal system is well demonstrated by the fact that I could legally use and be addressed by both my family names when I was in Kerala, without any sense of a fractured identity. Today, it enables me to recognize any person with the *taravad* names Chettur or Thottekat as being related to me, even if these names are hidden in an initial preceding the more widely used Nair, Menon or Pillai surnames to indicate the caste. This is quite different from the North Indian practice of nearly always using a caste name such as Sharma, Singh or Yadav to define the person's main identity. These cultural contrasts came to mind quite often when I settled down to a long life in North India.

Meanwhile, even within my own matrilineal household, there was a subtle distinction made between descendants from the Brahmin line and those from Kshatriya mothers. I experienced the disquiet of discrimination without understanding it when some of my cousins parted company from me at mealtimes to eat in a separate dining area. The banana leaves were laid out on the floor in a similar fashion; the food was cooked for everyone by the Brahmin cook and served by the same assortment of maidservants. The girls all bathed together in the natural water tank or in the large bathhouse and slept side by side, giggling and whispering till the elders rebuked us. Yet, those of us who weren't of pure Brahmin parents could not eat with the others. When I repeatedly asked why, my mother would scowl at me for asking embarrassing questions while her Brahmin cousins looked away.

2

MALABAR MATRIARCHY

Experiencing My Roots

AFTER INDEPENDENCE, THE STAY AT the summer capital of Simla ended. The government remained in Delhi. That gave my mother the opportunity of going to Kollengode to her cousins, or to Trichur (now Thrissur), to her brothers and sisters, during my summer holidays. She continued this practice even when my father was sent abroad to head the first Indian Liaison Mission, and then Embassy, in Tokyo in 1950. Thanks to this new summer routine, I could continue with my almost passionate attachment to all things Malayali. It allowed me to avoid practising 'The Blue Danube' on the piano, snacking *only* on *chole bhature* or Bengali Market's *pani puri*[*], listening to *ghazal*s and watching kathak performances. The latter never caught at my heartstrings the way Guruvayur temple's *vadyams* or *chakyar koothus*[**] did.

The completely different way of life practised in a matrilineal *taravad* of Kerala became the foundation of childhood memories that defined my identity. It was embodied in many things. For instance, *mukkeri*, the gritty, black tooth powder wrapped in small square pieces of newspaper, which were wedged between *ierkala*s, the finely stripped, split lengths of flexible cane, used as tongue cleaners. They were laid out on the edge of the verandah with shining brass water containers for us to brush our teeth every morning. The elders and young ones lined up together to brush their teeth and clean their tongues with these homemade toiletries. The tart flavour of *kadugu manga* pickle with crisp *dosa*s and freshly set curd, or white spongy *idli*s dipped in *podi* and melted ghee for breakfast, the

---

**Chole bhature* and *pani puri* are forms of popular Indian snacks.

***Vadyams* refer to musical instruments. *Chakyar Koothus* are a kind of performance art in Kerala that involve monologues containing narratives from Hindu epics. These are usually performed inside Hindu temples. The stories are narrated by a single individual dressed in distinctive attire.

delicious soft mush sucked out of the *murungyakaya* in the *sambar*, with chunky unpolished red rice, raw banana vegetable, and finally tomato *rasam* and small puffy papadams crumbled into the slightly warm and slightly sweet curd at the end of the meal, mapped out my taste buds forever. The waxy feel of the two foot-long banana leaves on which we ate, the clang of the brass tumbler being put down on a stone parapet, the sweet smell of dark green body oils and the rasping sound of gas lanterns being pumped to life at dusk—are special markers of a Malayali memory. I recall the beautiful quietude while the lanterns lit up the long corridors flanked with huge teakwood pillars, deep red floors and elaborately carved doorways over thresholds that were a foot-and-a-half wide. The Vengunad Palace in Kollengode, or the imposing Kollengode House on Museum Road, next to the zoo in Chembukavu in Thrissur, became the worlds in which I gathered my memories of belonging rather than of transition.

At the sprawling house full of elders and cousins, Shakuntala was our special playmate.* She was a pert, pretty, fair-skinned maid, full of fun and stories. She was so brisk at her work that all the aunts called for her to oil their bodies and pour water on them in the bathhouse. We too would insist that she help with our baths which for us was often the main event of the day. These were often elaborate two-hour affairs with time for swimming in the women's side of the water tank with either just knickers, or *torthu mundus*, garments wrapped around the upper halves of those who had begun to develop contours. It was a time when sweet-smelling oils like the greenish *neelibhringadi*, the garnet-red medicinal *kuzhambus* or pale yellow coconut oil, each with its own distinctive aroma would be applied on us. This was followed by a good scrub with *kadalamavu* (or gram flour) which we loved to mix into a paste ourselves. For those under ten, Shakuntala did the scrubbing. We hated it when it was done by the crabby older maids who would put oil in our eyes. Ugly, dark green Hamam soaps, melon-red Lifebuoys, or Mysore sandal soaps, meant only for the elders, were kept at hand in case anyone wanted fashionable toiletries. We had to oil and wash our hair every day; otherwise, it would not have been a proper *kuli*, the Malayalam for bath that was inclusive of hair-wash. The evening bath, not requiring a hair-wash, was a *melgarugal*, which translates into 'a wash

---

*Shakuntala's story and my experiences with the ouija board were also part of an article titled 'Memories of Kerala', *The Daily Star*, 10 January 2009, http://www.thedailystar.net/news-detail-70568

of the body'. Malayalam is full of these subtle definings. We were allowed to avoid a *kuli* only if we were sick. We considered each other filthy pigs unless we had a bath in the morning and a *melgarugal* in the evening every day. After dusk, following the prayer-ritual towards the family deity, the priest came over to everyone with the oil lamp for the ritualistic obeisance. We all had to have finished our *melgarugal* and settled down to more contemplative play for the evening. Bathing was almost a complete pastime in itself. Sometimes, wrapped in *torthu mundu*s, we would practice dance steps or enact plays in the bathhouse in which the king and queen were given large-sized 'English' towels to wear as capes.

One dull summer afternoon, while the elders were napping, Shakuntala introduced us to the Ouija board. She told us that if we wrote out the alphabet with chalk in a circle on the floor, upturned a glass at the centre of the board, put our fingertips on the glass very lightly, decided on a question for which we wanted an answer, closed our eyes tight and concentrated on a dead person, the spirit of that person would come to tell us the answer. We were enthralled. It was scary, mysterious and fun. It also made us fight raucously, accusing each other of pushing the glass and cheating—and that made it even better.

'Did Gopalan steal Venu Mama's pen?' we asked the spirit of Napoleon. There had been a big commotion one morning about an uncle's lost pen.

'No,' replied Napoleon through the Ouija board.

'Who did, then?' we wanted to know.

'Ammalu Amma,' the glass spelled out.

'Will Ettamma* allow us to stay up all night at *Arattu***?'

'Yes,' assured the Ouija board.

'Where is June's Achan going to be posted next?'

'Rangoon.'

Of course, we already knew that, and had only asked the Ouija board to check whether Napoleon really knew the correct answer. He seemed to understand Malayalam and no one else knew French except me.

---

*Etamma is a little used form of address applied in our home for the younger grand aunt. Valiachan, to come later in the chapter, literally means big father and refers to the husband of my mother's elder sister. Valiamma means bigger or elder mother, used to address my mother's eldest sister. Some use it to address their grandmother. Achan means father. Forms of address for relatives alter according to the region in Kerala. These are from North Malabar.

****Arattu* is a ritual of giving a temple idol a holy bath. The ritual also includes bedecked elephants surrounding the idol.

For many afternoons, we frowned, concentrated, shushed each other, and asked the Ouija board many things. The favourite ones were about the love affairs of the servants or famous movie stars. Shakuntala would feed us the questions. She loved to tell us about who said what to whom in the kitchen or bathhouse. She also told us how she and Gopalan, who, according to the Ouija board, was the one who had not, repeat, not stolen Venu Mama's pen, were, well…going to get married. They had to save up some money first. This got us so excited that we ogled and giggled knowingly at Gopalan every time he walked past us on his way to uncle's quarters. He seemed to not notice us at all.

For almost two months we were totally engrossed in this delicious and mystical journey into the unknown spirit world; Shakuntala was the driving force. Then suddenly, things changed. Shakuntala began to make excuses to stay away from the game.

Where are you going? Why are you not playing with us? Are you going to meet Gopalan on the sly? Have you fixed a date for your wedding? What is keeping you so busy? We interrogated her ceaselessly. Her answer was always a vague smile. She would promise to be back in a minute but not return. Sometimes her excuses did not ring true. Now we saw her only at bathtime or when cleaning utensils and mopping floors. She seemed to be looking downwards while doing all these chores and not at us. Her spare time was no longer ours. The fun and laughter seemed to have gone out of her. Yet we noticed that she put more kohl around her eyes, and a couple of extra gold bangles around her wrists. Her blouses were getting too tight. The elder cousins speculated if her romance with Gopalan was so 'hot' that she could not play with us anymore. She's just too fat and getting lazy, we younger lot offered. But by then, the game had taken possession of us to such an extent that we were lost among an eclectic set of ghosts like Queen Victoria, the mahout of the old family elephant Kesavan who had died two years ago, Subhas Chandra Bose, a distant uncle's first wife who had died at childbirth, and anyone else we could think of. The very idea of a glass that lurched a few inches this way and that, was enough to make us believe that we were in a special world of spirits who would be at our beck and call if we concentrated hard enough. The thrill was often all-permeating. In the evenings, I would be scared to go alone up the main staircase to our sleeping quarters in case one of the spirits had decided to stay back and follow me.

One afternoon, during our Ouija session, a cousin went off to the toilet, taking a rarely used route through the long outer corridor. She returned, agog. She had spotted Shakuntala slipping through the half open door, looking about to ensure that no one had seen her. We speculated on this for a bit but it did not hold our interest for long since we were busy coaxing the Ouija board to give us our exam results. As usual, the glass was moving in various directions and giving garbled replies that spelt nothing. Shakuntala's absence irritated us when this happened. When she used to be around, the answers would come quickly and clearly, despite everyone swearing on god that they were not moving the glass themselves.

A few weeks later, we heard raised voices from the main verandah where the aunts usually gathered in the evenings to socialize and discuss public problems, family news and administrative matters relating to the retinue of servants. Today, they sounded very angry. We crept up along the low parapet wall to see what was going on, but kept out of sight. To our amazement, the objects of our aunts' ire were Shakuntala, standing teary-eyed, and Gopalan, looking sullen, as he usually did, and slightly defiant.

'Useless woman! No time for work? Only time to spread your legs?'

This was a common accusation hurled at the young maids from time to time, in which the older maids often joined in.

'I haven't done anything wrong. Gopalan and I are getting married,' Shakuntala's voice quivered but she was trying hard to defend her dignity.

'So, Gopalan, when do you intend to marry her?' asked aunt Radha.

'Why should I marry her? I do not know for sure that she is carrying my child,' Gopalan became more distant and surly.

Shock among the aunts.

'Girl, what do you have to say to that?' asked aunt Thangam.

Quietly, Shakuntala replied, 'Thamburati, this is his child. He is refusing to own it. But it was he who told me to earn more money so that we could set up our home sooner. So you better ask more superior menfolk why they call me to their rooms in the afternoon,' she spat out bitterly.

There was a deathly silence among the aunts.

'Who will touch her?' asked Gopalan quietly, with a sneer, with no change in his sullen expression as he walked away.

Shakuntala was ordered to leave immediately. Gopalan stayed. The elders never discussed the subject in front of us.

There were only a few days of that holiday remaining before my mother and I set off for Rangoon (now Burma) to join my father and a new school.

'There was a letter from Kollengode today,' my mother said some weeks later as we sat at the end of the verandah of the Indian Embassy residence in Rangoon. I was in the midst of doing my homework.

'Remember that poor young maid Shakuntala? They say she hanged herself from a tree outside of town.'

We gathered at Kollengode again during my next summer holiday. One afternoon, a cousin remembered the Ouija sessions. Someone thought we should call Shakuntala's spirit. After all, she had taught us the game; surely she would return to play with us. But the glass refused to move and we soon lost interest. We were also a year older.

Despite the undermining and subtle exploitation of women, there were some unusual and path-breaking occasions at Kollengode that created history in their own way. One was the visit of Acharya Vinoba Bhave during his famous Bhoodan movement when he traversed the country persuading big landowners to give up large portions of their lands to be distributed to the landless. My mother's first cousin, Padmanabha Rajah, Appu mama to us, was by then holding the title of Rajah of Kollengode. (My mother would chuckle under her breath at the continuing use of the title by others when it was actually only accorded to my grandfather by the British and was not an inheritable title at all.)

Appu mama announced that Vinoba ji was coming to Kollengode and had to be welcomed graciously. A few lands were also to be ceremonially handed over but we children were not enlightened with the details of all that. I was asked to prepare and deliver a speech in Hindi on behalf of the family, since no one else knew the language. Although I was merely a twelve-year-old girl who could speak Hindi, I was given a major role to play that day. I died a hundred deaths at having to speak in front of such a big gathering and yet I did it. All my uncles and aunts treated me like the star of the show because they had been able to produce someone who could deliver a speech to Acharya Vinoba Bhave in Hindi. My cheeks were hot and red when it was over but Vinoba ji gave me an appreciative hug. Does a little thread of destiny run through our lives? Did that little speech in Hindi in the heart of Kerala form a thread of an unchangeable pattern of life's events that had me addressing thousands in rallies more than forty years later although I had never planned it that way?

My grandfather's eldest sister, Dhatri Valiya Rani, Ammu Amma to all of us, was a tall, elegant woman with a regal bearing. I remember seeing her draped in *kasavu mundus*, the two-piece gold and cotton dress, in a way that they never looked crumpled. She produced wonderful oil paintings and water colours, and encouraged the arts. She was the female head after Pati died but did not follow her mother's predilection for changing husbands. In her seventies, Ammu Amma suffered a paralytic stroke which cruelly arrested her grandeur and confined her to bed, practically speechless. She shrank in size and spoke in a garbled manner but insisted we sit by her bed every day and talk to her about all kinds of things. Sometimes she would turn over on her stomach, lean over the edge of her bed and write words on the floor—a bit like our Ouija board—except that these were questions, and not answers. If our replies delighted her, she would laugh loudly with saliva dribbling from the side of her mouth.

Ammu Amma particularly loved Kathakali. This ancient and highly sophisticated dance form was a special love of the family. The Rajah's High School had decided, through Ammu Amma's encouragement, to offer a full scholarship to any student who learned Kathakali. Although popular among the people, economic and social transitions of the time, particularly with communist rule, had deprecated the value of this art form because of lack of patronage. The family felt that Kathakali had to be revived. The school employed the best teachers and provided the finances for the costumes, the musicians, and everything required to conduct regular performances for the townsfolk. This dance form was traditionally performed exclusively by men. Even the women's roles were always enacted by men.

Programmes started after dusk with drummers standing in the open ground drumming vigorously for an hour or so to announce the evening's performance. A tall oil lamp would be lit just before the performance was to begin and the *tera*, a multicoloured silk ceremonial curtain, would be held up by two assistants when the artists came to take their places. The excitement would be palpable as people from all over town gathered after dinner for a show that they would watch till the early hours of the morning. The drumming would make our hearts beat faster. The heady mix of flashing eyes, elegant hand gestures, swirling costumes, the tiny nuanced twitch of an eye muscle to convey an emotion, the electrifying battles fought between Bhima and Duryodhana (characters from the epic

Mahabharata), the brilliant make-up of the dancers right down to the tiny seed placed inside the eye to change the white of the eye to red—transported us children and elders alike to the world of the gods.

Ammu Amma had earlier watched every performance and personally encouraged every dancer, but now she was stuck in bed. Undaunted, however, she decided that my cousin Vimala and I should be taught an item from *Kuchelavritham* and present a Kathakali performance for the Kollengode public. This most amazing ability to take a pioneering decision such as this by a speechless and paralysed seventy-year-old matriarch established the love for Kathakali and a 'women-can-do-anything' attitude indelibly in my life.

Vimala was to play the man's role of Lord Krishna while I would be his consort, Radha. No one complained about going against traditions; even Ashaan the master guru, didn't refuse to train young women. Our male cousin, Baby Ettan, who had been compelled by his grandmother Ammu Amma to learn Kathakali from the age of ten, was made to take us through our paces after Ashaan left at lunchtime. For two months we had lessons in the mornings, practised in the afternoons and lay in bed at night enacting our mudras in the dark and in our sleep. Our minds rang with the rhythmic beats and we endlessly repeated the accompanying shlokas and practised our steps in the bathhouse too, driving everyone else crazy. 'Kathakali Madness', the aunts reported to Ammu Amma, had consumed the two of us completely.

A dress rehearsal had to be held in Ammu Amma's room, by her bedside. Her eyes shone, she nodded her head and gurgled non-stop as she tapped her misshapen fingers to the drumbeats on the side table. She rewarded us with a set of fresh new *mundu-veshti*s, red silk blouse pieces flecked with flowers woven in gold thread, and a gold coin each. After the performance, as we went to remove our costumes and make-up, Vimala discovered that her monthly period had started. She was utterly mortified. In those days, women in such a state were considered impure and had to live in seclusion for five days till they had had a proper *kuli*. During meals, their banana leaves would be placed a little apart from the others', and a maid delegated to be in attendance separately would remove them, after which they would have to bathe. All hell could have broken loose that day as the entire paraphernalia of costumes had to be sent to the washerman and reconsecrated to remove the 'pollution', since the costumes transformed dancers into the manifestation of the gods and were thus sacred. Ammu Amma didn't bat an eyelid. She let it be known that the public performance would take place after the five days of mandatory separation of Vimala from the rest of us, and nothing more was to be said about it. And that is how it happened.

The townsfolk came to the open courtyard inside the palace to watch our presentation. Owing to Ashaan's impeccable and stern training, we managed a perfect performance. We returned the loud applause of the audience with *namaskaram* (palms folded in a formal ceremonial acknowledgement). We were filled with a sense of achievement and elation perhaps never felt before or since. There was no press or publicity, no printed invitations, no critic to write about how a bit of a history was made that day by a disabled old woman and two young girls because we were women and had performed Kathakali. Nevertheless, it certainly happened.

~

My mother's eldest sister, Kamalam, whom I called just Valiamma, was a tall, beautiful woman with large, mournful eyes and a slim figure that got more matchstick-like as she grew older. She deliberately flushed her dentures down the toilet at the age of eighty-five and died at ninety-one. She was a living symbol of the distortions that could creep into the system of matriliny. Valiamma was married to T.C.K. Kurup, a fair-skinned—always a special attribute—articulate, Oxford-returned, handsome barrister. She got married at the age of fifteen, and became a mother at sixteen when she preferred to play badminton and go for bicycle rides with her brothers. Her husband, Valiachan (as we addressed him), was a bully par excellence who had managed to crush his wife's spirit by the time she was twenty. It was because of her misery that my grandfather built the house in Trichur, so that his daughters always had a home in which the husbands could stay only if the wives wished. Matrilineal laws did not entitle his children to anything except affection at Vengunad Palace. One fine day, Valiachan decided to give up his practice and stay home to become a sadhu. He shed his barrister's robes and transformed himself into a bare-chested holy man, wearing only saffron-coloured *mundu*s (or *dhoti*s) with matching saffron-hued G-strings and wooden *khadaun*s which clattered loudly as he strode the floors in them, silently counting his rudraksha beads. It was quiet only when he was in his prayer room. For the rest of the time he roared at the maids or at Valiamma for some fault or the other, sending them scuttling in different directions. He insisted on bathing in water heated in a large copper vessel by the rays of the sun. The poor maids had to draw water from the well, carry the buckets a few hundred feet to where the copper vessel was strategically placed to catch the morning rays of the sun and then haul the heavy vessel to the bathroom every day. He would fling the banana leaf across the floor whenever he felt the food served was not warm enough, and hang his G-strings all over his room to use when he wished. The maids crinkled their noses and muttered in disgust at the sight of them. My outspoken mother had asked him why on earth he could not keep his wretched 'prayer flags' out of sight. He tolerated her taking liberties with him as he considered her the baby of the family. She took advantage of this till she was over seventy by ribbing him at every opportunity. When he finally died at a ripe old age, much to everyone's relief, we thought Valiamma deserved a medal for having fed this holy husband of hers and given him shelter for well over sixty years without a word of complaint. Some matriliny, you might say.

During all those years, Valiamma withdrew further and further retiring into herself and avoided contact with most of the world, and especially her husband, by disappearing into her prayer room from breakfast until lunch, and then from teatime until dinner. Only once, when sixty years old, did I see a glimmer of something different. I was cycling around the long gravel driveway at the centre of which is placed a mounted bust of my grandfather. She was taking a stroll to stretch her legs before going back to the prayer room. I asked her whether she had ever learned to cycle. 'Get off, let me show you,' she laughed. Before I knew it, she had hopped on to my cycle, smiling, and was pedalling furiously around the driveway, barefoot, dressed in a white *mundu*, with her *torthu mundu* instead of a proper *veshti* draped casually across her chest, her three-diamond nose-pin catching the light, and her big, horn-rimmed spectacles sliding down her nose. As she got off and wheeled the cycle back to me, pleased that I was gaping at her with astonishment, she unconsciously broke off a flower from the jasmine bush and tucked it into her always carelessly bunched-up hair knot.

Valiachan slept in a large bedroom on a decent sized four-poster bed, while Valiamma chose to sleep on a hard wooden divan placed in the open verandah just outside her prayer room. It was a bright, open spot. This was where I loved to sit, and read or write letters when we went to Trichur for part of the summer holidays. During the monsoon, I would watch the rain pouring down noisily, making deep rivulets on the red gravel below.

∽

All matrilineal families were not feudal, but all Nairs had a mode of living and a graciousness of manner which they practised even if they were not economically well-off. Neither were all men happy to sit around entertaining themselves in their wives' homes. My father, who was distantly related to my mother's stepmother, when he came courting at Kollengode, made it quite clear that he had no intention of living there as a man who was not expected to do very much amongst a gathering of women. It was another matter that he had come to view Gouri Valiamma, but had changed his mind when he saw my mother, her younger sister, and decided to marry her instead. According to my mother, this was much to my aunt's everlasting pique. She would attribute her sister's stiff, unemotional manner, her occasional lack of generosity and many other little flaws, to jealousy. Even in her eighties, my mother enjoyed believing that it was the early rejection of Gouri Valiamma by my father that had made her a bit sour, even though she was found an excellent partner in the shape of a talented lawyer, P. Neelakanta Menon. The latter went on to become a respected chief justice of the Kerala High Court. He was also the maternal uncle of a young boy called Balan, who became the famed Swami Chinmayananda, and set up many schools, colleges and hospitals; he travelled all over the world giving his famed discourses on the Gita to thousands of disciples.

∽

My father's side of the family, despite being highly placed and connected to one of the best known names in Kerala like Sir Chettur Sankaran Nair, was elevated intellectually. This, despite the fact that many of its members did not have enough money for bus fares. It did not really matter to anyone, since in those days merit and background counted for more than the social, psychological and material influence of money. Everyone, rich or poor, servant or master, of high or low caste, ate off banana leaves, sat or slept on the floor with equal ease, walked barefoot inside the house, and wore the same cotton *mundu*s and *veshti*s—creamy, with narrow coloured or gold borders when new, and bleached white after laundering. In fact, it is perhaps the only part of the country where men and women both traditionally wear plain white cotton clothes at all occasions, draped waist downwards in the same manner, irrespective of status or age. The equalizing factor offered by these aspects of Kerala's culture is far more important than anyone has cared to note.

Sir C. Sankaran Nair was a member of the Viceroy's Executive Council and my father's grand-uncle. He was elected Congress President in the 1897 Amravati session of the party. He was the only Malayali to ever hold the post. The government even brought out a four-rupee postage stamp on him some years later. He was an iconoclast of sorts who had his own ideas of how the freedom struggle should be carried out. He challenged Gandhi's views and strategies, but was no less a fierce nationalist even while working with the British. His sister's daughter was my grandmother, Parukutty Amma. They hailed from a tiny village called Mankara near Ottapalam in south Malabar. I only ever caught a glimpse of the small family house where my father was born, tucked behind heavy fronds of coconut trees, as the train from Madras, now Chennai, stopped for a few minutes on its way to Trichur. My paternal grandfather was a clerk in the Madras Secretariat and cycled seven miles to work every day from their small home in San Thome to Fort St George. Since they had no car, 'Sir C' would send his coach to pick up his relatives for Onam lunch at his home.

My paternal grandmother was an outstanding woman who was president of the Women's Association of Madras and a close associate of Annie Besant, the English woman who fought for India's freedom and rose to be President of the Congress party. She was the sheet anchor of the family and saw to it that her four sons, Govind Krishna, Krishna Krishna, Shankara Krishna and Rama Krishna—all famously known by their initials throughout their lives—received the best education possible. She was also proud to see each have a car, for which the porch of their small house proved too small.

In Tokyo, in 1951, as India's first Ambassador to Japan, when my father first bought a Cadillac, we went for a drive to get a feel of the car. He told me then, how he had walked to school as his father could not afford the bus fare. The wit with which he recounted the stories of his early days, and the dignity, refined taste and understated elegance with which he lived his life, never allowed his experiences of financial inadequacies to affect me negatively. That day, the joke (in the context of which my father told me about him walking to school) was about a young boy who boasted that he had saved his bus fare by running after the public bus to school, to which his father retorted, 'Foolish boy, you would have saved some more had you run after a taxi.'

Apart from creating a sensation while coming out on to the fields to play hockey and tennis at college, the young Chettur brothers—all above six feet tall, well-built, with thick mops of hair—were extraordinarily brilliant. My grandmother persuaded 'Sir C' to send GK to Oxford University where he published prose and poetry and was a friend and contemporary of W.B. Yeats and S.W.R.D. Bandaranaike of Ceylon; he was also a member of the Lotus Club in 1922 when Rabindranath Tagore visited it. He passed with a First but upon his return to India was so influenced by Sarojini Naidu, that he refused to sit for the Indian Civil Services (ICS) examination and went into academics instead. As Principal of the Government College in Mangalore he wrote *College Compositions*, a seminal text book that, I believe, is still in use to teach English to Indian students. He died at the age of thirty-eight of stomach cancer before I was born.

My father did not go to Oxford for lack of finances, but saw to it that his younger brother, SK, did. He returned from Oxford and entered the ICS. In 1942, as Collector in Trichinopoly (now Thiruchirapalli), he had to deal with a thousand students who had gathered outside St Joseph's College. They demanded the right to protest in solidarity with Gandhiji who had gone on yet another fast against the British. The situation turned ugly as the British Deputy Superintendent of Police (DSP) refused to allow the students to carry out a procession. The Principal telephoned S.K. Chettur. As the collector and the civilian authority, he was ultimately responsible. My uncle arrived and spoke to the president of the college student's union, Ratnaker Rai, who later became Inspector General of Police in Karnataka. Some students lifted him on to a wall to announce to the restive crowd his decision to allow the procession. The English DSP tried to argue with him and wanted to act tough with the students.

'Mr Martin, you have got your orders. Now carry them out,' shouted SK from atop the wall. The protest passed off peacefully as the students had promised my uncle. He went on to become the Chief Secretary of

Tamil Nadu and the author of the famous *Steel Frame and I* (1963), a must-read about the civil service. He consistently refused to ask for a posting to the central government in Delhi which he thought was a hot bed of bureaucratic intrigue, dishonesty and file-pushing to no useful end. He also wrote many short stories which were published and read widely. Some were slightly bawdy, which made my mother frown and grumble at her brother-in-law. He laughed uproariously, as was characteristic of all the Chettur brothers. He knew that with her Kollengode background, she wouldn't mind a bawdy comment or two, but only in the company of her own choosing, and only, if she was the author.

RK, the youngest brother, became a doctor and joined the army. He was the introvert among the brothers, and his frequent postings to remote places possibly caused a lack of communication with the rest of the brothers and their families.

After my mother died at the age of eighty-seven on 23 January 2000, I came across some newspaper clippings tucked inside one of her household account books. They had become pinkish-yellow with age; I had never seen them before. They were roughly torn-off sections from *The Spectator*, *Malayalam Manorama*, *Swarajya* and the *Madras Mail* of 13 February 1930. The last had a headline spreading right across five of its six columns: 'The Marriage of a Rajah's Daughter—A Brilliant Reception'. The caption said, 'AN INDIAN SOCIETY WEDDING—A brilliant gathering was held at "Kushaldoss Gardens" on Tuesday in connexion [sic] with the marriage of the daughter of the Rajah of Kollengode, Srimathi T. Meenakshi Ammal and Mr K.K. Chettur of the Indian Audit and Accounts Service'. Separate photographs of my mother and father in formal poses flanked one of my grandfather's sitting at a table for tea with my parents and a couple of obviously important English ladies in those fashionable hats of the 1930s.

These clippings, well-preserved and well-travelled, for almost seventy years, told me things I had never known before about my parents' wedding. We discovered that, 'the function was an unqualified success', that, 'although in the early part of the evening the weather was threatening, there was fortunately no rain', that 'Afterwards, refreshments were served both in European and Indian style by Messrs Harrison and Co, and a musical entertainment followed'. The *Swarajya* reported that 'The precincts were so tastefully decorated that it looked like fairy-land' and that 'There was a huge concourse of guests, including, Dr. Annie Besant, Dr. James H. Cousins, Mr. and Mrs. Jinarajadasa, Dewan Bahadur T.R. Ramachandra Iyer, Maulana and Begum Yaqub Hasan Sait', after which the guest list, which went on for another three inches of column space, ran out of breath and finally ended with, 'and others too numerous to mention'. I also discovered from the *Spectator* which had titled its story 'Wedding in High Life' that, 'After partaking of the refreshments provided on a lavish scale, the guests moved to the hall upstairs where the couple cut the wedding cake to the English fashion'. Rather conversationally it then confided to its readers that 'We understand the bride and bridegroom are going to England for their honeymoon'.

Coming across these pinkish-yellow scraps of paper fourteen days after my mother had died, almost exactly seventy years following her wedding on 12 February 1930, was like finding a family treasure. Amongst the hundreds of true, mythological, sad and funny stories she had told us all her life—some repeated many times over even if we reminded her that we had heard them before—my mother had completely omitted everything about her wedding day.

However, we had often heard some classic tales of a honeymoon that could only have happened to someone like her. On the honeymoon voyage, she asked my father whether the meals served in the opulent dining room of the British ship were made by Brahmin cooks. How could she eat if they weren't? My father told her she had better learn to do so as the alternative was to starve. She discovered a co-passenger, a conservative Tamilian gentleman who was accompanied by his Brahmin cook on the steamer to England. She decided to befriend the cook, until he confided that not being able to bear perching himself atop the English commodes in the tiny toilets on board the ship, he had found a way out: he would squat on a newspaper, wrap his deposits in it and throw the parcel overboard every morning when no one was looking!

My mother loved an audience. What made her get one easily was her vivacious and hilarious ways of recounting her experiences—the kind that always seem to happen to some people repeatedly and not to others. Maybe she just picked up the quirks and funny bits of life and knew how to share them well with anyone who was willing to sit back and listen. Friends, relatives, her only daughter, and her grandchildren, often rejected her tales outright as outrageous concoctions, but that was a part of the fun of listening to them. Everyone knew that she was incapable of fabricating a lie or hide a truth.

~

In the early nineties, Kollengode loomed large again in my life. A resident of the town, Sreedharan Nair, arrived in New Delhi at the doorstep of the office at 3, Krishna Menon Marg, with a bunch of files and an agitated air. He described how he and the citizens of the town had been waging a battle against the illegal dismantling of the oldest section of the Vengunad Palace. This section, known as the kovilagam, was where my grandfather and the subsequent rajahs had separately resided. The longer, more sprawling construction where all the fun and games took place was called kalari, and contained the quarters where all the women and their families lived. The kovilagam had a certain sanctity about it since the family deity was housed there in a small area designated as the temple. It overlooked the men's side of the bathing tank. The stone pedestal on which the image of the family deity was placed had an inscription saying it had been presented by Tipu Sultan. A priest was there full time to carry out the prayer rituals and it was he who brought the oil lamp, lit from the one in the sanctum sanctorum, to everyone in the household in the evenings after everyone had had their baths when I was little.

A cousin, the youngest daughter of one of Ammu Amma's sons, had entered into an unauthorized deal with a local person believed to be a big timber merchant, to dismantle and take away the entire kovilagam building, piece by piece, for sale elsewhere. The broad teak pillars, the beautifully carved wooden panels that ran along the pelmets, the smoothly worn wooden staircase with its elegant banisters—were all being systematically torn down. In a short while, there would be no building left standing there. She was not a part of the matrilineal line and therefore had no rights on the property, the same way as I did not. Her actions were thus unlawful.

Sreedharan Nair showed me all the papers describing the efforts of the people of Kollengode town in trying to save a portion of its architectural and cultural heritage. They had led impressive processions, blocked roads, and gone to court. He told me of his interactions with other sections of the family who expressed their helplessness in putting a stop to it. He had collected photocopies of old documents after painstaking research in the office of the local government authorities describing the historic value of the Vengunad complex. In between, they had won a stay from K.T. Thomas, a respected and upright judge of the High Court of Kerala. The opposing side had engaged the most expensive lawyers and had often seemed to be able to 'fix' things in the small registry rooms making the task of the citizens of Kollengode a Herculean one. But the small respite gained by the stay given by Judge Thomas ended when he was elevated to the Supreme Court of India. The stay was soon vacated by a more amenable judge, and the huge teak beams, valued at twenty lakh rupees each, started coming down again.

By a lucky coincidence, a trade union meeting took me to Palakkad. Thus I was able to visit Kollengode and see matters for myself. Things had changed quite a bit. The palace grounds had gone to seed and only a minimal staff ambled around. All the relatives had dispersed to the USA, Madras, Coimbatore, Ooty and Bangalore, visiting occasionally to see that all was well. Piles of massive teak beams lay waiting to be transported away at the cannibalized kovilagam.

Quite typically, I jumped into the fray with my sentiments and sense of injustice aroused. I assured Sreedharan Nair that I would stand by them and fight their battle. Never having had interest in owning property other than wanting a small and secure nest for myself and being clueless about the changing rules of matriliny and the intricacies of the succession laws, I decided that since I was a mere member of the public we would deal with this with a Public Interest Litigation (PIL). My approach was simple: I took the whole issue first to the Archaeological Survey of India (ASI) asking them to examine the historical value of the property and consider stepping in to save it for posterity. I believed it was a part of the valuable cultural heritage of the state which scholars, architects and historians could study and admire. Kerala needed such buildings to demonstrate its rich cultural traditions. Achala Moulik, then Director General of the ASI, and a batchmate of my former husband in the civil service, was very sympathetic. She studied the papers on Kollengode's history and the value of the old palace carefully. An ASI officer in Ernakulam was asked to intervene in the case being fought by the citizens of Kollengode but he never seemed to be able to reach the courts on time as there was always a bandh or a strike that obstructed him. I asked one of my Party colleagues in the Janata Dal who was a practicing lawyer to help out whenever necessary. When the stay was lifted, a dismayed Sreedharan Nair came to Delhi again. I took him to consult senior lawyers Ashok Panda and P.N. Lekhi at the Supreme Court. The ASI, in the meanwhile, examined the papers in further detail. They issued a letter saying they were actively considering adoption of the Kollengode palace building and needed three months to survey the property carefully to decide whether it would come under its protection. Armed with a fresh PIL, we approached the Supreme Court in an appeal to stay the destructive operations going on at a rapid pace in Kollengode. The letter from the ASI was extremely important as it recognized the value of the cultural property, and was a document from a responsible and concerned government body. We were sure it would give us a respite of three months till the ASI visited the site and decided whether it should be declared a protected monument of historic value that was more than four hundred years old.

On the day of the hearing, we entered the courtroom and took our seats. When our case came up for consideration, our lawyers who had not charged us any fees, began placing the facts before the judge. P.P. Venugopal, a prominent lawyer, stood on the other side and kept smiling calmly while our impassioned presentation went on. He did not need to argue. The judge listened briefly and looked contemptuously at P.N. Lekhi. He refused to open the file and take cognizance of the letter provided by the ASI. He remarked: 'These poor rajahs and maharajahs are out on the streets these days. Even if they have golden palaces, it is their right to sell them off if they wish and the public has no right to stop them.' He tossed the file aside and went on to the next case. We left the courtroom in a state of shock and the counsel left victorious.

My nephew, who lived in the USA and was legally in custody of the property, expressed his helplessness to act from such a distance and in fact, it was conveyed to me that he had been worried that since I had armed myself with a letter from the ASI, being a socialist, I was keen to remove the property from private hands and let the state take it over. I did not bother to argue that I had spent eighteen thousand rupees on court fees and other expenses from my own personal account—which I lost anyway. However, had we won, I would have saved the property from destruction for everybody with no material benefit to me. Sreedharan Nair returned dejected to Kollengode, and I, to my various other public causes with anger at my cousin's perfidy and the legal system's hollowness.

The same nephew has now come to an arrangement with the Casino group of companies to run kalari as a heritage health resort. It seems ironic that many people will now be paying a lot of money to have luxurious oil massages and baths that we used to have for free, years ago. It seems as if heritage is worth preserving only if there is money in it for everyone. Whether illegal acts are committed in the process, the ASI brushed aside, citizens' sentiments trampled upon and family relationships twisted, it does not seem to matter. At least the property will be well maintained, of course. However, the older and more historic portion is no longer by its side. Someone told me that the dismantled Vengunad kovilagam has been reconstructed in Thrissur as a heritage building by some private party. I intend to go see the building some day, to check the veracity of this piece of information. There is no hurry, since to mull over it would only bring a feeling of regret for the loss of what was part of my childhood memories.

3

DELHI AND GANDHI
Points of Return

DELHI WAS A CENTRAL POINT for my parents after their honeymoon. There seems to have been another trip to Europe, as I discovered after coming across a paper-cut silhouette of my mother done by a roadside artist in Zurich. It was carefully preserved in an envelope which had the amount she paid for it in francs written on it by her in pencil. She always kept meticulous accounts where even what she gave a beggar on the street is recorded.

Later, before I was born, they were sent on a posting to Rangoon where my father was handling a financial portfolio on behalf of the government. However, it was Delhi that saw us through the Partition days and Mahatma Gandhi's assassination. The capital of India took on many forms in front of my eyes over the period between the 1940s till this first quarter of the twenty-first century, changing its personality perceptibly as time went by.

∽

Delhi, new and old, had all become one. It spilled out into a maze of colonies growing upwards and sideways and joined together with tangles of electric cables like shabby black cobwebs. There was no sense of order to anything. Shanty clusters attached themselves like fungi against the walls of elegant residences guarded by dogs and men. These grew—unregulated, unnoticed and unlawfully—under the benign go-ahead of local mafia who then endeared themselves to the political class. Delhi became a city of cluttered marketplaces, shabby parks, food stalls on pavements and hundreds of small and big monuments, supposedly protected by the ASI only through a faded notice board that people never bothered to notice. In the centre, was the seat of power which made Delhi the capital of democratic and free India, a city of wheelers and dealers, power-brokers and con men all looking for self-aggrandizement and a slice of free profits. Stretching all the way from Gurgaon at one end to Ghaziabad on the other, from Rohtak to Rohini and Serai Rohilla, from Nizamuddin to Noida, refugees and other settlers were engulfed in a vast, cultureless, rootless, cauldron of mayhem. It took a while for the bullock carts, two-wheeled, horse-drawn tongas and cyclists to understand that the traffic lights were meant to regulate them as well. However, when it finally happened, the new labels stuck onto the rear windows of their cars as they drove through red lights defiantly said, 'SO WHAT?' All the chaos, aggression and lawlessness of Delhi's new soul was delicately camouflaged by manicured cosmetics only in the area tended by the New Delhi Municipal Corporation (NDMC). Here, diplomats, parliamentarians, bureaucrats, senior defence officials and senior members of the judiciary—in other words 'the Establishment'—lived.

This charmed area of New Delhi was created by the British who built parts of what came to be known as Lutyens' Delhi with its spacious bungalows surrounded by vast gardens and half a dozen servants' quarters. Its avenues were lined with flowering jacaranda and gulmohar trees. Tennis courts at the Gymkhana Club allowed browns and whites to play a few games together and share jokes over a *burra* (or large) peg. The Viceroy's abode with all its liveried accessories and regal embellishments that became the Rashtrapati Bhavan, the residence of the President of India, reassured the Establishment that whether India was a colony or republic, the pomp and style of the colonizers could now all be theirs.

One was a world of genteel comfort—the world of the rulers. The other consisted of people lurching in tightly packed buses, moving about on foot or in tongas—the world of the ruled. As within the Red Fort at Old Delhi, the capital was a division between the Diwan-e-Khas and the Diwan-e-Aam, the divided world of the chosen few and the commoners, the anointed and the rabble. It has remained this way from the days of the Mughal Empire, through British rule, transiting through the traumatic days of Partition, until today. For the washerman who still toils in the homes of the Establishment, freedom has brought with it some important, if only minor, changes. His son now wears blue jeans and runs a public telephone booth allotted to him at the recommendation of the politician-resident of the big bungalow. He launders his clothes for free in exchange for a servants' quarter. He still, however, acknowledges the master with a *huzoor*, *janab* or *sahib*. His emancipated son prefers to say 'sir' or 'madam' to skip the tenor of servility.

~

It was in a house like the one described above on Tughlak Road that my mother and father hid their Muslim friends till they could arrange safe travel for them to Lahore during the terrible days of Partition. Their hastily packed suitcases lay in piles in our storeroom till they could be sent by my parents, one by one, to their owners who had fled in disguise to avoid being slaughtered by rampaging mobs. One of their dearest friends who had to leave in a hurry was Apa Ghiasuddin who probably fussed over me more than the summer-only aunts of Kerala bothered to do. Aunty Apa had a pale green satin *sherara* stitched for me which I was made to wear on many festive occasions. It made no difference whether a girl of eight wore a Malayali *pavada* and blouse, or a north Indian *sherara* and kurta. Even as people found that the politics of both the British and a section of the leadership of India and Pakistan had created two countries instead of one, dividing Hindus and Muslims like never before, it did not necessarily have to be reflected in dress and language. The Hindu *kayasth*s and Sikh taxi drivers read and wrote Urdu, the Hindu cobbler greeted the Muslim tailor with a *Jai Ram Ji Ki*, and we all spoke Hindustani which was a comfortable blend of Hindi and Urdu.

Even after Aunty Apa left for good she regularly sent small parcels from Pakistan till we lost touch after the sixties. Fifty years later, in 1998–99, her daughter Nighat sitting in Lahore, regularly watched me anchoring 'The Woman', a weekly programme on Zee TV that went on for a whole year. She finally wrote to me, care of the television network, in April 1999, to ask whether I was June, the same person who was the daughter of Aunty Meenakshi, her mother's old friend. Enclosed in the letter was an old photograph of my mother and me with Nighat and Aunty Apa, taken in Delhi sometime in the late forties. Unexpected general elections and the Kargil conflict diverted my attention and delayed my reply which went only sometime in the winter of 1999. Overzealous authorities in one of our countries might have nabbed it along the way. I have never heard from Nighat again.

~

In the late forties, Tughlak Road led only to Safdarjung Airport, after which there were no buildings or serious habitation. A long Sunday drive with my father meant going all the way into the countryside up to the Qutb Minar and back. Everyone slept outside in the garden under mosquito nets, whether they were senior government officials or small- time farmers and shopkeepers. I was always a bit scared until my parents came to bed alongside me as I could hear the jackals howling in the night from the nearby grasslands at Safdarjung Tomb. Cows would wander in to the garden and snort into our nets. No gates were locked and armed guards were unheard of. For many years after Independence, even Prime Minister Jawaharlal Nehru rode from his official residence at Teen Murti Bhavan alone in the back seat of an Ambassador car, with only the driver up front. Preceding this car was a single outrider on a motorcycle. Ugly pomp and security systems were diseases that came to our democracy later, but feudalism, caste oppression and colonial voices still existed in the many clubs, offices, villages and towns of India, either blatantly or in different disguises, unfettered by the democratic spirit of freedom.

One morning, we awoke to discover that the entire cane sofa set that lay in our verandah overlooking the garden had vanished. The Tughlak Road Police Station was only a hundred yards away as you walked out of our gate and turned right. A complaint was lodged. My father was Secretary in the Ministry of Finance so the crime was solved with zealous briskness. My mother and I walked to the police station to identify the furniture. There was a pleasant-looking man in his late thirties nonchalantly sitting on our cane sofa, one leg perched on the other, smiling and conversing with the policemen who stood around him.

'Is this your sofa set, memsahib?' asked the station house officer.

'Yes,' said my mother. 'But how did you find it so quickly?'

'This fellow is a habitual thief,' the policeman explained with a laugh, pointing to the man sitting on the sofa. 'He was let out of jail just last week, but he says he has no job and nowhere to go. He steals only to be caught, so that he can get free food and lodging in jail from the government.'

The sofa set returned to our verandah, the thief returned to the lock-up, and the police notched up another solved crime. Everyone was happy. At home, we laughed whenever we sat on that cane sofa, remembering the sheer enterprise of the thief. The expression on his face had been so unforgettable that often we could almost feel the man sitting beside us.

Many years later, in 1996, I began an academic study of the socio-economic condition of artisans. It was to be published as a book named *Vishvakarma's Children: Stories of India's Craftspeople.** I found that the average earning of an artisan through his craft across the country was 2,000 rupees a month. For a family of five, this meant only Rs 13.33 per head per day. During the very same period, the Minister of State for Home Affairs, answering a question raised by a Member of Parliament (MP), informed the country that the state exchequer spent Rs 48.60 per day on each prisoner it housed in Tihar Jail in Delhi. I shared this information with a group of craftspersons. One of them looked at me with a bemused expression and said: 'That means it's better to commit a crime and be in jail than struggle to carve a stone idol, isn't it?'

After forty-eight years, the thief in Tughlak Road was sitting beside me smiling again.

Delhi was also where I discovered, lost, and gained from Mahatma Gandhi.

In the evenings, my mother would hold my hand, walk out of the gate and turn left. The road would lead to a roundabout so typical of Lutyens' Delhi. Turning right from there we would be at Birla House to attend Mahatma Gandhi's daily prayer meetings. For my mother, it fulfilled both her sense of nationalism and religiosity. I quite enjoyed singing the *bhajan*s as it reminded me of Kollengode and Trichur in the summer holidays. These *bhajan*s, however, were in Hindi.

On the evening of 29 January 1948, the crowd was particularly heavy. I sat a few feet away from Gandhiji. He saw me getting squeezed by a plump lady who was trying to edge her way forward. He put out his hand and drew me closer to him till I found enough room to sit comfortably. For a few moments, he stroked my head. When the prayer meeting ended, my mother hustled me out so that I did not get crushed in the crowds again.

The next day my mother and I had just set out for Birla House—a little late. We had reached the end of Tughlak Road when we heard a loud, sharp, short noise, like something bursting. It made the hundreds of mynahs that had settled on the trees along the Albuquerque Road for

---

* *Vishvakarma's Children: Stories of India's Craftspeople*, New Delhi: Concept Publishing Co., 2001.

the night, fly out in all directions twittering and chirping loudly. Loud cries came up from the direction of Birla House. Someone ran down the road shouting to anyone who was listening, 'Gandhiji has been shot!' My thoughts and memories are lost in the confusion that followed. Even the memory of Mahatma Gandhi gradually became distant and did not impinge on my life for many years. It was only in the late seventies when I returned to Delhi after living in Jammu & Kashmir (J&K) for fifteen years, that Gandhi came back into my life and provided the economic and social rationale not only for my work in the handicraft sector but also for the ideological moorings during my unplanned journey into politics.

∽

Some months after the Emergency ended and a new government was formed in 1977, my husband was posted to Delhi after serving as the Secretary and Commissioner for Industries in the J&K government. He was appointed as the Special Assistant to George Fernandes, the Union Minister for Industries in the new Janata Party government. He had been recommended to the minister by L.K. Jha, the then Governor of J&K, but who had been a deputy secretary working under my father in the Ministry of Finance in 1950. We found George Fernandes, the famous hero who had gone underground during the Emergency and the person who had, as we had heard, led the biggest railway strike in Asia. He was a man fiercely committed to democratic socialism as defined by Mahatma Gandhi and Dr Ram Manohar Lohia. Intensely energetic, single-minded about his work, and completely dedicated, among other things, to the protection and sustenance of the cottage and small sectors in the rural economy, he created the New Industrial Policy Resolution of 1977 for India that took serious note of the livelihood of the village artisan and handloom weaver. We had never seen a politician up close before, other than Sheikh Abdullah in Kashmir, who was by then like a benign father figure compared to the fiery Fernandes, who could fell people with his oratory alone. Both Ashok and I were happily surprised to find a man whose integrity and consequent fearlessness were remarkable, and who, although at a personal level rather shy and devoid of the ability to make small talk, was intellectually incisive and deadly sharp. This, despite the lack of a full and formal college education. He spoke at length about the importance of village industry and Mahatma Gandhi's ideas about sustaining rural India. He put it into practice by reserving 817 items in the small-scale and cottage sector from encroachment by the larger sectors. He spoke with Madhu Dandavate, who was the railway minister, about introducing earthenware pots in the railways to serve tea rather than the plastic or paper cups that had become fashionable.

~

In the mid-nineties, I was in the Tees Hazari Court for a short but sad final hearing for my divorce by mutual consent. As I came outside, I saw a municipal worker being let down a stinking manhole into thick, black, ugly looking water to unclog something that had lodged there, blocking the underground drainage system in the outer surroundings of the court complex. He had no special protection against filth or infection for his body or for his face and hands. A dirty, pathetic person from the 'scavenger' class, although no one used that word anymore by law, was being let down into this lethal liquid garbage with no consideration for his health or human rights. Despite being appalled at the callousness of the municipal authorities, I resisted the temptation of going back into the court and filing a complaint with the same judge who was present during my divorce hearing. He would surely have thought I was going through a temporary mental breakdown because of the divorce. He may not necessarily have appreciated that my husband and I had shared a common lawyer and I had neither contested anything nor sought any alimony as I believed that we should share earnings only if we were together. If we were to separate, I did not want to claim the right to anything and preferred to manage on my own without any demands or bitterness. Driving back alone to New Delhi, on a sudden impulse I stopped at Rajghat and sat under a tree on a gentle grassy slope surrounding Gandhiji's samadhi—where he was cremated—for two hours, reading from a small book of his most famous quotes. When the intense feeling of sadness and loss inside me subsided and I could face going back to work at 3, Krishna Menon Marg, and later home to my daughter, I found that I did not need to seek solace from anyone else. Gandhiji had somehow comforted me again.

In 1998, the Gandhi Smriti and Darshan Samiti held a commemorative programme for Kasturba Gandhi's centenary and asked me to deliver the keynote speech on Gandhi and the present status of women. I spent several days reading from Gandhi's writings and speeches over a period of twenty years and found a distinct transition is his attitudes and ideas from conservative to progressive, from casteist to liberal, and from patriarchal to almost feminist. I was keen to avoid the pitfalls of a clichéd approach to Gandhi. If one is examining anyone or anything objectively, one cannot allow it to be coloured by one's own likes and dislikes. This only leads to intellectual dishonesty, a very common characteristic among many Indian politicians who lay claim to intellectual ability. I found that Gandhi had the intellectual honesty to constantly reexamine his opinions and pronouncements, correct his earlier advice given to his followers, and indulge in self-criticism in order to arrive at a better understanding of himself and any issue that he was tackling. I had put all this down in a lengthy paper and delivered the address to a rather small gathering at Gandhi Darshan near Rajghat. Hardly anyone took notice of it until I discovered that the Gandhian institution itself had found it to be a 'brilliant new analysis' and printed thousands of copies to distribute as a lecture, they later published it in a book of essays on various aspects of Gandhi. I was particularly happy that the request to deliver a speech on him had led me to study and explore Gandhi's metamorphosis into a liberal supporter of women. I had delved into little-known letters of his to various women colleagues, and his own writings in *Young India*, and compared his hopes and aspirations for women with the rather miserable little the Westernized women's movement of India had done for itself in the contemporary scene.

I suppose it would be honest and correct to say that it was George Fernandes—referred to in those days as a stormy petrel, rabble rouser, and later as unreliable, inconsistent and opportunistic—who brought Mahatma Gandhi's life and teachings into my life. He has been both consistent and reliable in his advice that I should refer to Gandhi and Lohia whenever I needed answers to complicated political or moral questions.

I began to understand that my work among craftspersons did have a larger and more meaningful relevance for the development of India and that it encapsulated all the other things that Gandhi spoke and wrote about—the dignity of labour, the role of women in the village economy, the needs of the poorest man, the political and economic meaning of khadi, the handloom sector, the village potter, the ill-effects of alcohol, the importance of writing as a means of communication, the spirit of swadeshi, and the meaning of political freedom. While over the years, George Sahib (as I came to call George Fernandes often) demonstrated that politics had to be a combination of struggle, constructive work, and political party-related activity, it was Gandhi who became the guiding factor in my understanding of public causes and my moral guide when the deafening chaos of self-serving politics needed to be quietened.

In 2001, after the attack on me by *Tehelka* journalists in an ugly and fraudulent sting operation, I felt indignant and greatly insulted by the fact that I was being required to prove my moral integrity and honesty against accusations of corruption. One morning, there was an article in the edit page of a Hindi daily about the intrinsic characteristics of good and evil and how, quite often, the forces of corruption win because those indulging in it are ruthless, tough, rich and selfish, leaving the good weak, disorganized and ineffective. The article was in the context of the battle fought in Uttar Pradesh by a group of civil servants to identify corrupt colleagues, which came to naught. The closing lines of the article described an incident in Mahatma Gandhi's life when he was asked by a journalist what he had to say about the allegation that he had two million pounds stashed away in the Bank of England. He had replied that if his life itself was not a good enough answer to that question, his response then would not be of any use. I knew I had been put into a situation in which I was having to and would have to spend time answering many questions; I knew I had to face many more months of accusations, allegations and taunts by a section of the media and its friends in a section of the political opposition. Reading the article, I got strength from knowing that even Gandhiji had to face the ugliness of such evil. In comparison, I was nobody, but my life and the areas of concern in my work was there for everyone to see.

Gandhiji's words had found a way of soothing my troubled mind. I was also reminded suddenly of the day when his gentle hand had provided me with comfort. I wonder whether the incidents we remember of our childhood stay with us to give a meaning to later incidents, and thereby a sense of cohesion and continuity in life itself.

4

Japan Days
Insight into Diplomacy

Soon after Mahatma Gandhi's demise, my father had a disagreement with Prime Minister Jawaharlal Nehru. He had been asked to carry out some work which my father believed to be neither correct nor justified. His refusal on file annoyed the prime minister enough to order my father out of the country to head the Indian consulate in San Francisco. All the arrangements had been made—our living room carpet had been sold, we had said our farewells in Kerala, and I had been taken out of school, when the prime minister's sister, Vijayalakshmi Pandit, as we heard later, intervened with her brother to demand that a certain favourite of hers be sent to San Francisco instead. All of a sudden, our baggage labels pointed east instead of west. My father was appointed as the Head of the Indian Liaison Mission in Japan.

In the early fifties, it took three days to reach Tokyo from Delhi by air because aviation technology did not provide for such long hauls. The first stop was Bangkok, then Hong Kong and finally Tokyo. My father went ahead. My mother and I flew a few weeks later in the midst of the typhoon season. The aircraft was tossed about so much that the luggage fell from the top shelf, the crockery flew down the aisles, the airline staff belted themselves onto their seats, and the lights went out. The passengers were petrified but, innocent of new dangers, I kept reassuring my mother that the more the 'aeroplane' bumped, the sooner we would reach my father. The aircraft was forced to land at the Okinawa US Air Force Base till the typhoon abated. The passengers were crowded into a large tin shed, which served as an airport, along with a large number of American soldiers lying stretched out on sofas made of rexine, exhausted and mud-caked from the battle in Korea, waiting to fly home. The typhoon shrieked and buffeted the shed. The sky was black outside. The periodic flashes of lighting however, helped see the trees getting tossed in all directions, their huge swaying branches, being blown away into the howling night. Everyone sat huddled together on the floor waiting for the storm to pass. The rough and ready canteen at one end of the airport lounge had a juke box in which the American GIs repeatedly played 'La Vie en Rose' till I knew it by heart. It was the first popular western song I had ever heard and have not forgotten since. There were of course the nursery rhymes taught to me by Nanny Gwynne in the calm confines of the house on Tughlak Road that we had left behind.

We arrived at the Kato House residence in Kamifujimae-cho in Bunkyo-ku District of Tokyo in mid-July 1950 to be greeted by a gentleman housekeeper, three maids, two chauffeurs and a gardener. My parents had taken along Atholi Chandu, the bright, young scheduled caste cook who had worked in S.K. Chettur's house in Madras. My mother had come a long way from the need for Brahmin cooks that she had asked for on her honeymoon. Chandu had impressed my parents by going to night classes and doing well in his exams while spending his days as a domestic help cooking meals for my uncle's family. In Japan, they asked him to help out when Indian meals were required for dinner parties but paid for his studies at Tokyo University. This enabled him to pass his Grade B examinations for the Indian Foreign Service. Kato House became the Indian Ambassador's residence for many years till a subsequent Ambassador bought a new place. Today, that imposing double-storeyed house has been torn down and a school has come up in its place. Earlier, the house with its many rooms and passageways leading to various wings of the building, lent themselves to the curious for exploring, and in its vast garden one could gather enough snow to make many a snowmen.

Obviously, in such an establishment, my mother did not have to spend any time on housekeeping. Instead, she decided to dedicate herself to voluntary hospital work at the Blood Bank and in the General Hospital which were understaffed and full to the brim because of the Korean War. She had to wear a nurse's uniform. For a lady from Kollengode and an Ambassador's wife to wear a cap, stockings and a short dress may have been only mildly unusual, since trained Malayali nurses became as ubiquitous as Sikh taxi drivers all over the world. However, cleaning all kinds of messy substances off hefty American soldiers brought injured and unconscious from the Korean front, was another matter altogether. My mother would come back from hospital with a variety of stories to tell my father and me. The one that most pleased her was of how she had learned to light a cigarette and puff it a few times to get it going before holding it to the mouth of a soldier whose hands had been blown off. Many well-known people, decorated and liveried, came to donate blood at the blood bank. My mother would give them juice, stick plaster on and hold their hands before and after a pint of blood was transferred from their bodies to the bottles, and recount to us later with great amusement how some very important person had passed out flat on his back at the sight of his own blood.

In the meantime, I forgot all my Hindi and in three months learned to speak Japanese fluently. I even spoke Japanese in my sleep as a result of having forged an undying friendship with nine-year-old Noriko Sato across the road. Kiko-chan, as we called her, and her younger brother Kotaro, who played the violin well at a very young age, spent every waking moment with me after school work was done. We often slept nights together in one big bed. Halfway through the night my mother would hear a thud from the next room and come to find that one of us had pushed the other off the edge in our sleep. We bullied seven-year-old Kotaro most of the time and gave him no choice in the role he could play in our games.

One day, my mother bought me a toy electric iron, which only became mildly warm, from the American PX*. Noriko and I were terribly excited and set up 'house' under the dining table after which we got down to ironing anything we could find that was not absolutely flat. After ironing table napkins, handkerchiefs and other sundry things we could find around the house, we decided to pull off Kotaro's shorts and iron them as well, to discover that Kotaro had some protruding appendages underneath. We immediately decided that these too needed to be ironed. The hapless little boy had to lie still on his back, naked waist down, while two diligent and determined young housekeepers tried unsuccessfully to iron his appendages till they stayed flat! Today, Kotaro San has three children, and is a well-known musician and conductor of an important orchestra in Japan.

During the day, while my Japanese friends were at a local Japanese school, I was driven miles away to the International Sacred Heart Convent where I studied in English. Apart from studying hard, I collected cheap tin

---

*The American PX is the Army and Air Force Exchange Service, retailer of US Army and Air Force installations.

medallions on flimsy chains with the image of the Virgin Mary embossed on them to wear around my neck, and learned to sing hymns in the big school chapel. I also recall being curious to know what the flat, white biscuit that the catholic children ate at Holy Communion, tasted like. I had an American-style education but using typical Japanese stationery such as copy books with cherry blossoms painted on them, fluorescent pink plastic pencil boxes, bright green, sickly sweet-scented erasers, and long pencils with tiny wooden Kokeshi dolls wobbling at the ends. I had a set of American friends at school but when I returned home I would ask the maids to order two bowls of Soba from the nearby shop and telephone Kiko-chan to join me. She would arrive before the food, which was sent through a delivery boy on a cycle. The ordinary working class lunch there consisted of eating a big bowl of Soba—buckwheat noodles in a steaming clear soup, with vegetables and small pieces of meat thrown in. Delivery boys would cruise through the crazy Tokyo traffic balancing a pillar of up to ten bowls of steaming noodle soup dishes, somehow fitting one on top of the other in one hand, while holding the handlebar of the bicycle with the other. Thousands of people—officegoers, shopkeepers and school children like me—ordered wholesome, delicious, steaming bowls of Soba across the length and breadth of the city. Those talented bowl-balancers are no longer a part of the Tokyo traffic, but the bowls of Soba are still the cheapest and most nourishing meal for the working man. The poor, and there were many in those days after the War, ate rice mixed with shoyu, nori, the flaky dried seaweed, and a raw egg broken into the middle of it all. Sometimes I would sit with the maids and share their lunch.

One evening, during the Korean War, as my mother was returning from the hospital, she spotted a man lying unconscious and cold on the road. She ordered the chauffeur to stop, put him in the car and drove him to the hospital. She even borrowed all the money the chauffeur had in his pocket to leave with the derelict man. The Japanese are undemonstrative and outwardly unemotional people, but the news of this little act of kindness spread like wildfire and earned my mother a special place in the hearts of the people we knew in Japan.

The same short-statured chauffeur, Ikeda San, was nicknamed Chukri by my mother; 'chukri' was slang for 'titch' or 'tiny' in Malayalam. He proudly went about telling everyone that Madame San had given him this special name, without knowing what it meant. Ikeda San was brought by a big Japanese television network all the way to Delhi to meet her again in the mid-nineties. They had thought that their reunion would make a great story. They were both in their late seventies by then. My mother had been widowed for almost forty years. His arrival at my mother's home at Sujan Singh Park one sunny pre-winter morning and her hugging him with great excitement at her doorway after forty years was seen by millions on television all over Japan. My mother wore her favourite black and red sari when my daughter and I took them out to lunch at the India International Centre (IIC). After exchanging gifts and old memories and seeing a bit of Delhi, Ikeda San was flown back to Japan. We waited for a letter from him on his arrival back home. Nothing came for over four months. Finally, one day, an embarrassed and penitent Ikeda San wrote:

> *Honorable Madame San, I very happy to meet you and June-san again, and your beautiful granddaughter Aditi-san also. It was after very long time. But very sad to inform you when I reach home my wife very angry. She very, very jealous because I go so far away to see another lady. She saw Madame San and me on television and after that no talk to me very long time. Only now she is talking to me again. Till then I very lonely, go alone for fishing every day nearby to my house. Sometimes I play golf. But I never forget Madame San and my visit to India, Yours affectionately, Chukri.*

I don't blame his wife. My mother was so excited to see her dear Chukri after so long that she was beaming and looked quite beautiful that day, re-living her years as the gracious wife of an Ambassador. In fact, it was this image of hers with Japanese subtitles at the bottom as it appeared on Japanese television, that all the Malayalis saw in the *Malayalam Manorama* and on Kerala's *Asianet TV* when she passed away in January 2000. I did not inform Chukri of her death. Somehow, such situations have always left me paralysed.

These were small personal incidents, but there is much more that links the friendship between India and Japan at extraordinary times. With Japan crushed and demoralized after the Second World War, it stood friendless and condemned for Pearl Harbour, and deeply damaged after Hiroshima. India's Justice Radha Binod Pal was a member of the International Tribunal in Tokyo that was set up to assess the extent of Japanese war crimes and those responsible for it in the War. Much to the eternal gratitude of the

Japanese, Justice Pal wrote a note of dissent in his report and boldly went against the view held by the majority.

Fifty years later, the small but beautiful Pal-Shimonaka Memorial Hall stands in Hakone, a few hours outside of Tokyo, dedicated to the friendship between India and Japan. Yasaburo Shimonaka began life as a potter and went through life as a philanthropist and a widely respected leader of the publishing world. Justice Pal was a firm believer in Vedanta and resolutely upheld the integrity of the law. Along with Shimonaka he did much to bring to bear on Japan the teachings of Gandhi. So influenced was Shimonaka that at the age of eighty-two, he went back to making pottery, believing this was the way to re-establish 'the dignity of the Eastern Mind'*.

Prime Minister Nehru also committed India to extending a friendly hand to Japan after the War. He did this in a rather large and visible way by gifting Japan with a baby elephant, which he named Indira after his daughter. Maybe he had her in mind for big things even then. It was made into quite an event. The elephant was handed over to Tokyo's Ueno Zoo at an impressive ceremony attended by the royalty. Since I spoke Japanese like the locals, I was asked to address the children of Japan over the NHK radio network. A speech was drafted and I read it, presenting little Indira to them as a symbol of the strong and undying friendship between our two countries. As was the rather charming practice in those days, the radio station made a 78 rpm record of the speech to present to the speech-maker as a souvenir of the occasion. The record is warped and its plastic-coating flaking off, but the last time it could be played on those now-defunct old record players, you could hear a nine-year-old Indian girl ending her ten-minute speech with words of spontaneous congratulations, said with gusto, 'Mina sama no honto ni omedeto gozaimasu!' (I truly congratulate you all.)

Even fifty years later, the people of Japan remember the elephant that symbolized so much. Whenever I am introduced to a person from Japan, the elephant connection evokes an extra warm 'Ah so!' and a deeper, more respectful bow. Indira, the elephant, died of old age. Another elephant was sent by Indira Gandhi, when she was the prime minister, but it was not highlighted with as much enthusiasm because by then India's initial policy of friendship with Japan had turned cold. Despite protestations of non-alignment, the Cold War was at its height and India was firmly in

*See *The Unknown Craftsman: Japanese Insight into Beauty*, Tokyo: Kodansha International, 1989.

the Russian camp while Japan went under the US umbrella into the other camp.

~

Relations with Japan remained frozen until post Pokhran II when it took a further dive. India needed to woo Japan away from its hostile response to the nuclear tests conducted by the National Democratic Alliance (NDA) government in May 1998. Many friends in the political spectrum of Japan who had remained close to the socialists, particularly George Fernandes, the Defence Minister of India, took it upon themselves to make Herculean efforts to build new understanding. Among them was Senator Hosei Norota who was later honoured with a Padma Vibhushan by India.

In 1999, I suggested that a new elephant be sent to Japan to celebrate fifty years of Japan-India relations. George Fernandes, who had maintained excellent personal relations with many socialists in Japan, thought it was a good idea and arranged for an elephant. A young she-elephant was transported in a truck from the forests of Assam by its chief minister, Prafulla Mahanta, who wanted it to be named after his wife Jayashree. Tragically, the elephant was injured in the truck during the bumpy journey and had to be off-loaded at the Lucknow zoo for treatment. I was miserable about her plight and kept urging everyone quietly behind the scenes to do more to save her. Expert veterinarians were brought from Karnataka to treat her paralysed right leg. They struggled with her for over three months, but, unfortunately, she died.

George Fernandes became the first Indian defence minister to visit Japan in fifty years. In a happy coincidence, his only son who was working in New York was engaged to a Japanese girl. It delighted the Japanese that the defence minister of India—whose office was adorned with pictures only of the president and prime minister of India, an oil painting of Mahatma Gandhi painted by a refugee Burmese artist fighting for democracy in Burma, and a woven textile picture of the Peace Memorial at Hiroshima—was to be the father-in-law of a Japanese girl.

In 2002, another elephant was arranged, as the Japanese were by then very keen and enthusiastic about this symbolic renewal of ties. Friendship had blossomed again between the two countries. The celebration of fifty years of friendship between India and Japan was approaching. This time, George Fernandes spoke to the chief minister of Karnataka about providing another elephant. It was organized with better transportation and care, and the elephant reached Tokyo safely in time for the official visit of India's Prime Minister Atal Bihari Vajpayee. She was named Surya, since Japan was the land of the Rising Sun. Some snide commentators had already begun to spread the word that the elephant was going to be named Jaya, after me. So neither did I make known my role in initiating the idea of sending an elephant to renew old friendships, nor did I voice in the open my desire to accompany the prime minister's entourage. The whole event was more than extremely significant to me because of the old connection with elephant Indira and my father's unique role in the formulation of the India-Japan Peace Treaty fifty years ago. No one had discovered my ability to still manage a speech in Japanese with a bit of practice, but I kept silent because I was a woman in politics, and I did not want to give the scorpions an opportunity to stir any further rumours.

After 1952, I returned to Japan only in 1990 for an international conference on Tibet where I also met the Hollywood actor Richard Gere. This led to a warm and lasting friendship between us. At that time, I had no idea that he was such a popular star since I had not watched any movies for some time and did not tune in to the goings-on in Hollywood much. I treated him rather casually but the girls in Tokyo were going crazy and kept telephoning my hotel room constantly mistaking it for his. They refused to believe he was not there. Banners were strung up all over saying WELCOME RICHARD GEAR [sic]. He came up to speak to me after my speech was over and complimented me for what I had said. We became comrades in solidarity for the cause of the freedom of Tibet. I invited him to visit us in Delhi. When he finally did come to Delhi, George Fernandes had become defence minister and the NDA Government had just completed the nuclear tests in Pokhran. Pakistan had followed with its first test two weeks later. George Fernandes, who was also returning from a trip to Nagaland, had invited Gere to dinner. A large posse of the press, Gere and some Tibetan friends, and the three large dogs that lived with Fernandes, were all waiting to greet him as he arrived from Kohima carrying ceremonial spears, shawls, flamboyant head-gears and other gifts. However, the television channels and print media were so anxious to get Fernandes's comments on Pakistan's nuclear tests that they paid no attention to the handsome and popular Hollywood star and attacked Fernandes with a barrage of questions in the midst of which Fernandes was compelled to pay attention to the dogs jumping all over him in delight. An impromptu press conference took place right there on the back verandah of the large bungalow. Richard Gere was completely bemused at the whole affair. When we all sat down to dinner, he admitted that Fernandes's was a most unusual and eccentric political personality, but that he felt much more at home that way.

The next time Gere came to the same establishment, Fernandes was about to have a press conference on the eve of a historic visit to Vietnam. Again, Richard Gere was relegated to the background and had to spend some time sitting on the garden steps with some of us before he could get the attention due to him. The best part was that it was the passion and commitment to significant issues that enabled our friendship, rather than formalities common to being known personalities. It was also funny how Japan had brought me in contact with Hollywood again.

On my 1990 visit, I also met my childhood friend Noriko-san after thirty-eight years. In the lobby of our hotel she produced all the letters I had written to her after I had left in 1952, wrapped in a pale pink satin *furoshiki* cloth along with some of the small gifts I had sent her. We hugged each other, laughed and cried and talked in my room for hours in broken English and rusty Japanese. On a subsequent trip to attend the wedding of a young man who had lived in India for some months I accompanied Noriko-san to her dance class where she was learning Bharatnatyam. It was partly therapeutic, she explained. She told me she had cancer.

From age eight to ten, Japan for me was reading Popeye and Dagwood and Blondie comic books, dressing up with Noriko-san in kimonos and saris, learning Japanese songs and dances, listening to 45 rpm records of the latest hits by Rosemary Clooney and Doris Day played on the Victrola, attending very solemn tea ceremonies and Noh dances with my parents, skiing at the Akakura resort, driving to Mount Fuji or to Nikko on weekends and shopping for American goodies at the PX where only Americans and diplomats could enter. I was particularly drawn to the simple aesthetics of Japan's crafts. They had a minimal and stark quality quite similar to that of Kerala and other parts of India. The finely crafted bamboo vases; the *tatami*s (mats)—like the grass *metthapaya*s we slept on in Kollengode—covering the floors in the rooms separated by paper doors that moved with a soft shushing sound; the exquisite *kakemono* (scroll painting); indigo coloured *shibori* textiles; lacquered and painted music boxes; and the tinkling of handcrafted wind chimes—all laid the foundations for my understanding of aesthetics. It also helped in engaging with the economics and politics of all things handmade by skilled craftspersons who I believe to be the true repositories of a culture particular to my country.

Sometimes, there was a stir among the maids and I would discover that famous American violinist Yehudi Menuhin was coming to lunch at our home. There was also the excitement over going to see Errol Flynn, Clark Gable, Betty Hutton, Danny Kaye and other famous Hollywood stars at a special variety performance after returning from entertaining the US troops at the Korean front. There were so many of these 'stars' who I had come across in my life in those days that my autograph book never left my side. My mother would return from glittering functions hosted by General Douglas J. Macarthur and his gorgeous wife Penny, and later by General Dwight D. Eisenhower and Mamie, in which all these movie stars would be present. She told me and our excited young maids how their heartthrob Errol Flynn had got so drunk at the reception that he fell into the fountain in the lobby and had to be helped off the scene! An autographed photograph, giving me his love, is still firmly stuck in my photo album.

I discovered my father's contribution towards establishing truly significant bonds with Japan much later through a paper presented at a seminar in Delhi by Hiroshi Sato, a Japanese scholar. By chance, veteran journalist Inder Malhotra told me at a book release function in early 2003 that this paper had mentioned my father in very interesting terms. He sent me a copy the following day. It was a revelation that most Japanese were not aware of, which India never bothered about and I would never have known about, if Inder Malhotra had not cared to respect history.

The sources for this paper titled '"Courted Friendship": How Japan Negotiated with India for India-Japan Peace Treaty, 1952', are mostly from official Japanese records and the papers of two Indian scholars, Kesavan (1972) and Narasimhamurthy (1986). The paper examines the links between the San Francisco Peace Treaty (SFPT) and the Indo-Japan Peace Treaty (IJPT) and post-War Japan's Asia policies. In Clause 4 of the Indo-Japan Peace Treaty, the most significant aspect was India's waiving all claims to reparation of properties seized before the War. This gesture by

India contributed greatly to the favourable progress of Japan's reparation talks with Burma, Philippines and Indonesia. Sato's paper tells us that although India did not agree to sign a peace treaty supported by the US and UK, Prime Minister Nehru intended to enter into a negotiation with Japan for a peace treaty.

A draft was sent by India on 22 December 1951 borrowing in most part from relevant portions in the SFPT and reserving the right to the same claims as made by the Allied powers. Sato writes:

> Three rounds of preliminary negotiation participated by Mr. K.K. Chettur, the Representative of the Indian Liaison Office, Tokyo and Mr. V.C. Trivedi [later Ambassador to Japan], the Office Secretary was held and the differences were sorted out. It is noteworthy that the two Indian representatives stood firm with the line of the draft, probably without the mandate of the home office. Nevertheless, as we will demonstrate, their discussions with their Japanese counterparts were well indicative of what Indian side could have legitimately claimed. ....Then for five long months, ball was in the court of Indian Government in New Delhi, and finally on June 3, 1952, New Delhi Government sent a final draft, conceding nearly all the amendments proposed by Japan, including contentious issues of Japanese properties in India. Meanwhile, India and Japan established formal diplomatic relations on April 28, 1952 when SFPT came into force and Liaison chief, K.K.Chettur assumed office of the first post-war ambassador of India to Japan. Indian Government, with notification, declared the end of the war with Japan. (p. 3)

My father actually facilitated the final draft by allowing the Japanese to draft it themselves. As described by the same Japanese drafters, this was a gesture of 'extraordinary friendly consideration'. The select clauses of the treaty were:

- to co-operate in the promotion of common welfare and to maintain international peace and security,
- to waive all claims to the properties, rights and interests of Japan or her nationals,
- to employ negotiation and arbitration with respect to any dispute arising out of interpretation or application of the Treaty, and

- to accord a most-favoured-nation treatment with respect to customs duties in connection with important and exportation of goods.

After reading the paper, I spent two days at the National Archives of India at Janpath in Delhi searching through voluminous registers containing the indices of the material housed in it. Under the Foreign Affairs lists, I identified more than a dozen documents from those that were listed, including communications from my father from Japan during those years. I submitted my requisition slips and waited for the files to be exhumed. A few days later, I was told that these documents could not be found and had probably not been transferred from the Ministry of External Affairs. I listed them out in a letter and asked the Ministry to let me have a look at them. The informal reply I received said they were not traceable and must have been sent to the National Archives. I was back to where I started. I was surprised to note the Government of India's lack of concern for its own recorded history—lost in a bureaucratic runaround—while the Japanese meticulously explored that period in the diplomatic history of their country.

The story in Hiroshi Sato's paper has an important footnote that made clear to me, quite unexpectedly after fifty years, why we went to Burma after two years in Tokyo. In a paragraph following the heading 'Reparation and Burmese linkage', Sato explores how India and Burma maintained close links in the reparation issue with the help of recently declassified information from diplomatic records on Burma. He writes,

> One interesting fact was that Mr. Chettur, who was the main participant in the negotiation during IJPT talks, was transferred to Burma in June 1952 after the conclusion of the IJPT. And he maintained close relations, not only with Japan's foreign officials in Rangoon, but with Japanese foreign office delegation headed by Eiji Wajima, Director of Asian Division with whom Chettur had negotiated in Tokyo. Chettur suggested to Weijima that Japan should proceed with its own plan of reparation, as Burmese administration was neither competent nor prepared enough with good homework on their own[12]. Chettur's report must have been valuable enough for Japanese officials to force a breakthrough in the Burmese reparation talks. Japan could almost force their terms for the settlement of reparation demands by Burmese government. (p. 7)

Sato further writes:

> It eventually facilitated the Philippines and Indonesia to take similar compromised stand on reparation demand. We cannot emphasize too much that it was in the agreement with Burma that Japan first succeeded in broadening the scope of reparation to include comprehensive "economic co-operation". "Economic co-operation" successfully mollified the stigma attached to "reparation" and it was under this new flag that Japan could progressively reconstruct her economic relations with former colonies and occupied countries in South east Asia. (p. 7)

One of the important aspects of India-Japan relations was that India chose to take a line independent of the one taken by the Allied powers. What was also significant was that my father was expected by the Indian government to continue from Rangoon the work he began with the Japanese in Tokyo. The aim was to extricate Japan from the position of underdog without fear of being overwhelmed by the possibility of Japan's economic resurgence.

~

Documents are certainly not easy to come by. In a country where routine but important and declassified material is treated casually but policemen arrest people for possessing material easily available on the Internet for contravening the Official Secrets Act, anything of historical importance that comes into one's hands is a treasure. If it concerns one's own family, it becomes a matter of serendipity. There are papers containing information about the handling of treasures of the Indian National Army of Netaji Subhas Chandra Bose in which I found notes and quotes ascribed to my father during his tenure in Japan. What is particularly significant about these notes is the propensity of government servants, even at that time, to loot official property and use it to make their own lives more comfortable. It also demonstrates another aspect of how little such people value history. The contents of the document give an insight into this through my father's words as quoted in a letter from R.D. Sathe in the Indian Liaison Mission at Tokyo to the prime minister of India in 1951.

According to the document, considerable quantities of treasures were given to Subhas Chandra Bose by Indians in the Far East as part of their war effort. While he carried a part of these treasures with him in his ill-fated flight from Saigon to Tokyo, the remaining were left in Saigon. According to photo-static [sic] copies of the documents, the following treasures are reported to have eventually reached Tokyo: 'pure gold in two wooden boxes and paper wrapper' weighing '7 kg 900 grms'; a packet of gold mixed molten iron, weighing 3 kg 100 gms; in addition 'Mr SA Ayer* handed over Y. 20,000/-.' Mr Sathe continued:

> The above treasures were handed over in Tokyo to one Mr Ramamurthy. Mr Ramamurthy [was] on several occasions questioned by the representatives of the Government of India regarding [the] treasures and it was only recently that he admitted that the treasures were in his possession.
>
> Mr Iyer recently visited Japan with the ostensible purpose of investigating the present position in regard to the treasure. Mr Iyer's activities in Japan have been rather suspicious.

And Mr KK Chettur's views regarding this are as follows:

> "It appears that Netaji had with him in Saigon substantial quantity of gold ornaments and precious stones, but that he was allowed to carry only two suitcases on the ill-fated flight. These two suitcases must have carried very much more than has now been handed over to us, and even if allowances are made for the loss of the part of the treasures when the plane crashed, it seems obvious that what was retrieved was substantially very much more than has now been in our possession. What is still more important is that the bulk of the treasures were left in Saigon and it is significant from information that is available that on the 26th January, 1945, Netaji's collection weighed more than himself. In this context you will notice that Iyer came to Tokyo subsequently from Saigon and that his statement at that time was that 'the gold was intact as I have brought it from Saigon, ... cash is the balance after changing Piastras into Yens and meeting my expenses during my stay in Japan since August 22nd 1945'. There is a party here who has seen the boxes in Iyer's room and who was also to buy off the contents of these few boxes. What happened to these boxes is a mystery as all that we have got from Iyer is 300 gms of gold and about 260 rupees gold worth of cash. You will no doubt draw

---

*Iyer is also spelt as Ayer in some other sources.

> your own conclusion from all this, but to me it would appear as if Iyer, apprehensive of the early conclusion of the Peace Treaty came to Tokyo to divide the loot and to salve his and Murthy's conscience by handing over a small quantity to Government in the hope that by doing so he would also succeed in drawing a red herring across the trail."

After quoting this pithy description by my father of the murky goings on concerning the treasures belonging to Netaji Subhas Chandra Bose, Sathe adds his own conclusion to corroborate what my father had said: 'Suspicion regarding the improper disposal of treasure is thickened by the comparative affluence in 1946 of Mr Ramamurthy when all other Indian nationals in Tokyo were suffering the greatest hardships. Another fact which suggests that the treasures were improperly disposed of is the sudden blossoming out into an Oriental Cargo export of Col Figges, the Military Attache of the British Mission in Tokyo, and the reported invitation extended by the Colonel to Ramamurthy to settle down in the UK.'

The letter signed by R.D. Sathe on 1.11.1951 was initialled by 'J.Nehru' on 5.11.1951 with no comment at all. It is decidedly strange that such important and historic material should be treated so lightly and its fate, unknown. In 1978, Subramaniam Swamy charged the same J. Nehru with accusations of melting down Netaji's gold for his personal needs and demanded a full-fledged inquiry. The files are still secret, the fate of the treasures unknown, and, at the very least, the corruption involved in someone misappropriating some of the treasures was completely ignored by the same J. Nehru.

Theories that Nehru wanted to obliterate the importance of Netaji, that Netaji did not die because there was in fact no air crash at all, that Netaji lived as an ascetic in Uttar Pradesh for many years and that the Government of India hushed all this up, was the subject of an enquiry by a commission headed by retired Supreme Court Judge Justice Manoj Mukherjee. There too, there are many classified documents that have not been made available, and many questions that lie unanswered. When eventually, the commission brought out its findings, the Manmohan Singh government disagreed with them. This raised doubts about Netaji's death and there are many, who, after the release of some classified papers in 2016, have been demanding declassification of all the papers concerning him. I was one of the public who demanded this since it concerned my father. It made me very proud that a story in *India Today*[*] at that time referred to my father as the first whistle-blower of free India.

These incidents, covering a span of many decades, revealed to me the strong moral and humanitarian positions my parents took whether they were in India or a foreign country. It also brought home to me the fact that truth is a crucial ingredient to understand history.

As for my love for Japan, it keeps returning. Once in a while, a television company from Japan comes to India and does an interview with me, and I am able to reiterate my old links and loves.

*Sandeep Unnithan, 'Who Shrunk Netaji's Fortune?', 14 May 2015, *India Today*, http://indiatoday.intoday.in/story/netaji-subash-chandra-bose-wealth-lost/1/438113.html

5

BURMA TO MYANMAR

Engaging in Transitions

IN 1952, MY FATHER REACHED Rangoon before us. My mother and I arrived only after visiting all our relatives in Madras, Trichur, Ernakulam and Kollengode. We prayed at all the big temples there so that the next posting would be blessed with success, and life would be safe and smooth. My mother needed some time with family, and conversations with all her sisters, brothers, cousins, aunts and family friends before isolation would conquer her life again.

Rangoon felt like India with its crowded, dirty bazaars, high-decibel conversations, rickshaws and brown-skinned people. Except for the green paddy fields, it was a world away from Japan despite the influence of Buddhism. In Japan, the people were introverted, courteous, genteel and slowly succumbing culturally and materially to the domination of the USA following the Second World War. In Rangoon, human interaction was noisy and often violent. In Japan, the women were soft-spoken and self-effacing but in the crowded marketplaces of Rangoon, women smoked fat cheroots and were in control of their lives. They wore delicate, transparent aengyis with beautiful lacy bodices underneath, and opened and retied their *lungis* vigorously when their anger rose in the midst of a fight about space, prices or the unholy practices of their competitors—all this amidst the overwhelming smell of durian, a fruit that was sold in every market. It looked like our own jackfruit but was unbearable to approach. I fell instead, for Burmese kawswe, a spicy dish of noodle and meat cooked in a soup to which a fiery paste of red chillies, onion and garlic is added. In the end, there is also gram flour and coconut milk till the whole broth thickens somewhat. Kawswe has at least ten garnishes to sprinkle on for varied extra flavours—lime, fried onions, raw onions, fried garlic, green chillies in vinegar, red chilly powder, coconut bits, prawn balchow, shredded fresh coriander, crumbled hard-boiled eggs and dried fish so that each soup can be garnished according to a palate. For me, it was a smooth transition from the daily bowls of osoba (or Soba, a noodle soup) in Tokyo. In fact, the difference between Japan and Burma was at first simply like the difference between osoba and kawswe. One was subtle and lightly flavoured while the other was thick, fiery and intense.

The Indian Embassy house appeared to be even bigger than the one in Tokyo. It was a majestic double-storeyed white building that looked a bit like a half of the Western Court on Janpath in Delhi. The main rooms downstairs were large enough for ballroom dancing, medal-distribution ceremonies or banquets, and a staircase descended to the front hall the way you see in houses in movies about great aristocratic families. We had a 'mug' cook from Chittagong, which was then in East Pakistan, who cooked in a kitchen which was set apart from the main house and was connected by a long open verandah. My father, mother and I looked lost sitting at one end of a dining table that could seat twenty-four people. I usually preferred to eat in the way one would snack, in one of the smaller lounges while playing with friends or doing my homework.

U Nu was the prime minister of Burma during the period we were posted there (and after a brief interregnum, again from 1960 to 1962 when General Ne Win staged a coup and put U Nu in prison). He was a soft-spoken, ever-smiling, gracious man who provided the gentle healing touch that Burma needed after the assassination of their popular hero, General Aung San in 1947. He headed the Anti-Fascist People's Freedom League, and after independence became, like Nehru in India, his country's first prime minister. As a close friend and compatriot of General Aung San, he was highly respected. Later, with Ne Win consolidating his grip over a vast network of commercial interests linked to military colleagues, U Nu was unable to fight back. He left Burma and stayed for many years in Varanasi in India, and finally went back to Burma to take up the quiet, meditative ways of a Buddhist monk.

Speaking of General Aung San' death, it feels right to bring forth here the occasional visits of his widow and daughter Suu Kyi, to my mother whose generous and spontaneous bearing offered them a much-needed comfort given the trauma they had suffered. The mothers developed a warm relationship which continued later in the 1970s when Mrs Aung San was posted to Delhi as Burma's Ambassador to India. She spent several hours chatting warmly at my mother's house in Sujan Singh Park, and gave her a beautiful silk *lungi* which I still have with me. Suu was a quiet, young girl in the background, but this old link came alive in a totally unexpected way after she led the pro-democracy demonstrations in August of 1988.

In India, 1988–89 was a period of political transition. The sheen of the young, handsome, computer-loving Prime Minister Rajiv Gandhi was fast dissipating in the controversy over the purchase of the Bofors guns from Sweden. His finance minister, V.P. Singh, had jumped ship and was attracting various elements of the opposition who encouraged him to challenge Rajiv Gandhi's integrity and credibility, and take over leadership. Given such a scenario, India was too busy to bother about what was happening in Burma.

The National Front government headed by V.P. Singh came to power in 1989. Singh replaced Rajiv Gandhi, but was succeeded eighteen months later (in 1990) by Chandra Shekhar, who too had a short-lived spell as prime minister. Rajiv Gandhi was assassinated in May 1991. India's political scene finally acquired stability for the period under the Congress government headed by P.V. Narasimha Rao.

In 1991, George Fernandes was a mere Janata Dal MP. However, he continued to live at the same residence (3, Krishna Menon Marg) which he was allotted as senior Parliamentarian and Minister of Railways in 1989, during the V.P. Singh government. One day after the May 1991 general elections, a group of fresh-faced but dishevelled young men came to his residence to meet him. They were refugees who had fled Burma after the military refused to accept the overwhelming verdict in favour of Aung San Suu Kyi's National League for Democracy (NLD), and cracked down on the protestors. Suu Kyi was under house arrest. These pro-democracy activists were terrified that the Indian police would pick them up and send them back to sure death or incarceration in Burma. 'They will have to pick me up first before they will be allowed to do anything to you,' declared George Fernandes without a second thought. He walked into my office and announced that arrangements should be made to help them set up the All Burma Students' League.

I became 'Aunty Jaya' to all of them and helped them settle in. The young boys and girls, including truly dedicated ones like Kyaw Kyaw Htut, Shar Aung, Thin Thin Aye, Ma Thieu and others spent hours in discussing organization, the meaning of democracy, whether multinational corporations operating in Burma could help the development of the country while collaborating with a military dictatorship, ways of earning money through political and community programmes and organizing processions protesting military oppression in Burma. Noticeable among them for his sheer dedication and maturity was Soe Myint. But he had a serious court case against him for hijacking an Indian Airlines plane flying to Calcutta on 10 November 1990, which became almost intractable because of stringent international laws against hijacking in those days. It took almost ten years to extract him from the Kolkata High Court and persuade the government not to appeal or try too hard to look for witnesses who were not forthcoming. Soe Myint had merely held his fingers out like a revolver and covered them with a handkerchief, so it could not be considered a real act of terrorism. He had only intended to draw attention to the plight of Aung San Suu Kyi who was under house arrest in Rangoon.

Subsequently, Soe Myint wrote a book called *Burma File: A Question of Democracy* in 2003*, which was released by George Fernandes. During that book-release event, Soe Myint remarked that it was probably the first occasion in history that a defence minister of a country was releasing the book of a hijacker.

We organized solidarity meets between Tibetan and Burmese democracy activists and called meetings of MPs from all parties to support their campaigns. However, eventually, counting on individuals who would consider putting themselves out to sort the Burmese or Tibetans' issues, seemed not quite enough. The new crop of Parliamentarians was largely interested in their constituencies, elections and trips as part of Parliamentary committees to various parts of the country. Trips abroad were more in the nature of junkets and no one was keen to arrange a delegation to a country like Burma. Everyone was sympathetic, but ultimately it came to be left to a couple of NGOs, a few individuals and the socialist establishments connected to George Fernandes to support the cause of these refugees from Burma.

Burma, at the time we were there, was in an economic slump with continuing insurgencies among various ethnic minorities. We hardly ever

*Soe Myint, *Burma File: A Question of Democracy*, India Research Press, 2003.

left the confines of Rangoon to explore the country as we had done in Japan because it was simply too dangerous. Once, we were invited by U Myint Thein, the Chief Justice of Burma, and his wife, to spend a weekend at their home in the hill station of Kalaw. The government insisted we had to be accompanied by an escort of uniformed army men in open jeeps facing in all directions with weapons that were frightening to look at. As the vehicles crawled up the mountain roads, tense and alert, imagining insurgents to be all around, it hardly seemed like a pleasant holiday. It is not surprising that I remember nothing else of that short period away from Rangoon except for the pine trees that surrounded the wooden cottage we stayed in.

Mrs Myint Thein, a dignified woman, became a very close friend of my mother's. Later, when she suffered a degenerative muscular disease, my mother arranged for her to be treated with ayurvedic massages at our other family house in Trichur. While we stayed with her throughout the period of her treatment, Valiamma and the usually ill-behaved but saintly Valiachan, put their best feet forward to take care of her. Valiachan, of course, engaged her in highly intellectual discussions in English to demonstrate his superiority over the others who also happened to be around.

U Nu was very affectionate with my parents and always spoke to me kindly when we happened to meet, usually on Republic Day celebrations. My father worked closely with U Nu and Jawaharlal Nehru to prepare for the Bandung Conference of 1955. The importance of that conference seeped into my subconscious even at that age as the spirit of Asian-African nationalism was becoming a topic of active interest that my father discussed with my mother and to which I listened quietly. The sponsoring nations in the conference were India, Pakistan, Burma, Indonesia and Sri Lanka. Its grand finale saw the adoption of Nehru's five principles of peaceful co-existence on the lines of the Panchsheel Treaty subsequently signed between India and China. All 29 countries that participated in the Conference, lent their voice to the joint declaration to fight colonialism in all its forms which was supported by a moderate-sounding Chou En-Lai, the Chinese Premiere. U Nu went to Imphal in 1953, and in October 1954, Nehru visited Rangoon on his way to China. Much effort and preparation went into the historic Bandung Conference that remained in my memory, but the success of the Conference soon dissipated. Within a decade, China had forgotten all about cooperation, and marched into India in 1962.

Another vivid memory of mine helps recall the visit of Vijayalakshmi

Pandit in Burma. That she was a keen shopper wherever she would travel to, was well known. Hence my mother was expected to take her shopping, and of course, everyone who went to Burma had to acquire the 'pigeon-blood' rubies for which it was famous. They found a jeweller who made the most exquisite ruby bangles, some with rubies graded in size but all as large as pomegranate seeds, and others with tiny dark red rubies cut into squares the size of large grains of sugar. Sure enough, a pair of bangles worth nine thousand rupees were bought. The price of the bangles was certainly far more than my father's salary for the month. Nevertheless, Vijayalakshmi Pandit left Rangoon without paying the bill. My father paid for it eventually. My mother grumbled about this while my father, typically, chuckled quietly, and let the subject rest. As for me, I was getting acquainted, in a very nuanced manner, to the misuse of status by people in power but I was too young to come to any firm conclusions at that time.

Every week, my father would take me with him to a bookshop on Phayre Street near the Schwedagon Pagoda where we would pick up the latest magazines and buy a couple of books. My father loved books and liked nothing better than spending time browsing in bookshops, and reading. Books became a necessary part of my lifelong intellectual nourishment apart from being the only constant companion to a child who did not have siblings. There has not been a day that I have not been engrossed in a book at hand. The characters and places I inhabit when lost within the pages of a book provide me with a sense of comfort and security. The feel of paper while reading has always held a special fascination since an incident where a French school book got wet and its smooth shiny pages became wavy. As I read it, I remember being absorbed in running my fingers back and forth unconsciously across the bumps on the top of the pages in utter fascination. Over the years, the texture of paper, the unmistakable aroma of a newly printed book, the gentle rustle of a page turning in the silence of the night apart from the wonderful other worlds and people within the stories themselves, have continued to come together to stimulate my senses. The exercise of reading for me is not just one of absorbing information or being told a story, it is an all-embracing experience, which changes the extent of my knowledge and understanding of the world just that little bit. This feeling re-visits me every time I pause for thought after having finished the last line of the last page and come to rest at 'The End'.

In Rangoon, it was Enid Blyton's 'Famous Five' and Agatha Christie's Hercule Poirot that held my attention. We were at an age when countless hours were spent with friends admiringly gazing at double-page colour spreads of American swimmer Esther Williams's legs, actress Betty Grable's blonde curls, and actor Tony Curtis's dark eyes in movie magazines imported from the USA. We avidly collected all the small posters and publicity flyers that were distributed those days at the cinema halls. They were usually two-colour printing jobs, with all the details of the movies and photos of the stars. Magenta-hued stars acting in the *Thief of Baghdad* or *The Count of Monte Cristo*, Farley Granger's pouting lips in emerald green, and occasionally, if we were lucky, we would even come across a four-colour folder announcing the arrival of movies starring Piper Laurie or Janet Leigh. I had nearly a hundred of these wonderful papers, collected, hoarded, exchanged and gloated-over lovingly for two years. They do not seem to have surfaced anywhere else in collections of movie memorabilia and would probably be worth a fortune now in the hands of those who auction such stuff.

When we were packing to leave Rangoon for Brussels in 1954, I insisted that all these movie posters, my voluminous scrapbooks full of photos of my favourite movie stars, and boxes containing a vast collection of sheets of decorative silver paper—a fad of the early fifties among schoolgirls in Rangoon—be packed carefully and sent to Belgium. I kept following my mother around the house as she supervised the packing, reminding her to pack my bulky collection of valuables. She kept saying 'yes, yes' in an irritated and absent-minded way, but I did not find them in the trunks that we unpacked in Brussels. I felt terribly cheated, and remained furious with her for a long time for having been so callously disregarding of my treasures. However, I forgave and forgot when, following a full two years from the time of this incident, I lost my father at the age of thirteen. Suddenly, I had to grow up.

6

BELGIUM AND ENGLAND

Lessons in Loss

My father went ahead to Brussels as India's Ambassador in 1954 accompanied by our Lhasa terrier, Trixie, while my mother and I followed later. We went by sea from Colombo to London after staying for a few days with Sir John Kotlawala, the Prime Minister of Ceylon, at his residence in Temple Trees. My father complained, partly in amusement, that Trixie had to go to office with him every day as she refused to stay at the Embassy residence among unfamiliar people. She had wet the carpet and chewed up some pencils, horrifying the office staff who had 'never seen this kind of diplomat before'.

The Indian Embassy residence in Brussels was a beautiful rented house set amidst a dense forest between Brussels and Waterloo where the famed battle of Waterloo was fought. The battle sight was a fascinating stop for tourists who got to see a vast panorama of the battle in a big exhibition hall. Our house had a thick thatched roof, tall windows in every room that allowed a view of the tall pines, a huge sloping garden with a tennis court at the bottom end and so many rooms that our small family of three could spread ourselves across five of them for various activities during the day. I preferred to read, write, draw or dream while sitting on the main carpeted staircase, usually getting into the way of all those who went up and down. We had an Italian couple, Marco and Maria, as concierge and cook, with Balan and Meenakshi from Kerala to cook the Indian dishes and look after my mother's daily needs. The old Kerala habit of aristocracy needing a personal maid was still a part of my mother's psyche at that time. My father fell so in love with the house that he negotiated an excellent deal with the elegant landlady and bought the property on behalf of the Government of India, which still owns it. The landlady sent me chocolates in a huge box with a deep red velvet cover and gold baubles and ribbons in celebration. Today that box contains old photographs, including one of my father, playing golf with King Baudouin of Belgium.

Brussels was dominantly under the influence of the French-speaking population, with the Flemish comprising the working class. The former were sophisticated, slim, well turned out, occupying important positions in government, while the latter were bucolic, and seldom seen in the company of those who belonged to the upper classes. The European Commission was an idea that had taken root as the coal and steel amalgam of Europe, but Brussels was still a mere cultural adjunct of France.

I was enrolled in the Convent of the Sacred Heart there, which was a forty-five-minute drive from our house. My first term at school coincided with the onset of winter. I had to wake up at six and be ready to leave for school by seven in the morning, when it was still dark, to reach before eight when classes began. I was driven back by the chauffeur when school finished at four when it was already getting to be dark again. By the time I reached home it was like night-time. I never got to see my home in daylight until the weekend.

At school, all lessons were in French. Since I wasn't good enough at it, many special classes during the day went in learning French so that I could catch up with the others in class. It was terribly dreary, as in the classes meant for the local students I could not understand what was being taught. Our uniforms were white shirts with stiff detachable collars, navy-blue pleated skirts, and a navy-blue and green plaid pinafore over these. We had to bow and curtsy to all the nuns we passed by in the corridors. Lunch was served in a vast high-ceilinged hall with long wooden tables. The hall was very stark and grim. The drink served to all the students along with lunch was pale brown and bitter tasting, with froth on the top. '*Qu'est-ce que c'est* (what is it)?' I asked. '*La bière*' (beer), was the cheerful answer. My parents did not know whether to be shocked or amused that this prim convent served beer, albeit a mild one, to the students for lunch. It added to the reasons why they decided to send me to a boarding school in England.

~

On a map, if you connected London, Ashford in Kent, and Canterbury, where the great cathedral and the Archbishop were, it would form a neat triangle. Ashford had the famed Ashford School for Girls, and this was where I was deposited, with my grey felt hat, red- and grey-striped tie, pinafores, long grey socks, warm and cold underwear, alongside everything I possessed, including my toothbrush, with labels containing my name attached to each of the things I brought with me. The principal, Miss Brake, was popularly called Cherub, and looked like one, but apart from her, there were no soft contours to boarding school life in the Great Britain. Life was regimented beyond imagination. From the home of a diplomat, with every luxury available to me and the warmth of my parents' presence, I entered a grim world of lights out at nine; baths permitted to each student only twice a week, with the tubs allowed to be filled only quarter of the way; and stiff, rough, toilet paper in the loo with no water tap or mug for our Indian ways.

On Sunday afternoons, we had to go for 10 mile walks even if it meant walking through deep snow. My feet froze with ice around them and I developed huge chilblains. During one long walk, one of my tiny diamond earrings fell into the snow. It caused a big commotion among the teachers since I had needed special permission to wear them in the first place. They even asked if a search party should be mounted for it. Imagine looking for a tiny diamond in the sparkling white snow! I wanted to close the subject and forget I ever wore earrings.

Common Place was an excellent system followed at Ashford which required each student to read at least twenty-one books each term and write a synopsis of each of them with critical comments. They could be novels, travelogues or biographies. For those who loved to read, it gave the discipline of intelligent appraisement. I never ceased to thank Common Place for giving me the facility to review a book for newspapers or magazines. When I came back to Delhi in 1977, editors of national newspapers slowly discovered that I could write.

At Ashford, apart from studying, we had to scrub bathtubs, clean toilets, wash dishes and dry them, lay the tables for dinner, and run many errands for the senior girls. Even when I had chicken pox and was lying in the sanatorium along with others who caught the epidemic spreading in school, we had to get out of bed and sweep and mop the floors before the fever subsided and the scabs fell off. Other than being visited by a hugely built, loud-voiced male doctor who loomed over us, peering over his spectacles and asking, 'Are you feeling bettah?', we were pretty much left to mend ourselves without any fuss.

My mother fretted while my father grumbled at her for having decided to send me away to a place that sounded like a Siberian work camp.

However, they reassured themselves that I was fine by telephoning me every Friday night. This was highly embarrassing for me as no other parent ever telephoned their children and some girls sniggered about the special treatment I received. But it was 1954. British life was dull and staid, without the cosmopolitan sensibilities it acquired later. While the effects of being a colonial power had not fully worn off, the country had yet to recover from the damages of the Second World War. Even in a school like Ashford, most families were not from an aristocratic stock, and came instead from small towns and families with modest means. Many girls asked me why the palms of my hands were pink when the upper portions were brown. I had no answer and felt miserable about being different.

During the Easter holidays, I took two friends home to Brussels. The huge embassy house, the Cadillac car and four servants made them envious and unpleasant although generally they were sweet girls. They insisted on washing the masala off the chicken pieces in the curry under the tap before eating them, and upon our return, spread rumours in school that my father sat in office with his feet up on the office table. I felt hurt and betrayed although I never discussed it with them.

In my second year, a witty, defiant and brilliant girl from British Guiana (Guyana) joined my class and we became close friends overnight, cursing white ways under our breath and vowing we would never marry English men. We both did exceedingly well in our studies and I was happy that apart from getting good marks in all our subjects we could spice up our conversations with 'shoot, man!', 'bloody limeys' and odd bits of West Indian talk and accents. Many years later, the girl, Patty Ann, sheepishly confessed in a rare letter that she had married an Englishman, John Lloyd, after all.

∽

On vacation, my parents welcomed me home with a hired television to watch the wedding of Grace Kelly, the American actress, to Prince Rainier of Monaco. Television opened up a magic world, but most times our ears were glued to 'Mrs Dale's Diary', a radio version of the soap serials on television today. On weekends, my parents would often go to Luxembourg to attend official receptions since my father was the accredited envoy to this charming little country as well. Its cobbled streets and old town houses were charming facets of the typical European landscape. I entertained myself with sightseeing, listening to music in record shops and eating chocolates, while my parents went about their social duties.

I remember one occasion though when my mother decided to sulk about something and caused my father both irritation and distress. In a way, my mother was quite childish. She wanted to be fussed over and cared for like she would have been in Kollengode, and if my father did not do it just right, she would not forgive him for days. As a twelve-year-old, this annoyed and troubled me greatly as I somehow always found myself sympathizing with my father and wondering why my mother wasn't satisfied with things as they were. She let him choose the books she read and the clothes she wore for evening parties, but I began to notice that she never really cared to keep him company, or express pleasure when he came home from office. She grumbled to me about his keeping company with his office staff. This was particularly the case with a cheerful, gentle, warm-hearted young woman named Sophie de Croy, who was a social secretary in the Indian Embassy despite coming from a highly aristocratic family. I loved being with her as well. She took me to her family castle to meet her little cousins, to bookshops and ice-skating shows. Sometimes my father would also come along, but increasingly, my mother grew more sullen and cheerless. She would even refuse to join my father and me for a walk in the garden where he would tell me the names of all the flowers and share with me his deep love of gardening. There was nothing between Sophie and my father, but my mother chose to make it a subject of contention, seeking the attention she was actually simultaneously rejecting. Meanwhile, it was almost a relief that the Easter holidays were ending.

Mid-April, in 1956, my father decided to take me to Paris for a week before I went back to Ashford. My mother stayed behind. We drove to the Ritz Hotel where bookings had been made. The Indian Ambassador and his daughter were received with bows and flourishes and led to an opulent room. We enjoyed the style of it all until the omelette at breakfast came with a tag that worked out to sixty Indian rupees. It was like a six-hundred-rupee omelette today. We made an effort to behave like suave aristocrats but deciding to share the omelette and eat the rest of our meals in cheaper restaurants in the city. We had to express our dismay, suppress our laughter and make alternate plans in Malayalam so that the waiters would not understand.

On 26 April, my father decided to come to drop me back at school.

He was to retire at the end of April at the age of 55 but had been given an extension by the Government of India and was to be posted to Venezuela as Ambassador for India in July. The thought of going to South America was terribly exciting. It was to be my last term at school where the only thing that was going to be sad was leaving my friends, especially Patty Ann from 'BG'. I proudly showed off my father to my school friends and teachers and took him to see my classrooms, dormitory, friends and playing fields, to which I had finally become quite attached and familiar. My parents had also discontinued telephoning every weekend as I was now well settled and confident.

My father returned to Brussels on Saturday, 28 April 1956, and went out on Sunday morning, the 29th, to play golf. At noon, I received a message to go to the principal's office. She told me my grand-uncle who lived in Croydon was coming to fetch me as I had to go back to Brussels. At the London airport, he said I should be brave. About what, I wondered.

At the airport at Brussels, Sophie met me and told me that my father had had a heart attack while playing golf, and had died instantly. He had not suffered. My mind went blank. The only thing that engaged it on the long drive to the Embassy residence was that all the traffic lights along the way were green.

~

My fourteenth birthday was just six weeks away, but I grew to be an adult overnight.

The Embassy shutters were down, the drawing room was full of Indian ladies sitting around my mother, bedraggled and wailing. The atmosphere was horrible. The dining room had been converted into a European funeral parlour with black drapes and white flowers, and my father was laid out on his usual bed, as if peacefully asleep. He was embalmed and scheduled to lie in this state until the cremation on Thursday. I stared at all who faced me in silence. Then I asked my mother to go upstairs, wash herself, change her clothes, comb her hair and lie down. I asked for a doctor to give her a sedative, and requested the visitors to leave her to rest for a while. In the days that followed, I met every dignitary who came to pay his respects, saw to the kitchen arrangements, and attended the cremation while my mother stayed home, screaming from the window. The guilt of having harboured so many petty antagonisms against my father, and of having been the one to separate him from his beloved daughter, by deciding to send me to boarding school, must have compounded her agony. She never really let go of that guilt completely, and I never could discard my grouse against her for making his last days unhappy.

The sight of my father's body gliding on smooth tracks into the furnace finally made me start shaking. Sophie led me out towards the car. After a while, when I turned to look back and saw smoke coming out from the tall chimney of the crematorium, and realized that that was all that was left of him, I broke down and cried like the child I too had left behind.

7

DELHI AGAIN

But a Different Life

AFTER MY FATHER'S DEMISE, WE had to leave Brussels and return to India. I had packed the entire house while my mother grieved at each object that brought my father's loss back as an intractable fact. The trunks were in a storehouse somewhere, and our Cadillac sold at a loss by my mother's brother who had no head for business. We boarded the SS Himalaya for Delhi in late July 1956. This was one of the last ships to pass through the Suez Canal which was closed soon after. The closing of the Suez Canal was a short-lived but highly significant event in which Egypt, to retaliate against the attack on it by Israel, UK and France, closed the port to any traffic and thereby trade by these countries. This affected consumption patterns in these countries heavily, especially in France and Britain where supplies of milk and tea stopped. Everything had to go around the southern cape of Africa, causing the prices of petrol and other commodities to shoot up. As I learned to adjust to a huge change in the pattern of my life, these countries suffered huge losses too. A coming together of events linked it all together. It was the last of my cossetted and fairly luxurious life just as it was the last of these important journeys along the Suez.

Khushwant Singh's family was on the same steamer, and Rahul, his son, and I were a part of a group of young teenagers who spent most of the time swimming and running along the decks and innards of the vast steamship, irritating the more staid passengers who wanted to lie back on their deck chairs and doze off. It seemed to us as if everyone on the ship was over seventy.

In Delhi, we came to live with my mother's first cousin Gouri Bhadran, whose husband was in the Indian Forest Service and posted in the Ministry of Agriculture. Suddenly, there was no home of our own, no luxuries and no feeling of independence that a child has when living in her own home with her parents. My aunt and uncle were extraordinarily kind and loving in their own way, and it must have been hard to accommodate a widow and a child used to life abroad. The systems in the household were different and all that was my own here was my bed in a room that I shared with my mother. My mother made friends amongst the neighbours and had my aunt for solace. I had no one, and hid my sorrow in silence lest my mother became upset. I joined the Convent of Jesus and Mary and soon made friends who are as close to me now as they were at that time. The government of India gave my mother a meagre pension since my father had died 'in saddle', and allotted a bigger house to my uncle so that we could be accommodated more conveniently. So we shifted from Bapa Nagar to Humayun Road where my mother hired a piano for me to learn. I hated it. I wanted to learn Kathakali instead, but did not dare insist upon my wishes.

School became the mainstay of my life, and I was soon among the highest scorers in class tests. As young teens, we made eyes at the boys at St Columba's adjoining the girls' convent school, spent hours chatting to friends on the telephone exchanging notes on what to wear, who said what to whom, which our favourite song was on the Friday night radio programme, *A Date with You*, and cycling to Khan Market for an ice cream in the afternoon heat. My aunt's maid and cook from Kollengode and valet from Darjeeling, had not seen such activity in this childless household. They regularly reported to my aunt about the length of my telephone conversations, who, in turn, lectured me on how onerous her responsibilities were in looking after a fatherless child.

When my uncle retired, they left Delhi and the government allotted my mother one-and-a-half small rooms in the barracks of Kotah House on Shah Jehan Road, two minutes away from where we were earlier. I was desperately keen that we should have a home of our own. The houses in the nearby Golf Links cost a lakh and a half rupees at that time. It was a quiet and beautiful residential colony. However, my mother said we did not have the money to buy a house there, that my father's entire legacy was equivalent to that amount. I argued that we could rent one floor for an income and live on the other floor. She refused, saying she could not see herself in the role of a landlady. I asked why we could not have a home where there was a kitchen. She refused again and said she was not prepared to spend her time counting out the daily rations of rice, oil, salt and cooking coal. Anyhow, my mother intensely disliked cooking and had never been interested in even making a cup of tea. Thus ended my quest for an independent home of our own.

Perhaps at fourteen, I had not fully grasped the economics of our situation and no one cared to explain the details to me. I adjusted reluctantly to the reality of life in Kotah House. Khan Market was nearby and school was no farther, but now there was no servant, no kitchen and no car. I had to get used to sharing a 'single meal tray' that came from the main dining room of Kotah House. My mother ate the rice and dal while I had the rotis and vegetables. Sometimes we switched. We set dahi or yogurt on the shelf of the linen cupboard in the bathroom, and I cooked our dog Trixie's meal on a stove on the bathroom floor when I got back from school in the afternoons. Once, she tipped the entire vessel over in her excitement. There was greasy meat soup—globs of meat and bones—all over the floor. I cried bitterly as I cleaned up the whole mess, wondering why my life had to change so drastically and what I had done to deserve all this.

A year later, a maid came from Kerala. She cooked delicious sambar, rice and vegetables for us on that same tiny heater on the bathroom floor near the linen cupboard. At least we now had fresh hot meals, the dog, and we were cared for.

~

By 1957, my mother had taken up the post of Social Secretary to the American Ambassador, Ellsworth Bunker, as a means of getting her mind off the tragedy of my father's death. This is the first time in her life that she had ever worked in an office for a salary. We both adjusted to our new circumstances in our own ways: my mother tearfully but courageously, and I, silently. Occasionally, I shed a few tears too on my pillow at night when my mother was asleep. I wondered how life had taken me so suddenly from elegant mansions and vast manicured lawns with tennis courts, to a single room where, to escape from the summer heat, I had to set a block of ice in a vessel and place it between me and a table fan. In the early days of my life I never experienced the presence of an air-cooler; an air conditioner entered my home only when my son presented me with one forty-three years later.

Nevertheless, despite what could be perceived as a comparatively impoverished way of living, life at Kotah House was fun. Shankar Roy and his younger brother Bunker, who later became a pioneer of professionalized non-government development work, and I, became close friends. They went to Doon School in Dehradun, but in the holidays we raced around Kotah House on our bicycles, haunted Khan Market and saw movies together. As boarding school approached, they would leave their extra pocket money with me like they would in a bank, with dire threats of retribution if I dared to mention this to their mother. Sanjeev Mukherjee, son of Air Marshall Subroto Mukherjee, was another friend. His father died choking on a piece of meat during an official visit to Japan. The dread of revisiting a scene of a father lying lifeless paralysed me. I could not get myself to visit Sanjeev and his mother till many days later.

~

In 1958, I passed my Senior Cambridge examinations with a first division and high marks in English Language and Literature. Most of us chose to join Miranda House at Delhi University, and divided ourselves between English, History and Philosophy Honours. With good grades, upper middle-class backgrounds and fluency in English, we soon became the 'power bunch' among the first-year students. Anjoli Ela Dev, later famous contemporary artist, Lalita Katari, daughter of the Chief of Navy Staff, Barota Dey, daughter of S.K. Dey, the Minister for Rural Development, were the seniors we emulated and befriended. They looked askance, rather arrogantly, at the 'pass course types', who followed a simpler and more generalized syllabus requiring lower marks for admission. These students could barely speak English.

In college, a part-personality-part-beauty contest faced first-year students; these were pre-feminist days. We had to walk on to stage where a desk with four or five judges from among the seniors sat to ask each of us freshers some questions. Then we were asked to turn around slowly just once, for the audience of students to examine our dress and posture, join our hands in a namaste greeting the audience, and walk off. The decibel of applause indicated the level of approval. The exercise was quite timid; neither sexy nor glamorous in any way, and everyone revealed a sense of shyness rather than any kind of competitive spirit or vanity. I was astounded when they announced that I had been chosen Miss Miranda 1958. Soon after though, I was brought happily to ground in the excitement that followed when someone asked me to demonstrate whether I had nice feet to match my face.

While in college, I was one of the few who cared to read the newspapers set out in the reading room. Perhaps my education abroad contributed to this interest in the world outside the confines of our college. We were all young then, and were expected to just do well in our studies and not think too far into our future in the world we were being prepared for. My work in class was of a high standard, thanks to the time I spent at Ashford School for Girls. English, in all its nuances, came easily and naturally to me. With a deeply ingrained love for books and writing, studies were a breeze at Miranda House, considered the most progressive women's college in Delhi at the time.

8

SMITH COLLEGE, USA

Savouring Literature and Freedom

It so happened that Ambassador Ellsworth Bunker's sister and brother-in-law, Katherine and John Parsons, came to visit India. My mother was keen to take them all on a visit to her beloved home, the palace in Kollengode. With the help of her cousins, a ceremonial reception with caparisoned elephants and attending fanfare was organized for them. My mother was proud to show off her background and they got a taste of India they could not have had as easily. On their return to Delhi, they invited me for tea, and casually asked if I would like to study in the United States of America. Equally casually I answered in the affirmative. The Parsons set the ball rolling on their return home.

Bunker, and John Kenneth Galbraith, the succeeding US Ambassador to India, actively encouraged by their wives, oriented me for an education there. I was to apply for a full scholarship to either Smith or Vassar Colleges. I had to fill in a fairly simple form of which the important part was an essay on why I wanted to study in the USA. There were no formidable application processes with complicated acronyms in the late fifties. Eventually, I was transported to one of the most eminent women's higher educational institutions in that country. Amidst a world largely dominated by men, what Smith College in Northampton (Massachusetts) fostered was, as they put it in their own brochure: 'an uncompromising defense of academic and intellectual freedom, an attention to the relation between college education and the larger public issues of world order and human dignity, and a concern for the rights and privileges of women.' These were principles I was to later imbibe.

I would like to believe that my education at Smith, although not for the full four undergraduate years, played a major role in my personal and public attitudes, and actions throughout my life—far more than any other educational institution I have attended. Even the writing of this book, highly modest and miniscule in comparison, draws from the qualities that an institution like Smith College helped develop. It gave the world great authors like Sylvia Plath (*The Bell Jar*), Betty Friedan (*The Feminine Mystique*), Gloria Steinem (*My Life on the Road*), Julia Child (*Mastering the Art of French Cooking*) and Margaret Mitchell (*Gone with the Wind*). Other ladies who are 'firsts' in other ways, are first ladies Barbara Bush (wife of George H.W. Bush) and Nancy Reagan (wife of Ronald Reagan), both of whom stood out as symbols of poise and independence. Today, there are heads of financial institutions, neuroscientists, CEOs of major corporations and other pathbreakers who have added to the illustrious list of the Smith alumnae. Published in 2010, *Orange is the New Black*, a bestseller based on which a television series came to be produced, was written by Piper Kerman, a Smith alumnae who went to jail on drug charges and wrote brilliantly about those experiences. I thought, in a few moments of dark humour, that I may now be another Smith alumnae who is under trial for charges related to conspiracy and corruption and might just follow in her footsteps. That would make this memoir quite a sensation.

Interestingly, Smith has steadfastly insisted on remaining a solely women's institution, priding itself on reserving a preciously guarded space for women to develop freely and exclusively without having to compete in the intellectual field with louder, more aggressive, attention-getting members of the opposite sex. It was an oasis during the period between mixed high schools and the larger, often patriarchal, world. It worked just fine.

In my first few weeks at the college, I got quite a culture shock. I had to shed my shyness and bathe completely nude in a common shower room often with five other girls. No coy sari-wrapping as women did in public bathing places in India. Most girls smoked in those days, and felt unpopular if they didn't have a date on a Saturday night when they got out of their shabby blue jeans and dressed up. Girls needed one night a week to express their femininity, I guess. I would gather slots of evening duty at the reception for those who went out but once got chased by a boy around the room with a pair of scissors as he had decided to amuse himself by threatening to cut my long plait off while waiting for his date to come down the stairs. Very long hair, a funny English accent and brown skin were exotica in those days. I was also pursued by our Gillette House 'housemother', Ms Stillwagon, who was what was then called an Evangelical Christian; now, she would be called a 'Born Again' Christian. For her, my being a Hindu was the same as being a heathen who needed to be shown the light. She would often slip letters under my dorm door asking me to embrace Jesus Christ to be on the right path if I wanted to be saved from the burning fires of hell. Hugely amused, my friends and I joked about my plight, but I also studiously avoided Ms Stillwagon as far as I could while living under the same roof.

Students travelled and lived freely with their boyfriends, and Barbara Dodd, who was president of the Smith Alumnae of our class of '63, was a talented modern dancer who spent her summer holidays dancing at a famous nightclub in New York. Students married their professors and had babies during their student years but work pressure was the opposite to what students faced in Indian colleges where we only got serious about studies just before the examinations. We had to learn to type, and often submit five or six originally researched papers every week no matter what other engagements we were involved in. Some did wilt under the pressure. I had to uphold my own self-respect so I worked hard, with a very modest $200 per term as pocket money from Ellsworth Bunker's sister and husband who were my local guardians. I couldn't afford to eat out or buy anything extraneous to basic necessities but it was enriching to use one's mind creatively. I was selected to be Gold Key guide by the administration. These Gold Key wearers had to guide prospective parents around the college and were supposed to be an example of how good, well-spoken, diverse and presentable Smithies were. As the only Indian girl among two thousand students, I was expected to be an Ambassador for India as well. It was a huge honour which made me mighty thrilled. My friends would all tease me saying, 'June Jayalakshmi, how will our poor American parents understand your accent?'

Summer holidays were spent in Washington DC, as a family guest of India's Ambassador to the US, B.K. Nehru (Uncle Biju and Aunty Fori to me, as they were good friends of my parents). Jawaharlal Nehru was still alive at the time. Indira Gandhi, his daughter, and B.K. Nehru's cousin stayed there when visiting the US. I was the nineteen-year-old fly on the wall during breakfast when we all sat at the dining table in our dressing gowns. Indira Gandhi shared concerns and confidences about her sons, Rajiv and Sanjay. Although she had no complaints about Rajiv, she was troubled by Sanjay who had gotten into removing hubcaps from cars* in the company of his unruly bunch of friends. He was not interested in his studies at Doon School, and refused to listen to her, she complained.

It was at Smith that my sense of public activism first blossomed. The Chinese had attacked India in 1962. We were at war back home, and our soldiers were getting killed. Without any prompting from anyone, I decided to collect money for the Jawan's Welfare Fund or whatever it was called in those days. I wrote to the Indian Embassy asking to be sent a full-length Indian feature film—Satyajit Ray's *Devi*. In the meanwhile, I designed a poster and printed copies of it myself after learning screen printing at the college arts activity studio. They were put up all over college. I booked the large Sage Hall there, and screened *Devi* at a dollar a ticket following which I cooked an Indian meal to thank my friends who had helped with the arrangements. I had not been taught cooking but I managed a chicken curry, rice, spiced potatoes and even *jalebi*s taken out of a recipe book. I made the yeast-infused batter rise overnight in a bowl on my window sill for the crisp, tasty sweet, served later with ice cream. Everyone enjoyed it, and I realized that contrary to my mother's dislike towards cooking, I had taught myself how to cook.

I collected a thousand and seven hundred dollars which I proudly sent to the Embassy in Washington DC to be forwarded to the Indian government. I also collected a free body massage from my dorm mate Wendy Cutter, for working so hard to make the event possible.

∽

Smith College developed a sense of independence so strong in me that I did not want to return to India directly after graduation. Firstly, I had no real home to go to, and I dreaded settling back with my mother and other relatives, without the freedom to do as I wished. The idea of renting a small apartment of my own in Delhi and living independently, as many single girls can do these days, was unthinkable in the early sixties. I knew I wanted to get married to Ashok Jaitly who had been my friend from Delhi University days, but did not want to be unschooled in running a home of my own before that. So, I shot off a spate of letters for a summer job in

---

*This incident also finds mention in Coomi Kapoor's *The Emergency: A Personal History*, New Delhi: Penguin, 2016.

New York with many well-known magazines so that I could share an apartment with a friend and live without being supervised by a nervous mother or strict aunts. No magazine bothered to reply, so I set my sight on a gap year in London since Cambridge, where Ashok was studying, was close. My mother agreed to that since she was confident that Ashok was a 'good and responsible' boy who would not let me come to any harm, and who was in any case, going to marry me. After some effort and with my mother's family contacts in Air India, in July 1963, I got a job as a filing clerk in the Air India city office in the swanky New Bond Street in London.

I had illusions of becoming a stylish receptionist on the ground floor but my smart talk and literature degree from Smith College did not help. There was simply no vacancy. I was relegated to a tiny back room with a Sindhi and Gujarati woman for company as the junior staff member. We spent our days opening or dispatching letters, noting reference numbers in a register and filing away letters and documents. It was utterly boring with no intellectual conversation at all, but I earned nine pounds a week which paid for half my rent, meagre food and transport on the underground rail network. Subsistence level, but exciting and challenging.

I shared a flat in Bramham Gardens near the Earl's Court Road tube station with my old school and college friend Nanu (Pratima Bhatia Mitchell), veteran journalist Prem Bhatia's daughter. We remain close friends till today. Our building was dingy with a scary landlord named Mr Buckle, who was built in the dimensions of a large refrigerator. He had large, bulging eyes and wore the same brown tweed coat every day for the whole year. He had a looming sort of personality that intimidated us whenever he came to ask for the rent. He had installed lights that were programmed to switch off periodically in the corridors to save electricity. If they went off when he was with us, we were plunged into darkness, frozen mid-sentence, but with his booming voice he would always try to reassure us by shouting, 'You have nothing to fear!' Mr Buckle always reminded us of a character that should be in a scary story for children.

It was difficult in those days for Indians to find accommodation. The British thought we would make the place stink by cooking curry. The Indian 'take-outs' did not catch on till a couple of decades later. In that respect, our eerie landlord seemed kind and unconcerned about the personal lives or preoccupations of his tenants. Our upstairs neighbour was a tall, gorgeous blonde, who struggled bringing up a dark-skinned equally gorgeous baby boy with no sign of a husband. The gossip in the building was that the baby was illegitimate and belonged to someone from Pakistan's Bhutto family.

Both Nanu and I could only afford cornflakes and black coffee for breakfast. I bought a small carton of yogurt and a banana for lunch, and we cooked rice and a chicken or dal for dinner. It was a frugal but free life that taught me that I could manage my own establishment without any huge mishap except that work, exhaustion and too little of nourishing food made me faint flat out a couple of times. However, we were quite nonchalant about such things. On weekends, I travelled by train to Cambridge where Ashok and I would spend the weekend walking, eating out and going to the movies with friends like Kamlesh Sharma, Mani Shankar Aiyar and Dalip Mehta who all later joined the foreign service. I spent the nights on a mattress on the floor of Gita Patnaik's (Biju Patnaik's daughter, who became the famous author Gita Mehta, later to marry the publisher Sonny Mehta) single-room 'dig' at Cambridge.

Rajiv Gandhi was at Cambridge at the same time as Ashok. We moved in separate circles but met during our visits to cheap Greek restaurants or during informal social occasions. Rajiv Gandhi began courting Sonia Gandhi as we watched. She was then a shy au pair lodged with a local family to earn her stay and learn English at a local language school. She barely spoke to anyone. We used to joke among ourselves that since the female students speaking European languages were far more attractive than the University-going English ones who were largely studious and intellectual, some of our boys from India preferred to socialize with the prettier ones even if there weren't to be any deep conversations between them.

Anyway, getting back to my source of livelihood—the advantage of working with Air India was getting a free ticket to travel back to India after completing a year of work. We would not have had the money otherwise. I also got two free trips on an inter-airline transfer agreement to visit Brussels where I had a nostalgic reunion with all the places and people I had known when my father was still alive. I also managed an exciting trip to Israel after having read *The Diary of Anne Frank* earlier and wondering what creating one's own country would be like. It was incredible to see the fervour and energy of the people who, having experienced the horrors of Nazi Germany, were deeply dedicated to turning a barren desert into green and fertile land. I wished our Indians would work for their country with such commitment.

In Israel, our guided tours involved visiting a kibbutz, going to the Gulf of Eilat and discovering the streets and sights of Tel Aviv, Haifa and various sacred places. There was a British member among the Air India staff with me in the group of people from different countries of which I was the youngest at twenty-one. At one tourist site, towards the end of our trip, our elderly, wrinkly and red-faced Israeli guide, nearly three times my age at least, suddenly said to me that he was deeply in love with me and wanted to marry me. I hadn't bargained for this kind of situation on the side. All my co-tourists thought it was a joke. It may have been a great subject of fun but I had no idea about how to deal with this ardent but strangely respectful old man who kept trying to convince me that he was very serious. As we flew way above Tel Aviv, I wondered whether he did this to every young female tourist just to add a little spice to his life. It was surely a good story to tell when I returned to London, but nonetheless, quite embarrassing.

In those days many countries had not established diplomatic relations with Israel, or, like some Arab countries, were hostile to them. We had to have special passports made for the Israel trip so that it was not reflected on our existing passports and dispose of these upon return. Consequently, I have no proof now that I ever went to Israel.

~

During our year in London, John F. Kennedy was assassinated. And in 1964, Jawaharlal Nehru passed away. These were momentous events around the world, and momentous, even for us. As Indian students and young workers, we gathered outside the US Embassy, standing in line for hours, to sign the condolence book. We did the same at the Indian High Commission. After Welles Hangen's book titled *After Nehru Who?* which implied he was irreplaceable, it was a pleasant surprise to see a quiet, self-effacing Lal Bahadur Shastri take over as the Indian prime minister and I was even happier to see India managing the transition in a mature and dignified manner.

Ashok sat for his Civil Services exam from the London Centre for overseas applicants while staying at my cousin's home. We travelled back to India when his exams were over, and my stint at Air India ended, with me flying on my free ticket. We journeyed in a leisurely manner through

Paris, Rome and Beirut, seeing all the famous historical sites, eating bread and cheese on park benches, with money enough only for one good meal a day. In Paris, I remembered my Smith College professor's exquisite choice of words and gestures in explaining Marcel Proust's writings. In Rome, in the midst of sightseeing, when the afternoons were too hot to venture out, I buried myself deep in finishing *The Alexandria Quartet*, a set of three books with a fourth some years later by Lawrence Durrell, which I had begun to read while travelling on the train back and forth on weekends to Cambridge. Anyone interested in an intense, deeply philosophical and almost mystical story of the same event through different perspectives, seen through a set of four characters (which also form of the titles of the four novels), Justine, Balthazar, Mountolive and Clea, should not go through life without reading these remarkable literary works. I remember the effect those books had on me as I read them, more than I recall the low-budget romance on our journey back home.

Back in India in 1965, Ashok and I were met by our loving families who set about planning our engagement and wedding right away. I chose to design my own simple wedding card, refused to indulge in a trousseau, instead getting blouses stitched for all the saris I had with me already. My aunts collectively made a new red ruby necklace for me in a typical ancient Kerala design; I wore my grandmother's gold *odyanam* around my waist, a new gold-edged, Malayali, two-piece *mundu-veshti* for all small pre-wedding ceremonies, and a decade-old Banarasi tissue sari that belonged to my mother. We took my friends from Smith College who had come all the way to attend our wedding in Bombay along with us on a small tour of the Taj Mahal and other spots after the wedding. So, on this supposed honeymoon, the bride and groom ended up as tourist guides for their foreign friends.

Ashok had hoped to get enough marks to join the Foreign Service like his friends. However, we ended up, most unexpectedly, in the state of Jammu & Kashmir to find ourselves face-to-face with an extraordinarily different life.

9

'MY' STATE OF KASHMIR
Through War, Darkness and Light

THE STATE OF KASHMIR IS a conglomeration of histories and theories. Every person with an experience of any kind there, claims to have the last word on it. Add to this the 'opinions' of historians; political analysts; media personalities, who have become self-styled experts; interlocutors who became pompous about their intellects; and local writers, who have nursed sorrow, anger and angst. Then you also have the majority of ordinary citizens, who are gentle, scared, peace-loving, and hate the violent noise. They remain silent, being subjected to high- and low-intensity wars, and sandwiched between militant guns and the ever-present security forces. Ever since the three regions of Jammu, Kashmir and Ladakh became one political entity and acceded legally and legitimately to the sovereign Indian nation, the citizens of the valley and those living in areas bordering Pakistan, have had nothing but recurring cycles of peace and violence.

As the wife of a young Indian Administrative Service (IAS) officer, allotted Jammu & Kashmir (J&K) as his state cadre, I had my share of witnessing the wars, border areas, curfews, blackouts and democratic and undemocratic elections in the state. In between, I spent long hours among artisans; those were idyllic times. However, it was quite a contrast to life in London, New York and Massachusetts amidst progressive and peaceful times. Drawing from five decades of my own relationship with all regions of the state allows me to define 'my own state of Kashmir'.

My husband did not choose to be in the J&K cadre. IAS probationers are offered preferences. His were Maharashtra and Uttar Pradesh. No one knew that J&K was an option. There were only two officers who had gone there from the central administrative services before him. Someone in Delhi thought he was enlightened, well-educated and bold, and therefore well suited to J&K, a state that needed to be handled sensitively. We also heard that a UP Brahmin marrying a South Indian had something to do with being considered 'broad minded'. Having come from Cambridge, UK, and Smith College, USA, we thought this was quite a funny yardstick for assessment. Ghulam Mohammed Sadiq, commonly referred to as Sadiq Sahib, was the chief minister of J&K at the time. These were not the brightest of times in the political history of Kashmir where nomination papers of candidates from only one party were found to be legitimate. People often asked about India as separate from the state which seemed strange at the beginning but we started speaking that way ourselves when we realized that it was more due to geographical isolation than a feeling of political separatism. Anyway, the posting landed us and our Tibetan terrier Chinky at the *sarkari* dak bungalow in Anantnag in 1965.

∽

The annual Amarnath Yatra was due a month after we arrived in Anantnag. Multifarious arrangements had to be made for thousands of pilgrims to travel to the holy cave where the ice Shiva lingam was five feet high during the full moon of August. This task came under the civil administration of Anantnag. The District Commissioner appointed Ashok as Observer Officer but did not put him in charge. I could therefore accompany him on this five-day trip. We walked, or rode on ponies along precariously narrow mountain ledges, slept in tents in the extreme cold and passed crystal streams and quiet forests which suddenly opened up to patches of luxurious expanses of grass. For five days we were a part of a slowly moving stream of hundreds of sadhus covered in ash and flimsy loincloth, old people with sticks, men carrying *trishul*s, and young families with bottles and backpacks. Devotion seemed to carry everyone through. At rest stops, I made sketches and wrote my first article as a travelogue of the yatra which the *Statesman* published in full on the editorial page. While I was pleased no end at the proof of my fancy Smith education, I doubt if anybody in Anantnag even noticed.

While driving back to Anantnag from Pahalgam after the yatra late in the evening, the wireless in the jeep announced that 'Pakistani *huqamrans*' (infiltrators) had entered the district. The excitement of the journey ending in seeing the legendary pigeons representing Lord Shiva and his consort Parvati flying out of the Amarnath cave soon faded. We were instructed to put out our jeep headlights and keep our heads down. By the time we returned to the dak bungalow, we were in the midst of the first Indo-Pak war of 1965 with shots being fired in the vicinity. We covered window panes of the dak bungalow with newspaper. The freshly minted IAS officer now had a full-blown job on his hands. Prime Minister Lal Bahadur Shastri's calm sagacity and the *'jai jawan jai kisan'* slogan hailing soldiers and farmers, saw us through this tense time. Although the war did not last long, it was tense and dark. There were continuous reports of where the infiltrators had been spotted, on which portion of the highway shots were being fired, and where gunfire could be heard. I was confined to room in the dak bungalow, going outside only to walk the dog in the garden. It was not the time for women to be seen.

When the war ended, we went to Pampore in November to view the fields of saffron flowers in the moonlight. The fluorescent mauve aura created naturally is what people do through digital manipulation on their computer screens these days. The shimmering stillness made it hard to remember this was the scene of fierce firing between soldiers of India and Pakistan. When Shastri died in Tashkent two months later, it seemed that our part of 'India' absorbed the shock in uncomprehending silence rather than grief, as the country had hardly come to know him. The dominance of the Nehru dynasty following that, ensured the country forgot this great leader quite easily.

∽

At our Anantnag bungalow, electricity was minimal and the government staff were insular and slightly sullen. We had one room and a bathroom, with just a window sill on which to place our books and a small electric stove. The watery potato curry provided by the government cook needed to be supplemented by whatever I could cook on that narrow ledge. We could not afford non-vegetarian food with the miserable Rs 550 monthly salary of a junior IAS officer. Ashok had no car as he was only the Additional District Commissioner on probation so he went to office in a tonga. He couldn't maintain much of his dignity when once a goat took a ride under the tonga seat, and stuck its head out suddenly from between his legs. However, some of the people who had to wait outside his office for an appointment in those days were Makhan Lal Fotedar (later Indira Gandhi's powerful secretary), and the late Mufti Mohammad Sayeed, who became home minister of India in 1989, and later chief minister of J&K, twice. It was embarrassing to discover that even a very junior officer had the power to keep local politicians waiting for an appointment according to the IAS's scheme of things.

Daily life there was spent amid women in burqas, empty conversations about children or cooking, and tentative walks alone with the dog. The men had their work and badminton in the evenings. At the dak bungalow, I had to carry buckets of water from the end of the garden to our bathroom while the male staff looked on cheekily from a distance. Propriety demanded I go out in public only with women.

There were no bookshops in Anantnag. Even the occasional bus trip to Srinagar led us to a dim, poorly stocked bookstore. The low-voltage lights made reading tough anyway. Khalid Ansari, elder brother of Hamid Ansari, later Vice President of India, was the deputy commissioner of the district. His, in many ways lovely, wife Khadija, welcomed me when I carried a bundle of clothes to iron at their house across the road. Her delicious kababs and gentle affection made up for my otherwise restricted life. This was the only home I freely visited since they were from Hyderabad and were not conservative in their ways.

In Anantnag, which was otherwise a dusty old town with only make-do provisions and nothing to define itself, I discovered the fascinating wooden lathe work in which the artisan cuts tiny bangle-like rings on the outer part of a wooden baton without separating the wood from the original piece. The wood is coloured on the lathe in red, green and silver. These became baby walkers, cradles, *charkha*s, ladles and rattles. Such rare and special craft skills were never propagated in the way more expensive and ornamental crafts were. They often died from want of recognition or attention because they were made only for the ordinary people and not the elite.

~

Secretariat life for many years meant packing the entire house to the last light bulb for the bi-annual up-down transfer known as 'darbar move' from Jammu to Srinagar, every six months. This expensive and disruptive arrangement was put in place to balance the administrative and political interests of both regions. As juniors, we were allotted the dregs in housing and government furniture. We got chairs that had gaping holes in the seats where the cane weave had worn away. Our tiny semi-detached cement house in Gandhi Nagar in Jammu had such a small bedroom that only two charpoys could fit in it. When it rained, we carried an umbrella to the Indian style toilet located beyond an open courtyard.

The Jawahar Nagar government colony in Srinagar was not a very different story. Its bath was just a plain room with a cold cement floor, a single tap, and no washbasin or shelves. We rigged up a wooden plank dismantled from one of our wooden trunks as a shelf with an enamel basin and jug as seen in films about medieval England. We had one immersion rod and two tin buckets for hot water.

In this grim place, I had a risk of a miscarriage and was told to lie still in bed with my feet up to prevent it. However, on a sunny May morning, as is known to happen often in Srinagar, a sharp and fairly severe earthquake forced me to hop out of bed, run downstairs and jump out of the ground floor window as the front door had jammed. I lost the baby.

~

In 1967, we had our son Akshay, who was just three months old when Ashok was promoted. Posted as Deputy Commissioner of Poonch District, right on the border with Pakistan, his salary jumped from Rs 550 to the royal amount of Rs 1500 per month. There was nothing to buy except basic daily necessities brought by the cook, and so it did not matter. Poonch was a thirteen-hour jeep ride from Jammu, much of it on hilly roads through deep forests. If rains flooded culverts on the way, it took longer. We had to wait by the side of the road till the water receded. At such times, I breastfed my infant son behind a bush in isolated wilderness.

People were used to elderly Kashmir Administrative Service officers arriving on a posting in Poonch at the end of their careers with just a tin trunk and a bedding roll because of its proximity to the insecure border with Pakistan. Senior officials were geared to packing their bags and running if there was an attack from across the border. Poonchis were shocked to see a couple still in their twenties arrive with a newly born child and thirteen trunks of luggage of which eleven contained books, and the rest, kitchen utensils and household items. We didn't look as if we planned to leave in a hurry. If I went walking to the post office to mail a letter the news spread immediately, since wives of senior officials didn't do such things. Moreover, people in the bazaar who had not seen Ashok, would ask me discreetly whether the new DC Sahib was my 'Papa'. Since he had started balding prematurely by then, he wasn't amused.

An anecdote that stands out in memory when speaking of my life in Poonch surrounds the additional district commissioner (ADC) who was an elderly official from the state service, used to accepting a bribe or two on official visits to far-flung villages even if it was in the form of a hearty roast chicken for breakfast. Once, he was accompanied by an introvert Malayali IAS probationer who had been sent to train under Ashok. As they reached their destination, breakfast was offered as usual. However, the ADC discovered it was late and there was no time to have the chicken roasted. He solved the dilemma by ordering that the live chicken be put in the back of the jeep to take home. The greatest delight of the IAS probationer's life was his devilishly gleeful description of the incident, especially of what happened on their journey back, when the chicken managed to save its life by flying right out of the back of the jeep!

When I took Akshay for a ride in a pram every evening along the golf course-cum-helicopter strip below the DC's house, local kids would join me in a ragtag procession taking turns wheeling the pram or carrying him. Army officers told us that soldiers posted at the Pakistani and Indian pickets overlooking the golf course watched our little evening procession through their binoculars. The pickets were located on two heights separated by a narrow valley known as Naiwali Gali because a barber (or *nai*) shop was located there. This shop served as a peaceful no-man's land where soldiers of both armies would lay their arms down and chat about their families while having their routine haircuts.

The DC Kothi was a vast double-storeyed old *haveli*. Most of it was completely useless for comfortable living, but we had electricity for four hours in the evening. There was also only one air cooler in that entire house. Our only entertainment there was to sit in a special 'box' to watch B-and C-grade Hindi films that came to the cinema hall just below the front gate. We watched every film of Dara Singh's, wrestling his foes, and Helen's, wiggling her hips. If parts of a film were particularly entertaining, the *jawans* in the hall would cheer loudly. The operator in the projection room would take the cue and promptly rewind the film to show the scene again to another roar of approval from the audience.

I longed to go on tours with Ashok to Bhimber Gali, Surankote, Bafliaz, Mendhar and other areas of the district but he was stuffy and self-conscious and refused, saying there were no curtains in the dak bungalows where he would stay. Consequently, I had to remain home, often bored to death, practically in purdah because there were none. There were many picnic spots, forests and beautiful quiet lagoons alongside the Poonch River. For a twenty-five-year-old officer, however, the heavy responsibility of dispensing justice at and administering this very remote—in fact the smallest—strategic border district, while negotiating contentious situations between the army, police and civilians along the Line of Control, was an entirely new terrain that left little taste for pleasure.

Two years later, when we were shifted to Jammu, we were finally able to afford a car. The Premier Padmini cost Rs 21,000. We took a loan of Rs 19,000 from the government and made up the rest by borrowing from parents. Even though I got my driving licence in Washington DC in 1961, I actually got to drive properly only on the narrow crowded lanes of the Jammu bazaar. The DC's wife driving on her own and strolling in Raghunath Bazaar to eat samosas from a roadside vendor bordered on the sensational, if not the outrageous, for the traditional officialdom of Jammu in those times. I did of course manage gamely to do all the 'wifely' things like taking part in cooking demonstrations, playing tombola and dancing the *gidda* (a dance form from Punjab) with some officers' wives at the club. However, in my heart of hearts, it was an unsatisfactory forms of 'time pass'. I went to the local arts academy to learn sculpture and had a woman come to the house to teach me how to use a sewing machine just to avoid the urge of sleeping on hot afternoons and wasting time. I felt that it was far better to occupy myself in a useful manner by overcoming my ignorance of how to stitch garments, and by cultivating my artistic interests by creating sculptures.

~

Our Garhwali cook's wife Sundari had two small baby boys born in quick succession in Jammu. I had to stand by her side during the deliveries in the local government hospital since she refused to go back to her mother's home for them. She had not been pregnant for many years and thought that by coming to live with us, she had somehow been blessed. It was scary having to take on the responsibility of overseeing a baby's birth when I was young myself but it didn't seem as if I had an option. Both times, I had to hold the newborns' tiny, slippery bodies while the hospital staff did other things. The children slept in our bed and were fed on my lap along with Akshay.

At sewing class, I learned to make baby clothes. For practice, I created 'baba suits' for them all out of the same length of cloth. Since the boys would be dressed in the same way, most people thought all three were mine and began commenting on why I was having so many children so frequently at such a young age. Understandable, I suppose, since I was visibly expecting my second child.

A Rh-negative blood group problem required my pregnancy to be monitored in Delhi through regular Coombs tests which assessed the number of antibodies building up in my system. In January 1971, a strange thing happened. When I called the All India Institute of Medical Sciences (AIIMS) to ask for the results of the last test, they quoted a frighteningly high reading on the telephone but said they would not give it to me in writing as it was very alarming. My gynaecologist was shocked at this and had me admitted to the Holy Family Hospital immediately. A caesarean section was done and my second son came into this world, only to leave it twelve hours later on 30 January because of extreme anaemia. The antibodies in my system had destroyed his red blood cells and it was too late to save him through transfusions. One of the worst, to say the least, feelings in the world is when a parent loses a child. Relatives immersed the tiny shrouded body in the Yamuna, as was supposedly the custom with newborns, while I lay bereft in my hospital bed listening to healthy infants crying in adjoining rooms. Every year as the sad anniversary arrives, I have an irrational concern which flashes through my mind, but only just for a few moments: that my baby must be feeling very cold there, in the water.

~

Soon after, Ashok was posted to Ladakh with a slightly senior designation of Development Commissioner. It was considered a hardship-posting, so the cook's family had to return to Garhwal. It was difficult leaving behind the two small boys, and Sundari who was shy, loving and hard-working. This angelic woman had left her infant son at home all night to be with me at the hospital when my own child did not survive.

Years later, when she came to Delhi to visit us and stay with her brother who was in the police, she walked out of his quarters in broad daylight on Parliament Street and disappeared forever. There has never been any explanation forthcoming from anywhere for this completely strange act. For many years, I looked for her randomly and even drove to the eastern

Delhi border when I got a message that a deranged woman was found answering to the name of Sundari. I reached the police-post at midnight only to find out it wasn't our Sundari. Later, I sent a picture of Sundari to the daily *lapataa* (missing persons) programme on Doordarshan but we never found her. Since then, the sight of deranged women living on pavements is deeply troubling, especially when imagining the abuse and indignity they suffer with no power or understanding of how to prevent them. Meanwhile, this story remains without closure.

∽

In the early seventies, the Government of India did not permit tourists in Ladakh. There was the army, Ladakhis, Kashmiris, the Indo-Tibetan Border Police (ITBP) and civilian officialdom. Despite the intensity of cold in this high-altitude desert, we fell in love with the vastness of the mountains, and the expanses of desolate landscape occasionally disturbed by a moving figure climbing up a sharp slope or riding across the plains. The colours on the mountains moved like a kaleidoscope as the sun and clouds moved across them. Places like Zoji La, Khardung La, the Pangong lake and a host of distant monasteries became a part of our new world. A jonga ride over the frozen Indus River to Demchok, the last outpost before China, where the Election Commission had to set up a polling booth for the two inhabitants in the village, became a part of our travel destinations. We visited monasteries on ponies. There was no suitable school there, so I taught our three-year-old son Akshay at home. I also visited schools as part of my duties as a DC's wife. The local newspaper once reported, 'The DC's wife visited a local school where she wiped the noses of small children even though she was born with a silver spoon in her mouth.'

Speaking of spoons, I recall this very old and wrinkled woman called Ama Malo who would sit in the sun on the rooftop of her little hovel in Leh, known famously to grumble and mumble at everyone who passed below. She was an institution even though no one paid her any attention. Her curses were treated as routine greetings. Like many Ladakhis, she kept a steel spoon in her pocket. She would use it for her meal after which she would wipe it carefully with a cloth and put it away in her pocket to conserve precious water. Every day, as it became dark and chilly, she would climb down to her little room to sleep alongside her pet goat, but climb back up as the sun rose to start cursing the world. One day, word reached me that when she wasn't heard cursing, someone went to enquire and found she had passed away in her sleep, next to the goat. I decided to go to her funeral, which consisted of four pall bearers, six urchins, two street dogs, and myself. She so fascinated me, that a few years later I wrote a snippet about her and sent it to *The Times of India* in Bombay which published it. I received a letter from the editor expressing appreciation and asking for more 'middles' of this kind. I took it as a huge compliment.

I visited local pashmina centres, strolled through the Leh bazaar admiring gigantic cauliflowers and turnips from the rich fertile soil, brought in from the fields in baskets with *malchang*, the local willow woven by women. Visits to Ladakhi households meant lazy afternoons, warm, glass-enclosed 'sun rooms', and the soft-spoken graciousness of their hospitality expressed through repeated servings of *gud-gud* chai. While I loved this salted butter tea churned in a long wood and brass tube, most outsiders hated it.

Underlying the calm air in Ladakh was a quietly expressed antagonism towards the Kashmiri population who the Ladakhis felt was unduly spoiled. They had taken over most businesses in Leh and seemed aggressive compared to the soft-spoken Buddhist ways. They also objected to having development plans being formulated in faraway Srinagar or Jammu by a government that did not take them to be part of their own. This gave rise to the demand for the Autonomous Hill Development Council of Ladakh which became a reality much later in 1995.

Ladakh was too magical not to be shared with the world. As Development Commissioner, Ashok wrote to the Home Ministry recommending removal of restrictions of travel for Indians and foreigners, which finally bore fruit. It made Ladakh a truly magnificent spot on the tourist map of India and many Ladakhi homes opened up their rooms to provide guest accommodation.

The creation of Bangladesh in 1971 while we were in Leh—with the famous laying down of arms of the defeated Pakistani army coming across the radio, and Indira Gandhi's role in this historic incident—was the high drama in our lives. Our sense of patriotic pride, contained within one warm room in faraway Leh, expanded manifold. Ashok had to travel the district and stayed in the dak bungalow in Kargil over which missiles flew all night. In a cold room warmed by a bukhari (a coal-burning stove) in front of which my son took his daily bath in a tin tub, we listened to history unfolding and our four-year-old learned by heart Pakistan's surrender dialogue, commands conducted in the presence of Lieutenant Generals J.S. Aurora and A.A.K. Niazi. We went back to temporarily darkened windows while the usual civilian flights to Leh from Chandigarh stopped because the A-12 bombers reverted to wartime duty, stopping supplies of newspapers, bread and other provisions that were not produced locally. We were neither frightened nor worried. All things were simultaneously normal and abnormal as we had learned earlier, and life in J&K was a constant adventure.

Following India's victory in the 1971 War, her return to normalcy became visible when flights resumed and we had once again access to our daily bread. Normal life meant frozen raw eggs being boiled before they could be fried, and washed clothes frozen stiff on the clothesline as soon as they were hung. They had to be melted around the bukhari in the evenings before they could dry properly. At a minus 10 degrees celsius, the mug in the bathroom stuck to the top of the washbasin. No water flowed through the pipes and taps but unlike our first home in Srinagar, we did have washbasins.

Determination and persistence helps me pursue what I really want, and I knew I wanted another child despite the risk of facing another loss. In 1972, Ashok pursued and obtained a year's study-leave at Cambridge University. This gave us an opportunity to access advanced medical treatment in England. Ashok left a month before me. In those days, one needed permission and finances sanctioned by the Reserve Bank of India (RBI) to travel for medical reasons and expenses abroad for a year. The man at the desk at the RBI headquarters in Delhi quoted rules that essentially meant I could only apply when I was pregnant. I asked him, 'But how can I get pregnant unless I am with my husband and he is already there?' This conundrum so stumped the poor official that he quickly signed the papers without looking up again.

At Cambridge, I cooked and cleaned and cared for Akshay, became pregnant and went off alone into London every few weeks to St Elizabeth's Hospital at Hammersmith for tests and transfusions. The procedures were making international medical history but they were experimental. The process only had a 50 per cent success rate but I was willing to take the risk of another tragedy to achieve what I wanted. To save myself future pain, I studiously avoided looking into baby shop windows and made no concrete plans for another child. I could see the foetus clearly on the ultrasound screen but the position in which it lay, determined whether the transfusion could take place or not. Each time was a matter of chance. It never occurred to anyone to note the gender of the child. Forty interns looked on, taking notes during the procedure done by Professor Richard Dewhurst who was so eminent that he had a full page story on him in *The Times*. Our daughter Aditi was born as the successful result of this medical adventure with five intra-uterine transfusions, a caesarean section, a complete change of blood after birth, a few days in the incubator, and also after contending a post-birth bleeding crisis leading to further transfusions. This was done in Cambridge under the supervision of Dr Robin Coombs who had devised the famous Coombs test. The most highly experienced and qualified doctors in the world attended on me by pure chance and all for free, thanks to blessings from somewhere and the remarkable British Medical Welfare system. We returned to Srinagar from London with infant Aditi, as the first Iran-Iraq war began in 1980.

Oil prices shot up, creating a world crisis. Prominent J&K leader Sheikh Abdullah was released from detention and came to power supposedly through the benevolence of Indira Gandhi. The Janata government refused to accept the advice of some that since earlier, the elections here were believed to be fixed, this one should be fixed too. Charan Singh, the Home Minister, flatly rejected this idea, and the state saw its first free and fair election. The celebrations that erupted at his victory were euphoric and hundreds of *shikaras* (boats) decked with flowers, flowed down the Jhelum river through Srinagar. The Kashmiris felt free from oppression of a different kind. The first thing Sheikh Abdullah did, was exhort the Kashmiris to value their sense of self-respect and give up the subsidy that gave them rice at two rupees per kilogram. Everyone agreed. Sheikh Abdullah loomed tall in every way, and was all charm with young government officers and their families. At a government tea party, he had once asked me how many children I had. When I told him he smiled broadly and asked, '*Unme se zyada natkhat kaun hain*?' (Who is the more mischievous of the two?)

In 1975, Sheikh Abdullah was the first brave leader in India to denounce Indira Gandhi's Emergency. My friends from Delhi like

Khushwant Singh's son Rahul visited and argued in favour over dinner, saying the trains were running on time. We were angry and horrified at what was happening through the rest of India. News was controlled but people from Delhi brought us the latest happenings. Being in government, we could not express our views. The late political leader D.P. Dhar's son Vijay Dhar and his family were close friends. We spent the night of the election results at their house watching television since we did not own a set. By morning, it was clear that Indira Gandhi and the Congress had been defeated by the people of India. A few months after March 1977, George Fernandes became Union Minister for Industries in the freshly minted Janata Party government appointing Ashok as his Special Assistant. After twelve continuous years in J&K, we packed our bags for a new life in Delhi.

~

After barely two years in Delhi, Ashok was transferred back to Kashmir. Although this was against service rules that hadn't changed since British times, he had to return. I stayed back in Delhi since the children had settled into schools and I, had begun work with the Gujarat State Handicrafts Corporation as a design and marketing consultant. However, since Ashok was stationed away from home, the children and I kept visiting him in the years to follow.

In 1982, Sheikh Abdullah passed away. It was a foregone conclusion that Farooq Abdullah would take over. He came to rely heavily on Ashok. The relationship between us was never like that between politicians but of trust and camaraderie which Farooq based solely on his respect for Ashok's integrity and administrative abilities. Ashok was popular among the locals in Kashmir. He was unfazed with wearing his frayed shirt collar turned, and his modest salary. Only once did his driver plead with him not to embarrass him by sending him to have his jackets repaired from the *rafoowallah* and instead get some new ones. But of course, the trouble is, if one is honest and relied upon by those in power for precisely that reason, it does not sit well with rivals.

The state assembly elections were to take place in 1983. I often scribbled letters to George Fernandes in Delhi reporting on Kashmir, politically and otherwise. Although I had come to be quite politically indoctrinated by then, I was still immature. In one letter dated 3 June, I wrote,

The weather is wonderful. Kashmir is full of election excitement. Lots of red [National Conference] *flags everywhere. Farooq on whistle stop trips through all the villages. We got caught up in one of them so he grabs my hand from the Matador and yells, 'Do you think we'll make it?'!*

So far everyone predicts a tough fight and Congress (I) people are flexing their muscles as much as they can but I personally anticipate an emotional swing to the NC in the last days. Farooq's immaturity isn't helping but he means well. He has fought a tough fight.... All our friends who have been around with him say his popularity is immense and he is able to reach out warmly and directly to the people. Rural women go hysterical! They don't care what he says, they just love him.

The house is full as six of Akshay's friends have arrived to go trekking. Large new house with painters, carpenters, engineers all janaab-ing away to glory. Very disorienting being treated like a 'memsahib' again!

That year, the Congress had wanted an electoral arrangement with the National Conference which Farooq refused. They subsequently won 23 seats largely in Jammu while the National Conference won 46 in the valley.

I remember that at times we used to go to hear Indira Gandhi's speeches during the election campaigns. As families of senior officials on duty, we had seating fairly close to the stage. Once, after her speech was over, we saw her pass close by and in a few seconds she was in her car and away. The next morning we were astounded to read headlines from newspapers from Delhi saying 'blood and thunder in Kashmir'. Subsequently, former Governor Jagmohan described in his book *My Frozen Turbulence in Kashmir* (1995) that as Mrs Gandhi had left that meeting, a group of hostile Kashmiri men had lowered their pyjamas and shown their backs to her. This rumour spread like wildfire and became part of history. We had been ten feet away and can vouch for the fact that no such thing happened. When his book was published, I was asked to write a review of it for the Calutta *Telegraph*. I challenged many of his facts mentioning repeatedly that many of these details were untrue. Graciously, much later, when Jagmohan became Minister for Communications in the first NDA government, he fixed a chronic problem concerning my telephone by personally calling me to enquire about my complaint.

∽

In 1989, I visited Srinagar once again, to identify artists and crafts in the state for a book I was writing on the crafts of Jammu, Kashmir and Ladakh.[*] A photographer friend, Kamal Sahai, and I travelled to many remote areas combing through their intricate by-lanes to engage with and photograph the finest artisans and their crafts. We followed the Gujjar and Bakarwal trails, examining the crafts these nomads practised. We focused on crafts that were not even considered worthy of attention earlier, like the simple *waggu* mats woven from wild reeds collected from the Nagin and Dal lakes. By the time the book came out in 1991, Kashmir was aflame and the serene, idyllic scenery we had photographed for the book, was soon to be a thing of the past. By then, the tranquil groves that had embraced our embroiderers, had become shelters for militants with AK-47s.

Kamal and I witnessed manifestations of violent militancy following our departure from the Coffee House just above Preco Studios in Srinagar one day. No sooner had we left the premises, than there was an explosion in the toilet of the Coffee House. The people of Kashmir were, and still are, peace-loving, sentimental and hospitable. They have always been deeply religious but never radical. They lived in peace with Hindus but did feel a sense of injustice when they saw them occupying high posts in the bureaucracy over the years. The Congress-National Conference electoral tie-up in the previous Assembly elections had made space for an opposition in the form of the Muslim United Front. Victory in some constituencies was denied to them unfairly despite a legitimate election. By 1990, the violence erupted in full force and the Hindus were forced to flee while Muslim youth who were unemployed took to guns distributed by a number of militant groups that were increasing in number every day.

My book on the crafts of Jammu, Kashmir and Ladakh was released on the lawns of Prime Minister V.P. Singh's official residence in late 1991 and not at a public venue for security reasons as the National Front government was already in trouble because of the Mandal agitations. The book release function in Delhi proceeded in the usual fashion, with all the stock formalities and important guests. However, it was spoiled for me by a remark from the prime minister. He said, 'The book is so beautiful that now we do not have to go to Kashmir to see its beauty!' This was at a time when Kashmir's craftspersons were bemoaning the fact that tourists—their

---

**Crafts of Jammu, Kashmir and Ladakh*, Ahmedabad: India Mapin Publishing, 1990.

life blood—were staying away from Kashmir because of militancy, affecting an important source of their livelihood. I hardly wanted my book to serve as an alternative.

I stayed away from Kashmir during the years of militancy that followed.

After nearly twenty years, in the early part of June 2008, I travelled to Kashmir again. Signs of militancy had subsided by then. It was an enlightening and emotional homecoming to a state of which I had been part from 1965 to 1977, and then off and on until 1990. I had been a witness to the Amarnath Yatra, and the first Indo-Pakistani war in 1965. I was in Ladakh when the second Indo-Pakistani war took place in 1971, and rockets whizzed past the dak bungalow in Kargil. It was with a heavy heart that I had left Kashmir in 1977. It had been my home where my children had grown up eating apples and cherries off the trees in our garden, and Gee Enn baker down the road had baked all their birthday cakes.

During the 2008 visit, I witnessed a Srinagar that was filled with a sense of freedom and casual abandon that the locals agreed had not existed for nearly two decades. Twenty years back, craftspersons would not come out of their small workplaces. However, the next generation was more forthcoming. Upon my arrival, they came with cars to receive me, all excited and warmly welcoming. As we drove out from the airport, a policeman stopped us. The person driving got out and was asked to move away from earshot. When he returned, he recounted what had transpired. The policeman had advised him to squeeze a lot of money out of his visitors and demanded a little 'something' for refreshments. It was unfortunate that the local police were extorting minor bribes from their own people so openly.

Curious to know what had changed since my departure from Kashmir, I soon became aware that the route from the airport into town certainly had. Further, an unending row of houses, busy commercial areas, and hoardings showcasing international brands had replaced paddy and rice fields with the occasional house and a small string of shops encountered every now and then. There was hardly any greenery in sight. There was traffic along the way. Pedestrians, private cars, taxis and buses, tourist coaches and SUVs, *shikarawallahs*, army jeeps and random hawkers all inched forward on the roads without any discipline. It was frustrating, but underneath the exasperation I felt happy that Kashmir was bustling with tourist activity, and the people were experiencing freedom from fear of militant attacks and the tension of curfews. In intimate, frank conversations with *shikarawallahs*, craftspersons, former bureaucrats, politicians, proprietors of tourist establishments, school teachers, doctors, former judges, taxi drivers, pony-wallahs, cooks, and local elders, I heard the same words over and over: 'When there was militancy', 'when militancy was at its height', 'in the days of militancy'. It was remarkable that everyone spoke of militancy in the past tense. No one was pessimistic, negative, or harboured ill-will towards anyone. They were ready to get on with normal life. What was most striking to me was that Kashmir looked more busy and prosperous than it had ever before, and it was this factor that motivated me to explore the legacy of this twenty-year phase of militancy.

In Srinagar, it seemed to me as if the J&K Bank was running the state, not the government. Bank branches that were quite impressive to look at were all over. The Bank was responsible for the conservation of heritage places like the Badamwari, a park full of almond trees that had remained unkempt for years. Kashmiri housewives were seen picnicking there and basking in the sun. The Bank sponsored eco-friendly practices and projects that improved the condition of public spaces and the environment, and had enough money, through sound financial management, to invite a sense of confidence and security in its presence. All this happened throughout the years of militancy, thanks to the dynamic leadership of Kashmiri officers heading the bank, and the fact that the local people continued to propagate and encourage progress. Similarly, the Delhi Public School, set up by the D.P. Dhar Memorial Trust, was probably the best educational infrastructure the capital town had ever had. Facilities for three thousand children including a swimming pool, a golf course and a medical centre to be shared with the public were part of its future plans.

Areas at the foot of Hari Parbat, along the Airport Road and around Nagin Lake, and others were crowded with palatial mansions built during those troubled years. 'Many wealthy people have lost money, but many who had nothing have become very rich', my Kashmiri craftspersons informed me. 'Where has the money come from?' I asked. 'That is the point. It is obviously from illicit activities,' they replied awkwardly. By 2008, large tracts of government land were seized by militants and sold for tidy sums; officials were pressurized to process the papers, and the government was helpless, unable to control the proliferation of large structures that had come up quite illegally. But what was interesting to note was that no other region subjected to militancy had had such growth and obvious demonstration of wealth. New shops had opened and commercial areas were cultivating a distinctly cosmopolitan air.

In the bazaars, I saw Kashmiris preparing for the wedding season so that it could be over before elections were announced. Local *waza*s, who prepared meals for feasts, were charging Rs 50,000 to Rs 1 lakh for an evening. People commented with amusement how earlier, after a feast, no one used to be given anything. Yet now, baskets containing a large bottle of Coke or Pepsi, mineral water bottles, post-dinner mints, Pan Parag, wet, scented towels, a dry towel, toothpicks and soap were being presented to guests. This added to the expenditure of providing hundred to five hundred guests fifteen meat dishes (at Rs 180 per kg) where two kilograms were served to four people sharing a *thrami*—a large dish on which food was shared by four people at a feast. Milk and curd were being served in copper bowls instead of those made from old earthenware. Elaborate expenditures could only be possible when people had the means, and were comfortable spending it.

In traditional Kashmiri households, it is a norm to stock homes with enough rations for at least three months. This was in order that they could always be ready to offer their hospitality in the most unanticipated of situations. Yet, it was this very habit that aroused the suspicions of security personnel from Tamil Nadu or Bihar who went searching inside their homes for militants. They accused people of storing up for a jihad or feeding militants surreptitiously, and, as they suspected, quite likely, militants would arrive in the night and insist on being fed. My local friends described how agonizing such nights had been. 'Could you recognize any of the militants?' I had asked. 'No, they were all from other areas, and ran away after a while. Our friends and neighbours would never indulge in wrong activities. Why should we when we have the capacity to live with dignity?' they answered.

'What were the changes in your lives during this period?' I asked a group of craftspeople after we had shared a hearty lunch with Kashmiri dishes like *tabakmaaz*, *kabab*s, *rista*s and *gushtaba*s at the home of a papier mâché artisan. All of them were under the age of forty. They had been in their teens when militancy had started in their region. They narrated how some of them had fought with their parents so that they could be allowed to go away to see Delhi. Dilli Haat, the crafts marketplace in New Delhi (opened in 1994) gave them a means to earn. They also had opportunities through governments, NGOs and private organizations to travel as part of exhibitions to Goa, Mumbai, Bangalore, and later Madagascar, the UK, Germany and the USA. Their voices were unafraid and frank.

'The world opened up for us.'

'We learned a lot by going outside the state.'

'Did you know that over 30,000 Kashmiri girls are studying in educational institutions in the rest of India?'

'My daughter could go to college and is now doing her PhD here, thanks to opportunities I got to sell my crafts outside the state through your crafts bazaars.'

'We discovered that neither was Kashmir so badly off, nor was the rest of India a bad place.'

'We have also seen for ourselves that conditions in India are far better than in Pakistan. Look at what has been happening there.'

We drove to congested parts of old Srinagar, walked along many narrow lanes and visited homes and workplaces of artisans practising copper engraving, *waggu* mat-weaving, papier mâché art, walnut wood-carving, the finest embroideries, and *tilla* (metallic thread) work. Their shops were full to the roof with *pheran*s embroidered and ready to be worn at weddings. These were like defiant symbols of women who were determined to adorn themselves and celebrate the good times. The areas in which I spent the most time were Wantpora, Rajwari Kadal, Nowhatta, Mashadi Mohalla, Rangar Stop at Khanyar, Fateh Kadal, Haba Kadal, Kamarwari, Safa Kadal and Rainawari. My crafts-friends remarked that if I gave this list to the security forces they would not believe it. These had all been militant hotspots. The only anachronism to this amiable atmosphere I could find were the ugly rolls of barbed wire and security men inside bunkers. Outside the bunkers, there was utter calm. The men were largely ignored and looked as if they had overstayed their welcome. While it is true that they were the unwanted face of the Indian security forces, and human rights violations had been committed, my friends agreed that without firm action, militancy would have bled and ruined Kashmir forever. Word from the simple inhabitants of Kashmir demonstrated how Kashmir had progressed and prospered both despite and because of militancy. Others, of course, have chosen to draw a picture that may oppose this perception. Areas such as Mandibal, Zadibal, Kathi Maidan, Gulshan Bagh, Badamwari, Kathi Darwaza, supposedly less affected by militancy in its heydays, were no different from the 'heavy militancy' areas mentioned earlier at the time. Money flowed in from right and wrong sources, work went on, what people lost in earnings from the absence of tourists was made up from the security forces and their expenditures. In spite of how much Pakistan and others tried, the ordinary people of Kashmir had shown that they could not be crippled.

The 2008 visit to Kashmir was a lesson in microcosm for me. And it is what must be learned in the macrocosm by our politicians, both in the state and at the Centre. Unfortunately, things turned abnormal again in 2015. Indecision, lack of vision, vested interests in issues of daily governance, a heavy influx of Pakistani-funded militancy and cheap electoral politics was to take over this beautiful region again in 2015. With political parties cultivating election fodder, the wedding feasts were to be overshadowed by electoral machinations before the innocent public could see it coming. Artisans could not leave their homes because of curfews, stone throwing and firing. Security personnel stiffened up in their bunkers. Sentiments were being stirred from across the border and misinformation and violence were back in the vocabulary of troublemakers. In 2017, the mischievous involvement of India's western neighbour has become more than evident. The atmosphere in Kashmir is festive and normal in most parts except for areas where militancy still prevails. The people, luckily, are longing for peace.

Kashmir is India, but Kashmir is also Kashmir: When will 'India' learn to feel its pulse and truly engage with it?

10

A TRYST WITH CRAFTS AND THE 'CRAFTY'

Gurjari and Dilli Haat

FROM MID-1977, SETTLING INTO A faster paced life in Delhi, did not mean much to me beyond getting the children into schools and arranging our minimal baggage into our government home in Bharati Nagar. The whirlwind was around Ashok who had the time of his life keeping pace with George Fernandes who wanted to be everywhere and do everything all at once. Like George Sahib, his staff never had enough sleep, between staying up till 2 am to deal with files, or landing somewhere at 6 am to catch a flight at 8 am. Work for them consisted of creating a new industrial policy, setting up the District Industries Centres, laying down the nation's laws for IBM and Coca Cola to follow, and reserving goods for production by hand. George Sahib was disgusted that there were quotas for gas connections, cement, telephones and even the Bajaj two-wheelers. They worked to increase cement production, gave electricity supply contracts to the private sector, allowed private hotels to come up, and yet were accused of being illiberal socialists. Life for the minister and his Special Assistant was a series of jet lags, time lags and an over-frantic work pace. Ashok related to us how for a few moments George Sahib could not recall his own name when he looked in the mirror at a hotel abroad when they had gone for a conference.

In contrast, I was quite bored. One half-hearted attempt to participate in an IAS officers wives' meeting was short-lived. I found them discussing how little work their government *mali*s or gardeners did (this was forty years ago) and how some were trying to move to better housing. Better look for some work, I thought, and wrote to Brij Bhasin, an unusual police officer who loved Kathak dancing, and opted to revive the sinking handicrafts corporation of the state of Gujarat. I had only met him once briefly but he called back and said if I would work for them, he would create a job for me. I was to be a consultant in design and marketing. In those days, degrees didn't matter and I hadn't used 'pull', so I was thrilled at the 750 rupees I was offered monthly for the part-time work.

Continuing in my ordinary Kashmiri style of living and not expecting government cars to ferry me anywhere, I took a bus every day from the Dayal Singh College bus stop and walked from Jantar Mantar to Gurjari, the Gujarat State Handicrafts and Handloom Corporation showroom. Most times, the cheeky DTC (Delhi Transport Corporation) bus drivers would rev up the engine and speed away on seeing a young woman waiting at the stop. It was a game for them. I was so angry one day that I took an auto to Udyog Bhavan, marched into my husband's office and let forth a tirade about the rotten Delhi transport system and how bureaucrats and ministers did not care for the common people since they never used it.

'Calm down, *yaar**, have a cup of coffee,' Ashok offered, and laughed.

But he still did not offer me our old personal Premier Padmini car which he needed to drive to work every day. We never used government cars for our own work. Today, the opposite is the norm.

Soon, I had gathered a bunch of sympathizers at the bus stop across the road where the Dayal Singh College boys also waited every day. They had been watching my frustration and should have enjoyed it as they were considered the '*goonda*** college' of town, but when I grumbled loudly since yet another bus had zoomed past with the driver grinning at me in evil pleasure, this gang stood in the middle of the road when the next bus came along and blocked its passage till the driver allowed me in. I was more thrilled with my first brush with a successful agitation and people's power, than I was at being the wife of a supposedly important IAS officer who was very close to a minister and could thus avail of any undeserved comfort. When his anti-establishment minister—with silly tag names like agitationist, stormy petrel and rabble-rouser—heard this story a few days later, Ashok told me he was mighty pleased.

~

Gaining acceptance at Gurjari was a funny process. The manager at the time thought I had come to displace him. To put me off, he gave me several

---

*An informal way of referring to someone; *yaar* literally means 'friend'

***Goonda*, as in 'goon'

large sheets with multiple columns listing code numbers of items, stock positions, prices and totals to fill in by hand from bill books; I took these home and worked on them till midnight for many days. He had hoped I would get fed up and run away. I was not given a chair or desk to sit for the first year and a half of my job, and so I sat at the end of the sales counters. It was only when I hesitantly raised it before the managing director at the quarterly meeting at the head office in Ahmedabad that a small space was cleared for me in the Delhi showroom in a corner behind a pillar.

The manager had his own unique expressions when speaking. For instance, fabric that wasn't stiff was 'limping', according to him. When the highly popular film *Satyam Shivam Sundaram* came to town and Zeenat Aman was sizzling on the screen, everyone including our manager went to see it.

'Picture *kaisi thi*?' (How was the film?) I asked the following day.

'Bas, sirf tie and dye, tie and dye, aur kuchh nahin, Jayaji.' (It was just tie and dye, tie and dye, and nothing else, Jaya ji.)

Since Zeenat's sexy outfits in the film were mostly in Gujarati bandhni fabric which is tied and dyed, he thought it was the most suitable film review he could give me!

I travelled all over Gujarat in an exhilarating decade of artistic discovery: Bhuj, Dhamadka, Morvi, Mandvi, Hodka, Deesa, Rajkot, Wadhwan, Surendranagar, Jamkhambaliya, Dang and Bharuch. In fact, there was no place the designers and I did not travel to, often in searing heat in a matador van without any thought of air conditioning. There was more often no electricity or running water in villages where we stopped for the night. We bathed behind scrub bushes with a small lota (a pot made of brass) of water and a gaggle of curious dusty children watching. In Dhamadka, from where the now-famous *ajrakh*-printed fabric emanated, was a regular working stop where we arranged sari layouts in dim lantern light and slept on bales of unbleached fresh cloth in the printer's home while work was done. I noticed the adjoining farm had an electric line for its water pump to work. Mohammad bhai Siddiq bhai Khatri, an *ajrakh*-block printer, explained that farmers were given a line to run their electrical equipment. Around that time, Prime Minister Indira Gandhi had asked industrialists in the country what they required to double production. I asked him the same question.

'If we had electricity, we could work from 6 pm till midnight. If there is a storm, we can shut our windows and continue to work under light bulbs. With one power line we could double our work time and double our production,' he explained. I wrote an article about this simple logic and sent it to *The Indian Express*. Many months later, when I visited Dhamadka again, Mohammad-bhai greeted me with an even bigger smile than usual.

'See, Jaya-*ben*, we have lights now! I have a bigger workshed. We earned more so I built a comfortable *sandaas* (toilet) which you can use.'

Apparently some sensible soul in the Gujarat State Electricity Board had seen my article, and encouraged by my inquiry about why an artisan couldn't have an electric line like a farmer, had brought another line to the Khatri printers of the village!

Mohammad bhai's three sons, their wives and countless grandchildren are now all prosperous block printers in natural dyes, winning recognition and awards from all over the world. When I visited the village after the Kutch earthquake in January 2001, despite the death of his wife and granddaughter in the quake, the sense of enterprise of the family had not diminished. They had balanced their computer precariously on the debris and were sending scanned swatch samples to a client in Canada. Ismail, the second son headed a remarkable exercise in relocating *ajrakh* printers to a new village they proudly named Ajrakhpur. We should learn from them not to paste the names of political leaders everywhere. Even today, Ismail bhai telephones when he needs me to speak to someone in officialdom to expedite a file applying for a road, street lights and facilities for which he mobilizes funds from donors and the community itself. Their pride and self-reliance are great lessons that need to be learned by those who love to focus only on the woes of minority communities. The elder brother, Razzak bhai, voted for the Congress and had been Panchayat chief, while the younger brother campaigned successfully for a local BJP candidate, saying they give their vote to those who respond and deliver.

After the Gujarat earthquake, Narendra Modi was made the chief minister of the state. I often requested his office to expedite files to help them in the relocation of their village. This support was readily given. I was keen that the chief minister provide a date for meeting the craftspersons of Kutch so that he could honour their achievements across the region after the earthquake, and extend his support to families like those in Ajrakhpur who have achieved so much for the good name and identity of Kutch. Unfortunately, I never got a positive response from his office. A good opportunity to highlight the excellent skills of this region and emphasize communal amity slipped away.

~

Women in rural areas started many quiet revolutions. For me, the advantage of being a woman was the ability to enter their innermost living spaces and see their embroideries and skills to guide them directly instead of having to work through an intermediary. When women were encouraged to have bank accounts to save earnings from their work, the men began to respect them. Roles were often reversed. We hid our smiles when we saw husbands carrying the children and parcels while the woman walked ahead to meet us at the camp office in Bhuj.

The Girasia jat community makes the finest embroidery pieces with pin-head sized mirrors embedded in the threads for their own garments. Once, they refused to undertake an order from one Mr Suri, an Indian businessman who supplied to Au Printemps, a well-known departmental store in Paris. He was desperate and telephoned me from Paris every morning to urge me to help him get the work done. I held a meeting in the village where women discussed how commercializing their work would offend their Mata, their female deity, and invite destruction upon their livestock or their village, and were therefore against their sacred beliefs. Though they were envious of the women in other villages earning from their embroidery work, the young women of this community were apprehensive. I left it to them to decide. Finally an old, wrinkled woman spoke up. She said, 'Our Mata will not bring harm to us if our hearts are pure.' She went into a long lecture, the gist of which turned out to be: 'Give it a go, let's do it!' This old woman had had the most progressive voice. They began work and the yoke pieces for Paris were dispatched. Unfortunately, a short while later, Mr Suri suddenly died of a heart attack in Paris. The women, however, continued to supply their fine work for sale. Did bad fortune visit Mr Suri instead? I wonder.

In hundreds of villages, we would explain patterns and new design layouts to make contemporary items for city use. From a drought-ridden economy to one held together by women's earnings, Kutch turned itself around and has now become a must-visit spot for tour operators, designers, craft lovers and even the city elite who go to these 'must-see' places not to be outdone by their friends. I patiently listen to tales about the crafts of Kutch and the wonderful skills these new enthusiasts have discovered. I keep wondering how many times a tale has to be reinvented, a place rediscovered, a path further trodden before people learn to create their own fresh stories.

~

Gurjari became famous. Its sales rose every month. It was a rage in branches that opened in Bombay, Calcutta and Bangalore (now Bengaluru) where I also helped with the renovation and interior decor to save the corporation money. Actors such as Smita Patil, Shabana Azmi, Naseeruddin Shah and Ratna Pathak, Teji Bachchan, social activist and mother of Amitabh Bachchan, even Sonia Gandhi in skirts and boots accompanying antique textile buyers from abroad, and budding actors from the National School of Drama like Neena Gupta—all made regular visits to Gurjari to grab the latest textiles. Teji Bacchhan, who loved to chat every time she came, told me that cultural activist and writer Pupul Jayakar had always got only three saris woven together on a loom; one for Teji Bacchhan, one for Indira Gandhi, and one for herself, after which the weaver was told not to replicate them for anyone else. But some of my experiences made me wish that the benefit of the craftspersons was uppermost in people's minds which was not always the case. For instance, I had once asked a well-known film actress who often shopped at Gurjari to consider wearing a collection of saris designed by us in any of her forthcoming films and had requested that a line in the credits at the end of the film be carried: 'Saris designed by the Gujarat State Handicrafts Development Corporation'. She refused, saying she would not like to have everyone else wearing the same things she wore.

I developed campaigns like 'What's new at Gurjari' and bags printed with 'See you at Gurjari', which were phrases often uttered by customers. Bank employees, school teachers and students all started wearing Gurjari-style clothes and shawls. Young Indian fashion took birth, and the silly word 'ethnic' which Britishers originally used for natives became a description for Indian handcrafted clothes. Not bad for a place I had discovered in a condition where 75 per cent of the merchandise was junk and the accounts were in the red. We were one of the very few public sector undertakings that fulfilled a social purpose and made profits as well. It also set the lead for other emporia to follow. Ultimately, *India Today* did a multi-page story on 30 April 1988 on the success of Gurjari, a government emporium no less. There was a small picture of me captioned 'the brainchild'. There I was at a danger signal which I did not recognize, as I was still in an innocent phase of public life.

A steady procession of managing directors at Gurjari were open-minded, courteous and positive. The organization progressed with better outcomes. In 1987, the Uttar Pradesh Export Corporation asked if I would be a consultant for their handicrafts division as well. Travelling to remote villages and discovering so much talent in miserable surroundings made it even more challenging and exciting to create new ways of improving skills and lives.

In my experience, Uttar Pradesh was more rigid in its attitude towards progress. Craftspersons were more apathetic towards any hope for betterment there. Feudal attitudes of the *mai-baap sarkar* were still dominant despite officers being well-intentioned. This showed in the patronizing and condescending manner in which they spoke to artisans. They made it clear that they did not want any physical discomfort while travelling. Officers who travelled with me carried briefcases and couldn't squat on floors because of their tight three-piece suits. When I took Laila Tyabji, a friend who had decided to work in crafts, on a tour, we walked through the dirty lanes of Ferozabad where the gutters overflowed with all manner of filth in a sudden downpour. Arriving at the Tundla station at 2 am to wait for a train at 6 am we found one waiting room full. We went to another one and lay down to sleep on a large dining table for want of any other space. A posse of policemen arrived and woke us up, shouting for us to leave and make way for the Director General of Police or DG Sahib. I could see the DG Sahib waiting behind the screen so I loudly remarked that his Sahib would not like to be found turning two women out onto the platform in the middle of the night for his convenience. The senior officer got the message and hurriedly asked his men to leave us alone. Unlike Gujarat, UP was full of this sort of officiousness.

∽

George Fernandes, who was by then a mere member of Parliament, sometimes dropped by at Gurjari after Party meetings at the Jantar Mantar office to inquire how I was doing. Once, while I was in Ahmedabad, he was touring Gujarat for May Day meetings with his trade union colleagues. He invited me along as it was a Sunday and our office was shut. We spent till the early hours of the morning travelling and attending meetings in villages around Baroda where I sat absorbing this new experience of listening to fiery speeches about the blood of the working class colouring the revolutionary flag red. When asked to make a short speech, I was utterly terrified and almost ran away. It took me years to develop the courage to become a confident public speaker since George Sahib was the hardest act to follow. We returned at 2 am to a small hotel where he and his old socialist colleague Somnath Dube, began to tell me of the events of the Emergency and the Baroda Dynamite Case. The room seemed bathed in moonlight as I listened to their stories till dawn broke. Nobody had slept, and no one, including me, had given a thought to the fact that I was a young woman amongst these hardened trade unionists in unusual circumstances. Sometimes, and I would realize this only later, I was the only woman on the stage listening to speeches in a hall of two thousand men. My matrilineal roots may have helped in my being completely oblivious to such exclusivity, and the consequent lack of any self-consciousness. This, of course, doesn't go down too well in the male-oriented world of politics. Once I foolishly asked George Sahib what someone would think. He snapped back impatiently saying, 'I do not think about what they think'. At the time, I didn't realize that he was indoctrinating me into the world of politics and his many fearless struggles for justice and integrity. It was the only world in which he cared to belong, and those who were with him had to be part of it.

∽

One day, in the mid-eighties, Madhav Singh Solanki, the then chief minister of Gujarat, visited Gurjari. We showed him pictures of various other VIPs during their visits to the shop. Some photos featured me prominently. I showed him how the tie and dye bandhni fabric opened up when the threads were unravelled to reveal the beautiful design. He became poetic, describing the bandhni dots on the sari like stars coming out in the evening sky. A short while after his entourage left, the emporium manager received a call from his office saying the chief minister wished that I should go to the guest house and bring along the photographs he had seen of mine. I didn't know whether to be flattered or embarrassed. And acting on the later, didn't go or send the pictures. This was the same gentleman who, as per the CBI, was later reported to be surreptitiously carrying a letter to certain authorities in Switzerland in an attempt to clear the Gandhis in the Bofors scandal.*

The famed dancer, Mrinalini Sarabhai, was chairperson of the Gujarat Corporation. Amma, as we called her, had a real presence and a magnetic personality. Her mother and siblings were well known to my mother and being from Kerala, there was a certain sense of affinity between us. We had once travelled to Kutch together where the locals called her 'Saraben' thinking the 'bhai' in her surname was like any other local name and was therefore detachable. For them 'ben', meaning sister, is added to the woman's name and 'bhai', meaning brother, to the man's name as a form of respect. Her dance troupe, with daughter Mallika and others, treated my home in Delhi informally. I stayed at their home when in Ahmedabad and Amma was sweet and hospitable in return. Once, Mallika and actor Kiran Kumar had held a chilled jug of wine to the soles of my feet to soothe my raging malaria, telling me I should be honoured that movie stars were tending to me. I had planned a tour to Kutch and decided to brave the heat for a change of scene despite my high fever. I asked Carmen Fernandes, a good friend and a designer at Gurjari, to carry lots of ice cubes and come with the matador van early next morning. We reached Bhuj by late evening where a bed was laid out in the office. Craftspersons brought *moong dal khichdi* with lots of pepper and cloves to cure the malaria. We worked despite the fever and vomiting, and I soon recovered as a result of their care and concern.

Much as I admired and respected Amma's dignity, her writings and extraordinary talents, I couldn't shed the feeling of discomfort while being around performers like her who inevitably carry the need to constantly be in the limelight. She often held back on according credit to us for our design interventions; it seemed to me as if heading an organization with several good designers was not quite enough and she had to somehow be at the forefront of its achievements. She, however, had a vulnerable side to her and shared many confidences with me about her life and family. I too was always frank with her. When the Janata government fell, and the old bosses were holding sway again, she handed me some publicity

---

*'Solanki tried to scuttle Bofors probe: CBI'; see http://www.tribuneindia.com/ 2003/20030419/nation.htm#6

material asking me to have them delivered to the who's who of Delhi's power structure. One separate envelope was marked to the well-known son of a powerful political figure who had no position in government. 'Amma, why do you have to do something like this?' I had asked her. 'He is not important in the legitimate hierarchy. You have stature and don't need to be pleasing him to get some favours.' After a moment's pause, she agreed with me and decided not to send that envelope.

ᔕ

The year 1984 was a traumatic year that detached me from everyday reality and Gurjari for more than three months. It was a nightmare and another world. But that is a story that comes for when I knew for sure I had to leave the world of comfortable office spaces, and empty, pseudo-intellectual debates, for the real politics of the street. There were, however, some occasional incidents when I participated in political activism even during my engagement with the handicrafts sector.

Since Amma's sister Lakshmi Sahgal was a freedom fighter and firebrand activist, she did not object to my taking part in politics with the opposition Janata Party. Milk prices in Delhi had been abnormally hiked. We called a protest against V.P. Singh, finance minister in Rajiv Gandhi's government. It was an all-party show by women with seniors like Pramila Dandavate leading us. Interestingly, when I suggested the easy availability of liquor as a counterpoint to the difficulty in accessing milk for children, even some women members of the Left parties rejected the argument. Our procession led to a serious scuffle at Parliament Street. I was beaten black and blue by policewomen whose hard, expressionless eyes showed how brutal they could be. At the police station where we were herded, I noticed a board that listed heinous and non-heinous crimes. Eve-teasing, as it was called then, came much lower in the list than bicycle theft. I showed Amma the still vivid expanse of bruises on my thighs. She took it calmly. I genuinely respected and cared for her and never held against her what eventually happened to me at Gurjari on her watch.

ᔕ

In 1989, Gurjari got a new Managing Director—T.S. Randhawa. He had a passion for photography. When he shared his plans to photograph the nomadic communities of J&K, I requested our old colleagues there to help him out during his stay. I thought it was friendly and courteous for me to pick him up in our car at the airport if he was coming for a visit on work. As an IAS officer's wife, I did this as a helpful gesture to a colleague in the services. Later, he wrote a report about me saying I had boasted that my husband was the Chief Secretary of J&K and could get anything I wanted done. I couldn't comprehend why he did so.

As a consultant, I gave advice on marketing plans and design developments to support the organization. Suddenly one day, I received a four-page letter from Randhawa rejecting all my plans and suggestions, which I defended as they were based on experience on the job and what I was paid to do. He responded saying, 'If you are sitting on your laurels it means you are not wearing them in the right place.'

He used his talents at photography to also create an album of dusty and untidy sales areas in the Emporium to prove how poor the quality of my work was. The staff told me he had taken these pictures at closing time on a very busy day when I was not present. In any case, supervising the cleaning of the showroom was not part of my duties. The fabrics had been opened by the staff and shown to the customers like any other day. Tidying up always happened before the shop opened to customers the next morning. The last photograph provided the perfect *filmi* ending. He had written 'The End' in the dust on top of a sales counter with his fingertips. He had been in the IAS for a total of eight years while I had worked at Gurjari for eleven years. I suppose this was the old story of the IAS being trained from inception like the British Civil Service to believe that they always know best and that anyone who may know better is a threat. Earlier, heads and colleagues welcomed and acted upon suggestions, but this showed the changing avatar of officers. Official credit cards were being used for entertaining and giving gifts from the Emporium to friends. This seemed to be the new norm to keep in step with corporate officials who were the only ones at that time to use them.

An instance of changing trends in the behaviour and attitudes of public servants was seen when S.S. Sherawat, a former captain in the army—tall, honest and decent—was the manager of Gurjari. We had a very good working relationship. At one point, the Mallika Sarabhai dance group began to expect him to facilitate their travel and shopping. This had not happened before Randhawa. Considering my old-fashioned and rigorous views on such matters, I advised the manager not to lower himself into having to shop with an old pair of Mallika's shoes as a sample just because she was the chairperson's daughter. He too felt uncomfortable.

A few days later, in April 1989, as I was sitting in Sherawat's room helping him open the day's mail, I came across a letter addressed to him from the Head Office saying 'This is to inform you that Mrs Jaya Jaitly is no longer working for us'. I thought it was terribly funny and began laughing, but the staff thought it was an earth-shattering event. They feared if this could happen to me, any one of them could be next. I tried to meet Amma in Ahmedabad to ask why the office couldn't have discussed any problems with me amicably and even tell me they preferred to have a change after a decade of my work. No luck. I met senior officials who sheepishly said they respected us both so much that they didn't want to take sides. They suggested I go to court! I did so, but only to show the staff that one had to always fight injustice.

A petition was filed before the Gujarat High Court. A few moments into the hearing, the judge harshly pulled up the corporation and quashed my dismissal, scathingly commenting that it was 'a shame this was happening in the land of Mahatma Gandhi'. Within two hours, the government went to court and obtained a stay. Typical of the Indian justice system, as I would come to experience many times over, the case dangled for twelve years because of the heavy load of pending cases.

In the meanwhile, my lawyer Girish Patel lost interest and became a prominent activist in the Narmada Bachao Andolan.* Kalpesh Jhaveri, a fine person with strong socialist leanings became my counsel. He is now a judge in the Gujarat High Court and is facing a piquant problem with fellow judges who complain that he disposes off his cases too quickly. I finally won my case twelve years later but the high court order said I should be reinstated at the same salary with no compensatory pay.

Socialism and 'pro-labour' judgements were obviously fading away. My victory was merely pyrrhic. If my honorarium was to be the same after twelve years, it was a status quo. It would have been silly of me to even think of going back. The 'state' eventually won, and misuse and corruption entered Gurjari as was the norm in most government establishments. It became a typical, rigid, state body no longer promoting quality or

*The Narmada Bachao Andolan (NBA) involved adivasis, farmers, environmentalists and human rights activists protesting against the number of large dams being built across the Narmada River flowing through the states of Gujarat, Madhya Pradesh and Maharashtra.

innovation, and its fame departed. I felt it had its time, served its purpose, and private establishments were opening everywhere. All the government emporia today need to be shut down or radically revamped as most have rented valuable space to the ever-present Kashmiri traders and have no motivation to promote the interests of craftspersons of their own state.

I had learned that many government establishments could not give all craftspersons a fair deal. Some needed a space like our traditional *haat*s or shanty markets to engage with customers directly without officials keeping them waiting, or finding fault with quality, price and delayed payments. As my work as a consultant in crafts allowed me time to follow other interests, in the early eighties, I decided to pursue a project to study the possibility of setting up a *haat* in Delhi, and was advised by Shiromani Sharma, Development Commissioner Handicrafts then, to give it a practical ending. We wanted to hold a weekly bazaar in the premises of Hanuman Mandir, across the road from Gurjari in the NDMC locality. This involved locking horns with the NDMC for a year and a half for permission to use the *tehbazari* space there that lay vacant except on Tuesdays. Nobody listened. In desperation, in 1985, I finally went to meet Jag Pravesh Chandra, an elderly gentleman who was then Chief Executive Counsellor of Delhi.

Chandra had a habit of giving appointments to visitors at 8 am while he was in bed in his pyjamas, still sipping his morning tea. I was the only woman there in a room full of Congress activists. Half-way through my impassioned appeal to him, he raised a finger to stop me. The tea was doing its job. He got out of bed, went to the toilet behind the curtain and, in everyone's hearing, loudly proceeded to unburden his bowels. His audience pretended not to hear anything. When he returned, I hastily concluded my final sentences and dashed out of his house almost in tears with embarrassment. This was a first in my hitherto pretty elitist life. Despite this eccentricity, Chandra was helpful and we were officially permitted to use the space. I invited him to celebrate the first year of our little *haat* at Hanuman Mandir, which he very graciously did.

My 'Dastkari Haat Samiti', a national association of craftspersons, was formed and registered in March 1986. Hanuman Mandir saw us through interesting times on the pavement every Saturday. There were bomb blasts and bus strikes, and our secretary, a tailor, had a stroke while sitting at the *haat* and died soon after. The NDMC confiscated the tea seller's cart because it wasn't something for which permission had been given. The penalty to have it returned was two thousand rupees. They also refused to beautify the place, not allowing a tea stall, or even a small stage where street theatre could be performed. They argued that if the place improved, rich commercial bodies would want it. In effect, we had better wallow in a mess amidst drug addicts, laddoos surrounded by flies, and no tea stall if we wanted to remain there paying five rupees per stall as rent. However, our organization grew, with monthly meetings held on the pavement, democratic decision-making processes formulated and a membership of ninety craftspersons from Delhi. Those who earned four rupees supplying dolls to a retailer, now earned twenty-five rupees selling them directly at the Dastkari Haat. That was the basic idea behind the market. We eventually learned that we needed storage space, a longer occupancy and definitely food stalls to attract customers. The concept of Dilli Haat was slowly evolving.

∽

Since Gurjari's time for serving craftspersons faithfully seemed to be over, the concept of a marketplace exclusively for them became the obvious answer to the need for sustaining their livelihoods. I took the idea to officials in the Delhi government for a couple of years but it proved to be too difficult for them to understand. The explosion of militancy in Kashmir in early 1990 triggered its initiation. I sought an appointment with the then Prime Minister V.P. Singh and provided the concept on paper to set up a permanent marketplace for craftspersons. 'Good idea. Do immediately', he wrote on file and passed it on to his Principal Secretary who called a meeting inviting various officials to the Prime Minister's Office (PMO). S. Regunathan, Chairman, Delhi Tourism and Transportation Development Corporation (DTTDC), took up the project with funds from the Ministry of Textiles with the late Ajai Shankar. It also had dogged support from one Mr Hakim, Joint Secretary in the PMO, who pushed it whenever it stalled, which is what happened when the project was to come up behind the Purana Qila opposite the Crafts Museum in a small triangular park adjoining Bhairon Mandir. These officials were from that remarkable breed who were positive, altruistic and cooperated with great willingness considering I had no political standing. In the midst of the planning, however, V.P. Singh's government fell and Chandra Shekhar became the prime minister.

Behind the scenes, some people felt threatened and used their supposed proximity to Maneka Gandhi to cancel the allotment of this location, claiming it would disturb the animals in the zoo. As we went back to the drawing board, another civil servant, Ramesh Chandra, the officially designated Administrator of the NDMC, telephoned me with a unique solution. He had discovered a law common to Chandigarh and Delhi that allowed municipalities the ownership of the space over sewers. Sarojini Nagar had a wide storm water drain running through it. He proposed to cover it with a thick slab of cement and soil and offer it for my project. I had never met him but he claimed he had seen my efforts from a distance. Nothing went too smoothly but that will be part of an exclusive book on Dilli Haat which I am waiting for someone to write for me. I had to call an urgent meeting of our organization to propose the simple name 'Dilli Haat' to avert the danger of Delhi Tourism christening it as 'Shilp-Ahar' as an incorrect translation of Food and Crafts Bazaar.

I asked Ashok Gehlot, the then Union Minister of State for Textiles, to lay the foundation stone for Dilli Haat in May 1992, and I was asked to set up a tiny bazaar on short notice for the event. He not only agreed, but actually came in early. Later, for its inauguration on 28 March 1994, no one had to 'put in a word' throughout. Only George Fernandes had to request Madan Lal Khurana, then chief minister of Delhi, to meet me when I had to bring to his notice that Dilli Haat had been ready for four months and was waiting to be inaugurated. Atal Bihari Vajpayee was the leader of the Opposition, so Khurana preferred to defer the honours of inaugurating the marketplace to his senior leader. On inaugural day, George Fernandes, then Janata Dal MP, and I, sat casually in the audience while ministers and officials from the concerned agencies occupied the elevated stage. Craftspersons had been persuaded to occupy the stalls. Vajpayee gave a typically playful speech in which he warned everyone that while 'crafts' were good, no one should become 'crafty'. My first twenty of twenty-four artistic maps documenting the crafts of India was released by G. Venkat Swamy, the then Union Minister of State for Textiles. As a fellow trade unionist, he spotted George Sahib in the audience and called him to join them on stage. After six years of sheer perseverance, I enjoyed my moment of accomplishment quietly from below.

After the function ended, I received a call from Venkat Swamy's office. He came on the line to express his dismay about the fact that the BJP and Delhi Tourism officials had been very thoughtless not to acknowledge my role in setting up Dilli Haat, or refer to me at all. I mumbled saying it did not matter, although it was true. Subsequently, he put me on the All India Handicrafts and Handloom Board, which, typically, never met at all during his period in office.

Interestingly, the entire set of fellow craft aficionados who still decorate Delhi's drawing rooms and sit on advisory boards to give expert opinions on policies for this sector, watched from a distance without offering to join my efforts in setting up the Haat. Some family members did not visit till the Haat became famous. I think both did not want to be involved in my 'politics', as they saw it.

I also felt that socialist leaders like Sharad Yadav and Nitish Kumar—who claimed to care for the backward classes, tribals, minorities and other underprivileged sections (craftspersons comprise 94 per cent of these communities)—could have taken more ownership of it as a major achievement of a party colleague. It never struck them to acknowledge, even informally, that a woman with no position or power could set up this infrastructure that brought about the economic revival of thousands of craftspersons. However, their personal staff never failed to recommend and quite often at that, some undeserving trader to me who wanted a stall. I wonder why they were stuck in the Mandal mode of quotas. I wish they had considered creative work to be politically worthwhile.

∽

In ten years, Dilli Haat became popular, both nationally and internationally. *Lonely Planet* and other guide books advised travellers to visit it. At one stage, impoverished Russians came in droves to buy inexpensive crafts, taking them back in gunny bags to sell in Moscow. It won awards and became a win-win for Delhi Tourism, the craftspersons and customers. I had devised concepts for regulations to ensure allocations and rents were fair. Regular meetings to monitor, evaluate and improve the complex were held between Delhi Tourism, Development Commissioners of Handicrafts and Handlooms, NDMC, Pradeep Sachdeva, my friend and architect of Dilli Haat, and me, as its founder and representing the Samiti and thus the craftspersons' voice. This lasted till a seniority issue between the managing director of Delhi Tourism and the handicrafts office ended in such meetings being abandoned. Success bred greed and corruption. Stalls were added and removed indiscriminately and at will by the Delhi Tourism without a heed to proper usage of space or a sense of aesthetics. Traders posing as craftspersons bribed, fought, used influence and manoeuvred through various dishonest means to remain as occupants of their stalls. In this manner, they managed to sabotage the concept of a fortnightly rotation of genuine craft practitioners.

Today, the banners outside may announce a bazaar highlighting a particular agency or state, but the sellers inside are largely the same faces. Five years of letters, meetings, videos, photographs and protests have not succeeded in creating a system free of corruption. In fact, it seems to be getting worse because of the collusion between traders and officials.

I had never asked for a position of authority in the management and I soon became a supplicant, begging for permission to hold a crafts bazaar run by my Samiti just once a year for a fortnight. Since the Development Commissioner had disallowed occupancy by NGOs, as many bogus ones had proliferated, we got thrown out with the bathwater.

Dr A.P.J. Abdul Kalam had released my book *Vishvakarma's Children: Stories of India's Craftspeople* (2001) just before he became President of India, and had dined on *appams*[*] and stew with George Fernandes and me a few times. His query to me and the small delegation of craftsmen, whom I had taken to meet him, was, 'Why are they troubling you instead of praising you? Please meet the minister for textiles and tell me what he says.' Shankersinh Vaghela, the then Union Cabinet Minister of Textiles, was sympathetic since he knew my work.

So, handicraft officials decided the Dastkari Haat Samiti headed by me could be the only NGO to be allotted Dilli Haat since I was its founder, but I had to provide proof that I was indeed its founder. That was like asking Sita to prove she was Lord Rama's wife! I gave them copies of ninety letters, notifications and minutes of meetings proving I was part of the team but it wasn't enough. Finally, they found a letter written to me by Manmohan Singh when he was the finance minister, complimenting me for having established Dilli Haat. I did not and still do not have a copy of

---

*Made with fermented rice batter and coconut milk, *appams* resemble pancakes and are a favourite and popular breakfast item in Kerala.

this letter. Since he was by then the prime minister, it worked. But this is not a happy ending: at least, not yet.

Dilli Haat has since been taken over by a group of traders who have changed its purpose, systems and integrity. They have a running campaign against my organization and, along with certain officials, have sworn to get us out. A letter was sent to the PMO accusing me of acting like a 'Jhansi ki Rani' with craftspersons, selling stalls to bureaucrats and traders for five lakh rupees each and taking exorbitant sums from poor craftspersons. An official sent it to me for a response. I found the complaint had no letterhead or date, and out of the two main signatories, one had died four years earlier and the second denied any knowledge of this. Other names were cut-and-paste jobs from the list of awardees available on the Ministry website. My reply noted that if the officials had done their job of at least verifying the identities of the signatories and the veracity of the letter it would have saved time. The same official who was new to his job sneeringly told me I should be magnanimous and walk away from Dilli Haat even if I was its founder. It was always puzzling to me as to why some bureaucrats who are meant to be public servants and therefore polite, decent and transparent when dealing with the public, should behave in this manner.

It is also puzzling as to why trying to ensure the continuance of Dilli Haat in a socially and economically just manner should be such an uphill struggle. Mark Twain had once said, 'It is better to deserve honors and not have them than to have them and not deserve them.' This has been my view too, but I cannot stop wondering why one gets opposition and trouble instead after one has done some work that is otherwise highly acclaimed in private. As if six years of effort to create this most popular and successful marketplace were not enough, I have now spent as many years in fighting the corruption crawling out of the woodwork from various quarters and combatting accusations of all kinds. As I said earlier, growing success and profits always bring greed and destruction to the best intended policies.

~

I understand that what has kept me positive and energetic even as time and age have advanced is the inspiration and pleasure derived from engaging with policies, ideas and creative projects that keep our craft traditions alive. It also helped its practitioners to be productive and hopeful. Every time I come across a skilled craftsperson, I am inspired to jump ten steps further into planning how to empower him with a means to a livelihood and also acknowledge their courage to step out of the shadows of anonimity. The fact that I have had such a deep, first-hand involvement in the nitty-gritties of politics, culture, heritage, gender issues and social movements across the country, helps me widen the scope of craft development work and take it far beyond the mere documentation of practices and people or superficial design interventions from ideas borrowed off the Internet.

At Gurjari itself, the bottom line in our approach to the communities we served was to never send away those people whose work, in their present state, was un-saleable. They needed the most help and if a government development and marketing agency was involved in addressing their lives and needs, it had to lift up the lowest rung rather than build its name on the skills of already well-established craftspersons.

In early 1990, when Sharad Yadav was appointed minister for textiles in the V.P. Singh government, Lakshmi Chand Jain, who had been Secretary of the All India Handicrafts Board, along with former MP and senior socialist Surendra Mohan, decided to meet him to suggest he appoint me as the new head of this Board. Pupul Jayakar, its long-time head under Indira Gandhi had resigned in protest against the violence in Rajiv Gandhi's constituency during the elections. They had not spoken to me before they did so or else I would have dissuaded them—not because I would not have wanted to take on such a challenging responsibility, but because I instinctively knew it wouldn't happen. Sure enough, they telephoned me after returning from their meeting with Sharad Yadav to say that the latter had not taken their proposal on board and that he said he was looking for someone of Pupul Jayakar's stature. From then till today, ministers with the textile portfolio have been disinterested in this practically defunct and useless body because they have not only never appointed anyone to take the place of stalwarts like Kamaladevi Chattopadhyay or Pupul Jayakar but allowed them to be forgotten as well.

I never give up my push for the benefit of handicrafts and handlooms. So, later I soldiered on by visiting Sharad Yadav with a long note for him with concrete inputs on how the Board could function usefully considering he had re-constituted it with seventeen people from his own community, some political associates who had no familiarity with the subject, and forty-five ex-officio officials who were transferable. After the meeting, he thanked me, adding: 'We shall keep talking from time to time'—in Hindi. Nothing happened eventually, as the Board did not meet even once, as far as I know.

~

The last days of the National Front government in 1991 were not uneventful for me. Ajit Singh was Minister of Industry and Commerce. The National Institute of Design (NID) in Ahmedabad came under his care. His office requested my bio data to be sent to him. I did not know why. I woke a few mornings later to read in *The Times of India* that I had been appointed Chairperson of NID but its top administrators had already met the President of India and requested this appointment be cancelled. Aditi and I were both amused and amazed as we read the news together over our morning tea. The news of my appointment was like a bolt from the blue and I found the desperate measures already afoot to stop it, terribly funny. It was difficult to take both seriously.

I planned to meet the Director and ask what their problem with me was, but he refused to let me step in to the NID campus to do so. I suggested a meeting at the India International Centre (IIC) lounge. He explained in a rigmarole sort of way that NID had aspirations to go big in industrial design. They preferred to focus on designing cars rather than crafts, he said. He indicated they feared I was already behind the unions that had been protesting outside their gates for months, and that I would upturn the work done by Pupul Jayakar. While not caring for the position, I felt I had to preserve my self-respect so I argued that a national institution meant serving it for the good of the nation and not a small section, and that, with my years of experience in both crafts and its administration, I had the capacity to be even-handed and objective. Moreover, I had no connection with their union troubles at all. I offered to travel to Ahmedabad and discuss things on campus. The Director asked me to desist for a few days. I found it all very odd but did not bother to run to Ajit Singh or do anything about it at the level of government. The media did hound me, and thus I gave some frank interviews about how ridiculous their position was in fearing I was going to be a monkey tearing up their flower garland.

The V.P. Singh government soon fell, Chandra Shekhar took over, and the people around Rajiv Gandhi prevailed upon the prime minister to undo the appointment in the first order it issued. So, Rajni Kothari, as a member of the Planning Commission, and me, as Chairperson of NID, were the first personalities to have our appointments cancelled by the incoming government. It was a hilarious honour.

I wondered if it's a general rule of life that anyone stepping out into public work must eventually prepare for conflict and controversy. Maybe India is more prone to this. Why do roadblocks inevitably come in the way? Or does it happen more to women? I don't believe in donning a mantle of victimhood and it is an established fact that women are greater targets of attack. Perhaps enthusiasm and energy in public life is considered excessive and unseemly for a woman. Or maybe there are just minefields of egos and vested interests out there waiting to explode if poked.

Apart from the creation of Dilli Haat, I was inspired by a hand-painted map I had seen in Thailand called Markets of Bangkok. I thought since India had so much more to offer than just a bunch of assorted markets in a city, a map of the Crafts of India would be a good idea. The project started very modestly in 1993, when typesetting and printing plates were the norm. Creating the map became a huge and intricate exercise that did not end till 2010. It resulted in my overseeing the documentation of all the crafts of each state in India and using local traditional artists' interpretation of crafts, culture and maps to point to locations of production and sale. Each such activity took six months to complete with a team of graphic designers, researchers and craftspersons involved in every part of the way. We drew from growing technological innovations as we progressed faster over the years. Then it took on a life of its own—the idea came alive slowly in the form of posters, journals, book marks, postcards and later a major exhibition that travelled inside and outside India, and a documentary film called 'Indian Crafts Journey' that can be now be seen on YouTube*. Enlarged versions of these maps finally rest on the walls of the Lok Kalyan Marg Metro station in Delhi and the Ashoka University in Sonepat (Haryana), while poster and folded-map versions are still available and bought by people all over the world.

In February 2004, the maps were mounted in an exhibition at Dilli Haat. The exhibition incorporated innovative modes of display. I had music composed out of the rhythmic sounds of processes involved in making

*See https://youtu.be/NDoIyWixtHs

crafts; there was a dance performance and a film show too. The exhibition also used unusual lighting methods to transform the look of the areas involved in the exhibition. All this was quite contemporary at that time. Dr A.P.J. Abdul Kalam was requested to inaugurate this event in the presence of sitar legend Pandit Ravi Shankar and well-known contemporary artist and Padma Shri awardee Anjolie Ela Menon.

The President had fractured his shoulder. His presence was uncertain. His orthopedic surgeon, who was a friend, assured me that if the President would go anywhere at all, it would be to my event. President Kalam came with a shawl covering his injured shoulder and was enchanted with what he saw, ordering artworks for the Rashtrapati Bhavan from the tribal artists there. Everyone from the cultural world was present and I felt thrilled that I had managed to get the President of India to visit Dilli Haat. We had publicized the invitees widely among the media. Well-known social commentator Suhel Seth had recommended a public relations company for this. We were at the time quite unused to such sophisticated ways of publicizing our efforts. Curiously, only half a dozen obscure travel journals covered the event; there was of course the mandatory photographs of the who's who among the guests that go in the society pages. However, there was no review of the entire map project or the exhibition in the media. Following this, I recall reading Suhel Seth's comments in a newspaper on the tragic consequences of political bias which seemed to have prevented my magical exhibition in the environs of Dilli Haat from attracting any attention. Interestingly, however, Sheila Dikshit, chief minister of Delhi at that time, was impressed enough to have Delhi Tourism take a part of it to be mounted at Trafalgar Square in London over a weekend. I was astonished at the costs involved in such an endeavour. Later, we were requested to present the entire exhibition at the Frankfurt Book Fair on behalf of the Ministry of Human Resource Development, where India was the guest country. The minister declined to visit this large and popular exhibition.

It was quite strange for me to observe how with the changing regimes in power—first the NDA and then the UPA government—the perception of my efforts to bring India's craftsworld to the fore, changed. Often my own government supported me the least. Life and governments are sometimes odd.

Later, we had to compile all the texts and rewrite them for a major publication titled the *Crafts Atlas of India** released in 2012 and selected for a 'Choice' award in the USA. Of the many satisfying uses these maps have served, the best was when the United Nations Development Programme (UNDP) told me they were used to target and deliver relief to artisan communities during the massive cyclone that hit Orissa (now Odisha) in 1999, and the tragic earthquake in Gujarat in 2001. Originally, the social purpose of these maps was to lead people directly to the sources of production so that middlemen and exploiters would not keep them hidden. They were also to make information on and locations of crafts available to travellers.

When the maps were part of an exhibition in Germany at the Frankfurt Book Fair in 2006, I began to be fascinated by the idea of India's multifarious ancient manuscripts, contemporary languages, and their scripts. Calligraphy formed a part of this fascination, combining my love of art, writing and literature. Alongside, craftspersons often came to me repeating their habitual, self-deprecatory line, *Hum gareeb hain, hum unpadh hain* (I am poor, I am illiterate). I didn't feel sorry for them; I felt annoyed. I did not want them to undermine and underrate the knowledge and skills they already had. They felt they lacked knowledge in computers and English and consequently felt inadequate. I wanted to teach them not to feel that way even if they did not have this knowledge. I decided to find a way of making them appreciate literacy through some new means to bring them out of their sense of inferiority.

A new idea formed in my mind. Why not combine the visual beauty of the Indian alphabet and scripts with calligraphy, and make them into designs suitable to be translated through a variety of craft skills into exhibit-quality objects? Over a period of two years, I introduced illiterate and semi-literate craftspersons to the idea of calligraphy and worked with more than sixty individuals to create 150 objects. My instructions were that the outcome should be such as to bring out a 'wow' from the viewer. We used fourteen languages and twenty-one craft skills from sixteen states of India. This resulted in a chic and very contemporary exhibition in Delhi in 2012, in Egypt and at the UNESCO headquarters in Paris the following year, and in Mumbai in 2015. It was recognized and acknowledged by

---

**Crafts Atlas of India*, New Delhi: Niyogi Books, 2012.

many, and was selected to be a part of the launch of Google's Art and Culture India online platform.

The best part of this exercise was the adoption of Indian scripts and calligraphy into many craft processes and designs. Illiterate craftspersons learned to read and write from their children's text books, school drop-outs who were fine artists honed their handwriting skills, and shy craftspersons learned to communicate ideas and cultural expressions through their own craft forms.

Personally, this period post 2009, was a strange and emotionally disruptive time in my life. It was a point when I had not only been forcibly removed from my part-time workplace (Dilli Haat), but also severed from the responsibilities I had in George Sahib's ailing life—this will come in another chapter. Suddenly, I had to myself the hours I had devoted to his care earlier. Being fully occupied with this creative and inspiring project gave me new vigour. It took on a full life of its own. It was relief, compensation and inner satisfaction far beyond anything that could have been offered to me by anyone else. Providentially, this catharsis came from my beloved world of crafts.

11

THE ORWELLIAN YEAR OF 1984
The Beginning

IT WOULD BE TIMID TO say that 1984 was just a momentous year. Not quite Orwellian but forever memorable for nothing that was pleasant. Farooq Abdullah's government in J&K was toppled, Indira Gandhi sent the army to the Golden Temple, Jarnail Singh Bhindranwale was killed, Indira Gandhi was assassinated followed by the blatant and public slaughter of Sikhs. Anywhere between 2,800 and 8,000 Sikhs were killed as per official and unofficial sources across the country, and as per the Sikhs, reportedly at the hands of Congress-I leaders, and workers and goons nurtured under the leaders' wings. I spent the last months of 1984 and part of 1985 running a relief camp with three thousand traumatized riot victims. This was also a period during which George Sahib was sharing with me feelings with regard to a particularly tumultuous time in his personal life; repercussions were to follow in the subsequent year. But I should slow down, and begin from the beginning.

It started with the turmoil in Kashmir and Farooq Abdullah's ouster, owing to perhaps the fact that he did not agree to Indira Gandhi's demand for sharing seats in the elections. Wajahat Habibullah, who was close to the Gandhi family and a good friend of ours, came over to commiserate when Ashok was ousted as Planning Commissioner in this process. He felt that if Farooq had courted Indira Gandhi when she was '*rootha rootha*' (meaning displeased), as he described it, she would have been all right. Instead, he was moving in the opposite direction and Ghulam Mohammad (Gul) Shah therefore, became a substitute. But this further encouraged Farooq to move closer to the opposition groups that were desperately finding ways to come together. The more he did this the more Indira Gandhi supported Gul

Shah, whose alleged involvement in corruption and nepotism made locals hate the Delhi durbar style of politics even more. Wajahat was himself shocked by the fact that even though Indira knew G.M. Shah was not quite the first choice, he was considered okay. He felt that years of her own good work had been undone.

Journalist Tavleen Singh has been an old friend who often met for a chat after visiting Kashmir. She had been to Kashmir to cover the visits of Opposition leaders who rushed to extend support to Farooq. Tavleen reported that besides I.K. Gujral and Tarkeshwari Sinha falling out of their *shikara* and getting soaked *a la* Hindi film style, the Opposition group's trip was excellent. Syed Mir Qasim (J&K chief minister from 1971 to 1975) too played a good role by saying that he would not be part of a voice that wasn't for India. Their fight was for democracy within their country. There were vivid reports of Farooq driving the opposition group in his vans amidst thousands of people shouting and cheering. None of this pleased the powers that be in New Delhi but it did bring new blood into the Opposition's efforts at unity. The waywardness of various leaders of the Opposition had reached epic proportions. Getting everyone on to the same page was a tough task considering the nature of people like Raj Narain, Chandra Shekhar, Subramaniam Swamy, Morarji Desai, Biju Patnaik and others. It kept them involved in an endless round of meetings and strategies to be united and get ahead yet cut down whoever seemed a threat to their own importance. As usual, George Fernandes was the persuader, spokesperson, mender and hurter of egos, scapegoat, who had to be everywhere, all the time, with no time for his family or rest. When he was out of town, and wanted something urgently communicated in those times of a badly functioning telephone system, I became a courier pigeon between him and other leaders.

It was at this time that George Fernandes and I started a system of writing notes to keep each other informed of what was going on politically since he was hardly in Delhi. Soon he found me to be the most dependable in terms of confidentiality, intelligent inputs and faithful reporting. It also led to a flood of exchanges on personal matters that had troubled him for some time. I became a sort of personal confidante and well-meaning adviser. I took care of his wife and son when needed, and my home too was open to them for any assistance. This went on till 1990. The letters eventually filled a whole suitcase.

Leila Fernandes, his wife, had been abroad in the USA and UK for some months. I was told she was having a severe bout of recurring health problems. George Sahib said he would go to see how she was and bring her back. He asked me to keep an eye on their son Sushanto (Sean Fernandes, also called Sannu) while they were away since he was acquainted with my children and did not have many other friends. He spent several days at our home, demanding my love and affection just as my own children did. He was sweet, funny and longed for a normal life.

Many things in life need discretion and privacy. The state of one's well-being is one of those things. Today, of course, people are more forthcoming about such things and this attitude of openness also helps others give the affected space, or assistance to see them through such difficult phases. Back then, things weren't so straightforward. I was often called upon both by George Sahib and Leila when she was in one of her lowest moods, and was unable to get out of bed and do anything. Contrarily, if the mood swung the other way she would be aggressive and hostile to me, or be highly critical of her husband in front of strangers. It was sad for the both of them. All I could do was unquestioningly be by their side.

In one of his notes to me during that time, George Sahib writes,

> *Had a long talk with Leila today. She feels she has 25% of her strength, and will need several more weeks of rest and recuperation before she is able to undertake the journey home....*
>
> *I'm at Hans Janitschek's on Fifth Avenue right opposite the Central Park. It's very cold out here and snowing. Lunch today was with an interesting group of artists, writers and journalists where George Gallup III was the speaker. Leila wants Sonny Boy to spend time at your home. She thinks it would be good for him. Please take him across even it means persuading him a bit. You have been extraordinarily kind to him, and it means a lot both to him and to me.*
>
> *George*

There are many who like to believe that I was the femme fatale, the 'other woman' who ruined people's marriages. Having grown up to be completely uncaring of and maybe even naive towards what I 'appeared' to be to others, I have gone ahead and done whatever I pleased in all sincerity without feeling the need to explain or justify myself as long as I meant no harm to anyone. Now, it is best to be clear about my role in certain relationships in those days.

Probably because George Sahib had been brought up in a strict Catholic household with five other brothers, he had no experience of personalized care or collective family activities. Having been expelled from home at the age of nineteen because he chose to leave the seminary where his father wanted him to be a priest, he spent years living on the pavements or trade union office benches in Bombay and married only much later when in his forties. By then, he was already a fierce trade unionist whose life consisted of public meetings, constant travel, negotiations and socialist politics with great personalities like P. D'Mello, Ram Manohar Lohia and Madhu Limaye. He had been to jail many times during workers' struggles and was thoroughly toughened both physically and mentally. He had a sharply honed sense of political nuances, strategies and struggles. He could size up anyone related to politics in a moment and knew how to deal with the worst of them. He could also get to the heart of any complicated issue and find a solution. In contrast, however, in comprehending personal and domestic issues, he was like Alice in Wonderland.

George Sahib had left some letters with me while he was away in the UK and USA; one was a carbon copy of Leila's handwritten twenty-page letter to her brother regarding her health problems and insecurities; another, a typed letter to George Sahib from his British socialist friend Richard Hauser reporting on Leila's health problems and also his advice. George Sahib had many mixed feelings about how to decipher them and how to mould his responses to Leila's general behaviour which was troubling him deeply in the midst of his political headaches. He asked me what I made of them. I shared these with Ashok, and in what I wanted to be a carefully thought-out, objective and frank reply devoid of any judgemental attitudes, I kept my response for when George Sahib returned. Since there was hardly a moment to meet or talk for most of those years, these notes would be kept in a cupboard until they could be read and put back. Many times, the reportage or queries became redundant as the notes could not keep up with the speed at which events occurred at the time.

Reading over the letters carefully many times over and trying to be responsible, perceptive, objective in my assessment, here are a few thoughts:

There is tremendous understanding and lucidity in Leila's view of herself in the letter to Dadabhai. The misfortune is that such clarity of thinking disappears when the 'problem' re-surfaces.

How much of these revelations are new to you?...

Her concepts and values are consciously built up westernized ones. She has a fear of keeping things simple and describes actions and thoughts in terms of theories, whether medical, psychological, sociological, etc.

You have really lived in a distant world of your own as far as she is concerned–and yet your world is as much the real world.

My appreciation is for Richard's letter where he feels as I do–Unhappy about the situation but knowing that your real marriage is to the people of the country and not to any one individual.

Individuals have to bear the burdens of their own circumstances, natures, past influences, present feelings and go their own ways. Where there is someone to go with you with understanding and support, fine. Where you can go with the other, that too is fine, but it is rarely that this happens within this socially created straitjacket called marriage.

You have both looked for things from each other which each was not capable of giving–some were imagined and didn't exist. You should at some point of time decide whether it is worth living in the same house as troubled strangers–and also how much each is willing to do or give to the other for his or her comfort, convenience and happiness.

No point evading or hiding under the carpet a problem that exists. You either have to tackle it or say once and for all that you can't.

I truly feel she will be happier being independent because you are incapable of being what she wants you to be. Her acknowledgment of your value, your greatness, doesn't sustain her happiness much. Can you discuss this with her thoroughly when the time is more opportune?

There is a contradiction between her desire to be different and unique and her desire to see everyone conform to her strongly conservative moral values.

She needs so much, I wonder where she will get it all. Her own nature rejects the sources that might begin to give her what she requires.

I wonder if I can be of any help to you? I don't want to confuse you or distract you with my opinions but I am there to help whenever it is needed.

Jaya.

In response, I received this brusque response from George Sahib, which made me realize I could not get through to him with normal, well-meant advice:

> *Adults are adults. Each knows what he or she is doing. I have always tried to mind my own business and let others mind theirs. I know your response to that. But, it is completely out of character for me. I cannot afford to waste my time on such trivialities. Sonny's life and future is the only matter of concern, and that's what I need to discuss. Anything she may need and where I can help, I shall do it for her, as I'll do it for anyone. Of course, there are some obligations, and I have not run away from my responsibilities. I have done more than anyone else in my circumstances or situation would have done. I don't know how to deal with domestic crises, and any help you can give me to deal with mine will be gratefully accepted. I'm not being formal. Anyway, I am totally confused on this, particularly after reading your note.*
>
> *This is only a confession of my helplessness.*

Some scribbles, as George Sahib started calling them, were just a lighthearted sharing of trivia which the political or trade union male colleagues who kept him constant company would not have found interesting. He was getting used to 'lightening up' occasionally, thanks to my habitually informal manner.

> *My doctor gave me a check up today. Said I'm the best preserved politician in the country. No problem whatsoever. Do you feel tired or exhausted? He asked. I said, no. Nothing tires you? I said, no. He gave me a sort of dirty look and said, nothing? I said, no. However, he feels that I should slow down a bit, particularly in my travels. Jet fatigue takes its toll, was his point.*

George Sahib was then 54 years old. Reading this now, as he lies disabled by the monster of all diseases, Alzheimer's, the last sentence sounds ominous.

~

Indira Gandhi's 'Operation Blue Star'* in the first week of June 1984 set off a

---

*Operation Blue Star was an Army offensive by the central government between 1–8 June 1984, to remove Jarnail Singh Bhindranwale and his followers stationed inside the Golden Temple, Amritsar. The offensive led to the death of not only Bhindranwale and militants but also that of civilians and army personnel.

chain of events that changed the course of people's lives forever. It also gave new energy to the efforts of the Opposition. Our notes contained a lot of political venting, speculation and comment. One of George Sahib's read,

> *The reports in the newspapers are so doctored that it is impossible to know what is happening in the Punjab. Have they finished the operations or are they still at it? Is Bindranwale dead or has he escaped?... S. Sahay writing in the Statesman thinks that [Indira Gandhi] may now weigh the possibility of an early poll. But Punjab cannot be the same again—not for a long time. Chandra Shekhar phoned a little while ago from Bombay. He has not met Morarji Desai and has no plans to meet him. He takes the 10 pm flight to Delhi. I'm taking the 5.15 to Bombay but it seems as if I may have to postpone it if some strategy planning is called for. The country is hurtling from one crisis to another.... Terrorism and violence will soon become an integral part of our political life, and I shudder to think of the future. The military action in Punjab is a water shed that will leave an indelible mark in our history. Generations may have to pay the price for the follies of one [...] woman and her ambitions. You mentioned about certain people who are prepared to give of their time and talent. I look forward to the meeting you will fix with them. But what about you? When will you take your decision? Keep well and smiling. There's a whole world to fight for and to win.*
>
> *George*

Sometimes, my notes would be anecdotal chatter that served as reporting.

> *Why is Charan Singh wanting the army to stay in Punjab till things are normal! What's normal going to mean for a Sikh?*
>
> *One of the hijacked boys (GS Rathore) is Mala's friend's son.** *He said the hijackers were excellent. They said "We hate Mrs Gandhi and want our demands met. But seeing you all here like this we haven't the heart to harm you." Some terrorists! That's probably why Doordarshan said that the External Affairs Ministry spokesman would not reveal the details of the negotiations.*
>
> *Jaya*

---

*A Srinagar–New Delhi Indian Airlines flight was hijacked and forced to land in Lahore, Pakistan, in July 1984.

George Sahib's relationship with Chandra Shekhar was full of camaraderie mixed with frustration:

> *CShekhar keeps complaining that I'm rushing him into prison. He also keeps proclaiming that he is coming under my spell in regard to political style and tactical lines. But this is only superficial. Unless he falls in line with me on socio-economic policies and programmes, there is precious little to be gained by either of us.*
>
> *We have many battles to fight and overcome, and, believe me, we shall overcome. Of course, I keep waiting for you to get into the mainstream of that struggle, and as you perhaps know, I am a man of immense patience and great faith.*

George Sahib regularly pushed me towards committing to more political work instead of spending so much time working for a government organization, but I loved travelling to Gujarat, sometimes taking my children along so they could see rural life in western India and what their mother was doing when she wasn't at home. They learned to draw water from wells and sleep on charpoys under the stars in the Banni desert; and my daughter learned to embroider flowers from little girls whom she taught drawing flowers with crayons on paper.

∽

Decades later, in 2014, George Sahib's brothers were fighting Leila Fernandes in court to be able to care for him. I had given an affidavit saying Leila had not been living with him for twenty-four years. In court, Leila's lawyer Meenakshi Lekhi (now MP), on behalf of her client, made allegations against me of neglecting my children during those years, implying the reason to be George Sahib. She was quite aggressive in the court proceedings on behalf of her client, and I was surprised that a lawyer would go to such lengths to offend the other side. Maybe, I was naive. I was surprised when her name was announced as the BJP candidate from New Delhi in the general elections. During these court proceedings I told her that although I was unhappy with her, I would have to cast my vote for her in the forthcoming election. Her father-in-law, P.N. Lekhi, had been a very good friend of George Sahib's who often phoned me if he needed small favours, including requesting me to ask George Sahib if he could use his garden for his son's wedding. I decided to vote for her anyway as I was committed to supporting the NDA. A lesson I learned over the years was to overcome a personal feeling in favour of a political necessity.

Without a doubt, I was getting politicized under George Sahib's influence. It had nothing romantic about it. The atmosphere in the country was already worse. Means to quell voices of dissent—like ours who had protested Operation Blue Star at civil society gatherings—in the form of tapping our phones, were being exercised. My association with George Fernandes could also have been, quite clearly, an additional reason for the interference since he was already viewed as a trouble maker by Indira Gandhi. Driving alone on heavily barricaded roads at night was scary. This angry note of mine shows how:

> *...I mentioned someone has been blatantly listening in on phone calls. Earlier in the evening the person cut into another conversation and was quite rude to me. He said he was from the exchange. After you rang off I kept holding on to the phone as I could almost hear him breathing—so he came on the line again saying hello, hello but I didn't say a word so he disconnected.... Please don't give exact news about your movements and travel plans on the phone. In a roundabout manner would be better. I'll understand eg if you are coming from Bombay reaching here at 7.45, say you'll bring Freddy's clothes over to the house at 7.45 or something like that. I don't want them to know where you are and what you are doing all the time. They are only welcome to hear our opinions about them and their leader and not what we are doing, even if it is only eating papayas.*
>
> *I wrote a letter to all the papers with a copy to Pratipaksh* [the Hindi journal edited by Vinod Prasad Singh on behalf of George Sahib] *about the crude invasion of privacy, describing the entire day's telephone eavesdroppers, the 'torn' register, etc. Very annoying and I'm getting sick of accepting all this quietly just because we take it for granted they are rotten.*
>
> *Hope Biju relished the crab curry.*
>
> *Jaya*

My life was still fairly routine, but for George Sahib who depended more on me as a sounding board or a 'base camp' to share a variety of thoughts.

The great sadness in the relationship between George Sahib, as a father, and his son Sushanto developed much later when his son grew older and perhaps shared his mother's antagonisms. However, during those days when he went to see him at Rishi Valley School, a few words reveal the love and pride George Sahib felt for Sushanto, and how I was a family friend who was around to help out whenever he was left alone:

> *I tried to speak to you on the night of the 8th. Sonny Boy is fine. We had a jolly good time together from 6.15 pm to 9.15 pm. He read your letter with grunts, smiles, laughs, and several yes and no to the questions you had posed. Then he read his mother's letter. He has scribbled a note to you and one to Leila and will be writing you longer letters in the week. The only moment of sadness was when it was time to part company. I told him that you will be visiting him which made him do a few of his goodie yippee noises. But he is longing for your visit as he is from his mother. One definite conclusion I've come to is that he is settling down well and fine and by the end of the month will have developed bonds with the school. He likes his teachers, he has friends among his classmates, he likes Radhika and believes she is fond of him. He likes his studies and believes he is 'head and feet' above his classmates.*
>
> *George*

Both Leila and Sannu, stayed for some weeks with us in Srinagar that summer of 1984, where George Sahib felt Leila recuperated, and Sannu was leading a carefree life in a house full of children and guests. My notes to George Sahib from Srinagar refer to my husband Ashok's ouster as Planning Commissioner by Chief Minister Gul Shah, and his loss of the trappings of officialdom which had impressed Sannu who seemed to love *sarkari bandobast* (government arrangements):

> *You must be with Sannu. I wish him all the happiness in the world. I am writing him a letter tonight sending photographs he took in Srinagar. Tell him Uncle Ashok now has no flag, driver, peon and authority but he is happy and fighting, and fighting for what is right, and being angry about what is wrong. Such tough things we adults try to teach him when all he wants is a hamburger and some fun!*
>
> *News from Kashmir House is that 6 Congi's have gone over to FA* [Farooq Abdullah] *so he has said he has a majority. No clear or confirmed news.*
>
> *Sometimes I think the only reason you depend on me is because I*

am a crazy kind of person who has said and done things for you which no one else does in your kind of life. Must be lots of people like me–nothing extraordinary–but you haven't had anyone tangle themselves up in your life the way I do–too informally, taking things for granted, putting myself wholeheartedly out there where others may not. I only see myself perhaps as silly, but helpful like my mother and with some grandiose ideas.

Jaya

George Fernandes's periodic nudges didn't have much impact on me although I worked to support him in his political endeavours. I was not ready for a more direct involvement in politics and thought that all I needed was to give my time to my family, and craftspersons. But what I saw and experienced later in 1984, was a major turning point in my life.

12

THE HORRORS OF AN ORWELLIAN YEAR

Towards No Closure

AS SAID PREVIOUSLY, IT WASN'T that George Fernandes's scribbled proddings were the only source of influence on me to get into active politics. It took some time and that too at a subconscious level for them to have any effect, if at all, on me. I clearly saw the need to influence public policy through politicians and the bureaucracy to save and preserve the livelihoods of millions of artisans and their traditional skills. No one ever raised their issues in Parliament. I was, however, still distancing myself from the political world, despite occasional activist forays.

Then came 31 October 1984. My niece Nandika and I were driving towards Chanakyapuri (in New Delhi) around 10.30 am. The roads were strangely empty and quiet. Typical of the shoddiness of the Public Works Department, a wrongly painted sign was hanging on a barricade across the entrance of Safdarjung Road. It said 'MENAT WORK' [sic]. It has remained in my memory ever since for the resemblance that innocent phrase had with what was to come, what we did not expect, what was to begin on the evening following the news of Indira Gandhi's assassination, and what, for some, is yet to end.

As we returned home, news spread that Indira Gandhi had been shot. Rumours, shreds of news, and tension built rapidly one upon another by the hour, until finally it became clear that she had been assassinated by two of her own security guards who were Sikhs. The danger of revenge and retribution seemed obvious to many of us. We also heard that Giani Zail Singh, the then President of India, awaited swearing Rajiv Gandhi in as prime minister. That was a lot to digest all at once.

There was an unfathomable anxiety, a sense of unease, but what we did not do was to worry about the Sikh community as a whole. After all, who worried about the Hindus when Mahatma Gandhi was shot by a

Hindu? We witnessed shock, sorrow, indifference, dismay, but mostly, we saw silence like an all-pervading pall on the streets.

We saw groups shouting slogans. Ashok and I decided to drive from where we were staying with my mother at Sujan Singh Park towards Lodhi Road to see what was happening. We saw three trucks full of men in white *kurta pyjamas* and white Nehru caps. (I have hated calling them Gandhi *topis* when Gandhi never wore any; this was Nehru's style.) They were driving past shouting, *khoon ka badla khoon se lenge* (we will avenge blood with blood) in unison. As far as we could see, there was no spontaneity about it as was claimed by the Congress party subsequently. There was a car in flames in the middle of the road in front of Safdarjung Tomb. Stabbing and stoning of Sikhs had started at 6.30 pm at the junction of Safdarjung Road and Lodhi Road too. Mobs of ten to fifteen young men aimed at vehicles carrying Sikhs. At 7 pm, we drove up to a policeman conducting traffic at this junction. Five vehicles were burning around us.

'Stop them from stoning,' we shouted.

'Don't worry,' he assured us soothingly. 'You are all right. They are only after the *sardars*.'

'Does that mean they should not be stopped?' we shouted again.

'Drive on,' he commanded. 'The police will come.'

Two Sikhs on a two-wheeler near the Safdarjung Flyover were about to be attacked in front of us. We protected them by escorting them to Sujan Singh Park and suggested we drop them home in Lajpat Nagar. 'Leave your two-wheeler at our place,' we suggested. As we drove them towards Lajpat Nagar, a huge mob was advancing towards us on the road. We told our passengers to hide in the back, turned the car around at top speed and drove back. The Sikhs crouched below the back seat till we reached the Tughlak Road Police Station where we insisted the police assure us they would be taken home safely in a police van.

Those men did not return to collect their two-wheeler from us for three months. We never asked each other's names.

In the meanwhile, we received phone calls that Sikhs were distributing sweets, and gurdwaras were celebrating with lights, and that the Sikhs had poisoned the water supply in Delhi. For that entire night of 31 October, the next day, the day after, and up to the early hours of 3 November, smoke filled the skies of the capital city of India. I recall M.J. Akbar, the well-known author and journalist, sitting with us at our Sujan Singh Park house and remarking that others would now realize what happens when specific communities are targeted for the misdemeanours of some.

I was upset to the extent that I felt like I had to do something more. George Fernandes informed me of a peace march organized by politicians like Chandra Shekhar, Madhu Dandavate, Swami Agnivesh, himself and a host of others. I joined them, and we traversed through the Ring Road, via Lajpat Nagar, Ashram and Bhogal, watching Sikh taxi drivers, shopkeepers and residents stunned and tearful their smouldering establishments. What comfort could we give them? What could we say? We were too shocked ourselves. Victims told us mobs had come armed with voters' lists deliberately picking out Sikhs. 'Iron rods', 'burning tyres', 'inflammable white powder' were repeatedly described in countless affidavits, as implements used to kill and burn throughout Delhi.

'Police?' We asked.

'Can you see anyone around?' was the reply.

Janata Party leaders went back to their offices and homes to make frantic calls to the President of India, the home minister, the police commissioner, anyone they could think of, and issued appeals to stop the senseless killing, looting and arson by calling in the army. Phone calls remained unanswered and no action was taken. Common citizens were forming protective groups; Sikhs did not attack Hindus. It was clear that the attacks were a diabolically organized, one-sided pogrom against the Sikh community by well-prepared mobs of lumpen led by local leaders. India has not been short of riots, and many of a certain ideological variety now like to speak of Gujarat 2002 in the same breath. As a first-hand witness from the very first hour of these tragic events, till the traumatized were at least physically, if not emotionally, rehabilitated, I can solemnly swear there can be no comparison. But that's a story for another chapter. This worse-than-fascist mass attack on a single community as revenge for the killing of their leader was something we had never seen before nor imagined could happen in a free and civilized India.

Meanwhile, some of us who were not directly in any political party gathered at Lajpat Bhavan and formed the 'Nagrik Ekta Manch' where we discussed what should be done to provide immediate relief to those affected. I also continued participating in actions planned at the Janata Party office by senior leaders.

On 2 November, Madhu Dandavate, Surendra Mohan and I went to the late Indira Gandhi's residence from the Janata Party office to speak to someone directly. The guards refused to let us in even though Dandavate had been a senior minister in the Janata government and a respected MP. After a while, Congress MP Arun Nehru came and spoke to us over the top of the closed gate. We asked him to call out the army urgently to stop the carnage. He muttered a few meaningless sounds like 'hunn' and 'haa' (translated to 'yes, yes'), meant to reassure us, and went away.

~

During this Orwellian year of 1984 till January 1985, I headed a relief camp—the Farash Bazar Relief camp—for three months. Thereafter, I had authored a report* with regard to my experiences around the riot victims on behalf of the Nagrik Ekta Manch. It is now a part of many archival sets on the Internet. Going through it brought back the immediacy of those days in vivid detail. Much of what I will relate here is a replication or paraphrasing of sections of the report. I still have my original, old, faded, cyclostyled, typed-on-a-typewriter copy, which has minor corrections and sub-titles handwritten by Ashok. The direct quotes here are in italics to which I have added some other remembrances.

> *On the morning of 3rd November, the government's focus turned to the funeral of Mrs Gandhi with every force and dignitary involved in the arrangements. As the funeral took place, some members of the Nagrik Ekta Manch came upon the horror of burned bodies lying in the narrow streets of Trilokpuri, a trans-Yamuna resettlement colony not far from what was still the industrial complex of Noida. We came across people hiding in the charred remains of their homes having had no food, water or protection from marauding mobs for two nights and a day.*

My son, Akshay, then 14 years old, stayed with me as we helped the police who had finally arrived and called buses to take the victims to a relief camp. At least our frustration and anger of the past three days could now be channelled into organizing clothes, medicines and food supplies for them.

Our team of volunteers took some victims to AIIMS, Akshay went with other volunteers who found a truck and took rounds in the city to ask for relief materials. Bundles of clothes, and sacks full of wheat flour and

*See https://archive.org/details/AReportFromTheFarashBazarPoliceStationReliefCamp

medicines were brought to where we were guided to proceed—the Farash Bazar Police Station complex (which housed the relief camp):

> *The Farash Bazar Naya Thana was a police station and residential police colony adjacent to Jhilmil Colony in the Shahdara area. It had 144 rooms, 72 kitchens and 72 balconies most of which were opened for the refugees, the others being full of stores and supplies. At its peak, the camp had almost 3000 people, which meant 20 to a room. Balconies and kitchen corridors were crowded with refugees—the new born* [my son helped to shield a woman behind an old sari in the lawns while she delivered her baby at midnight], *the sick, the old, and the injured* [men had their heads split open]*—but at least it was shelter.*

I must add and emphasize here what I wrote in the report about a certain police officer:

> *For all the absence of the police and the ensuing nightmare in Trilokpuri, Station House Officer* [SHO] *Daryao Singh showed he was of a different sort. He had sent his men to rescue the living on the 3rd and had brought them to his police station without any instructions from higher authorities.*

I have no idea whether one of the very few caring policemen, Daryao Singh, was ever recognized or honoured for his act of courage and compassion. It was unlikely under the very regime that caused the mayhem. Maybe, his deeds were conveniently swept under the carpet.

> *On November 4th we organized rations, a team of six doctors and collected out-sized cooking vessels from tent houses. A team began to work immediately on an aspect which proved to be of utmost importance—the listing of people (men, women, children, babies) in the camp, in each room. We compiled lists of missing persons and identified those needing immediate medical attention. We distributed rounds of clothes as they came in—one piece each, then sets each, extra woolens for the children, elderly and sick. Every one of the 3000 refugees had spare clothes, soap to wash off blood stains, a hot meal, drinking water, and tea by the end of the day (5th November). The Nagrik Ekta Manch had by then contacted the newly appointed relief committee official, the magistrate on duty, the Municipal Corporation, and the Red Cross*

arrived. Last but not least, unwelcome visitors arrived such as the SHO of Kalyanpuri and a local activist ...whom the refugees immediately identified as being among their attackers.

I recommend this report as compulsory reading for those interested in social and economic profiles of victims after a riot or pogrom as this actually was. Apart from listing names, addresses, relatives and losses, they are telling as portraits of distress as it manifested itself in the different strata of Indian society at the time. Trauma is not always a great equalizer, as I discovered. The rich felt they deserved more compensation than the poor. The rich went back to their comfortable lives soon enough. The poor suffer till today.

The poorest were in the rear block of the camp and comprised the core that was rehabilitated later, largely to Tilak Nagar in West Delhi. There were 225 widows; elderly couples, the earning members of whose family had been killed; the badly injured and the burned, whose ages ranged from six months upwards; and women who were pregnant. A pervading hopelessness, and a fervent determination never to go back to Trilokpuri were the dominant emotions.

The refugees in this section consisted of railway coolies, auto-rickshaw drivers, manual labourers and charpai (cot) weavers. We formed a team to collect affidavits about their ordeal from all the refugees at every camp. The ones I received at the Trilokpuri camp were the worst. Some like the ones I provide below still evoke feelings of anger, disgust and despair at the extent of inhumanity I was witnessing for the first time in my life. In most affidavits that contained names of the criminals, names of the victims were withheld.

One was short, but tells the story of another kind of Ram, one who obviously did not imbibe the virtues of the god-like character he played:

On the night of 1st November 10-12 persons came to my house after my husband who was beaten unconscious by the mob. They were armed with swords and lathis and threatened to kill me if I didn't comply with their wishes. Then all of them preceded to gang-rape me. It was dark so I couldn't recognise them. But I can identify one person.... He is a sweeper in Alankar Theatre, Lajpat Nagar, New Delhi, who also played the role of Ram in the Ramlila in Trilokpuri this year [sic].

A longer affidavit describes a horror story that was repeated with variations over and over. The stories never failed to stun me:

> *Trouble started in our Block around 10 am in the morning on 1st November, 1984. Through the day mobs were on the rampage burning and looting the houses of Sikhs and systematically pulling out the male members and burning them on the street. I identified several people in the mob. There was the local leader (also the Pradhan of Block 32) ... who was leading the mob and instructing it to kill all the male Sikhs of the locality.*

The affidavit mentioned a grocery shopowner from Block 31, a motor mechanic, the 'dholakwala', the butcher with his four brothers, and even the 'dhobi who used to wash ... clothes'—as perpetrators of the rampage.

> *In the evening, the local leader came with his hoodlums* (mentioned above) *and pulled out our neighbours Badshah Singh and Nanak Singh from their house. They gouged out Nanak Singh's eyes. They assaulted both of them with sticks and stones. Then they put burning cycle tyres around their necks, laughed and shouted jubilantly as Badshah and Nanak died a slow, agonizing death. I watched all this with my own eyes.*
>
> *At night this leader and his gang lit bonfires out of the loot in front of our house and stayed there through the night, shouting threats to Sikhs. They were also shouting abuses and obscenities. They asked us to give all the kerosene we had. They were also filling kerosene cans from the depot in Block 26 which was open all day and night to assist the miscreants.*
>
> *In fact, the morning of Nov 1, the Police was conspicuous by its absence. [A] police constable among them, gave the signal for the mobs to loot, kill and rape and went away, not to return till the next 35-4- hours [sic].*
>
> *...In the morning of 2nd November, a mob of at least a few hundred people came to my house. Our dhobi [who I have mentioned earlier] told the mobs that ours was a Sikh house. After this my husband was pulled out and attacked with lathis and spears. Burning articles were then thrown on my dying husband. He died in no time...*
>
> *Heaps of dead people were then burnt in front of my house by*

the leader and his gang of hoodlums. Even people who were killed in adjoining streets were dragged in front of my house and burnt with torches made of blankets and other inflammable materials....

... The police themselves were amongst the mob, identifying Sikh families and inciting them to kill all of us. Urchins from Block 27 also came, looting and killing people.

I never want to go back to Trilokpuri.

The gang leader who ordered the attacks and the butcher (who used his knives to gouge out eyes), remain in my mind, stuck like dirty tar at the bottom of a shoe. I visited Block 32 some days later since I had seen bail applications being prepared by the hundreds in the outer office of a prominent leader of the ruling party.

Someone led me to the butcher's front door at the end of the lane. It was chained and padlocked. I was told he had been told to run away to Banaras (or Varanasi).

As for the local gang leader mentioned in the testimony above, he was arrested on 9 November and released on bail five days later.

Victims at the camp told us that that local leader was well protected by '*netas*' higher up. The police regularly shared the loot collected by these criminals who harboured ill-will towards the Sikhs among them because they worked hard to earn some comforts and did not engage with them in their nefarious activities. The local leaders spoke to us too of their helplessness in the wake of the storm created by the death of their beloved leader. Others even mentioned a *hukam* (order) to go ahead.

I met one of those accused of leading the mobs in Trilokpuri. He began to lament over his inability to save the people. He even put out a poster asking Prime Minister Rajiv Gandhi to save these poor victims from blackmail by the police and begging them to return to their home in Trilokpuri!

I heard that a senior Congress leader tried to visit the Farash Bazar camp one day. I could feel the instantaneous hostility and fear, and requested the police to shut the gates. He stood outside awhile and went away. Mother Teresa came too and blessed everyone.

I also noted in the report:

It is remarkable how no personage [from the ruling party] came to show public concern, console the tragic victims, promise them anything, or

> *even wipe their tears for the benefit of Doordarshan as usually happens when there is a flood or drought.*

Actually, the Sikhs didn't want anything more than turbans to hide their cut hair and humiliation. One auto-rickshaw driver told me he had hidden himself in a tin trunk for two days. His neighbours begged him to cut his hair and beard which he did with tears flowing down his face. He told me it was the sixth day he had been unable to look at himself in the mirror. Another scene that I am reminded of when thinking of this Orwellian year is of a dog gnawing at what looked like a mound outside a gutted home. When I asked why it was doing that, I was told that the dog was trying to get at the melted flesh of burnt bodies that was still under the mud.

For many, their tragic stories have still not ended. They feel no sense of closure because the years that followed saw a series of cover-ups, whitewashed reports and callousness by the then ruling party. Each action or inaction has been a slap on the face of each victim. The helplessness continues. As for me—after the victims moved out of the camp, I spent my mornings at the Gujarat Emporium, a few hours at the Janata Party office dealing with relief and rehabilitation work through the People's Relief Committee that had been set up inside the Jantar Mantar office, and writing and editing a book on the crafts of Jammu, Kashmir and Ladakh.

With the intellectual opposition I bore towards the Emergency and my experiences during the 1984 saga made me certain that I would openly oppose the Congress on political platforms and dedicate my very untested and minor abilities towards that. It started with ten days in Bangalore helping George Fernandes campaign for the general elections of 1984. What more did I need as a baptism of fire to decide that I would not stand on the sidelines anymore, pretending I was apolitical and unaligned?

13

THE EMOTIONAL BECOMES POLITICAL

Towards a Bigger Public Platform

MY RESOLVE TO NOT REMAIN apolitical was final. Indira Gandhi's declaration of the Emergency, atrocities inflicted on Sikhs in 1984 following her assassination, and my commitment to giving craftspersons in India a platform to exhibit their immense talents, were factors that helped me make up my mind.

When George Fernandes decided to contest the 1984 general elections from Bangalore North, I decided to help him with his political campaign. Sadly, he lost the election to Congress candidate C.K. Jaffer Sharief by a margin of over 40,000 votes. George Sahib took the election results in his stride, as he always did. Victories of any kind evoked a fleeting smile, but his mind would be ticking overtime with plans for work. In defeat, it was the same but without the smile. After the emotionally draining work involving looking after the Sikh victims across Delhi and elsewhere, and the gruelling work put in during the campaign in Bangalore, seeing the huge Congress victory, though in a way expected, intensified my frustration. This was aggravated when I returned to the Sikh relief camp in Trilokpuri to see some of the senior leaders of the ruling party playing angels. My note to George Sahib expressed the misery I keenly felt:

> *3rd Jan '85, Delhi*
>
> *The effect of the early morning visit to the camp has loosened the restriction of the tight band of self control one has been exercising. I kept crying all the way in the car back and even now tears keep filling up in my eyes.* [I feel] *anger and misery* [over the fact] *that people like us who believe in ideals, principled battles, lifelong struggles, honesty, hard work should see these rotters brush everything aside and walk in from their comfortable niches.*

...You have fought all your life, been through hundreds of adverse mental and physical situations, we talk of building up ideological workers, slogging at it in constituencies—and what happens? ... money, media and muscle power and immorality wipes everything aside.

Don't think I am disheartened or am giving up at all. It's just the immense and intense indignation of seeing [an undeserving person] *walk in. Is the electorate also so ruthless or cowed down or self-seeking that they preferred this?*

[The people in the camp are now depending on handouts from those whom they feel had harmed them earlier.] *The debasement of the most fundamental human values and dignity is totally galling and unacceptable. Eventually, all that's left are flickers of individual conscience while the lowest and darkest of actions succeed. Are we so useless?*

I know we have faith, we have courage, we have hope, but can't help privately letting go of some of my pent up anger. We shall never give up—but I hope we have the ability to understand how to direct our strength and desires towards a successful path, "Success" here meaning the rightness of our hopes and visions, achieving the power to make them real, seeing the results of having faith, not having to suffer from seeing things done in vain.

Don't dwell too much on all that I am writing—and don't fear that I am losing hope. We all can be disheartened for a few moments before we get a fresh understanding of how to go about our fight, can't we?

Jaya

George Fernandes was a hard taskmaster and never allowed my emotions to get the better of me. His response to this note a few days later was like that of a kind but brusque schoolmaster.

Your note had me disturbed. True, it brings out your immense humanity and love for the people as well as your concern for the country. But we cannot afford to be overwhelmed with the problems, including the wretchedness of the mind of our people.

I don't know how much of our history you have read. We are a strange people—a people divided against themselves. 5000 years of built in cruelty and injustice of the caste system is the most important bane of our national existence.

You really need to read a lot more than you have been doing. Books are good companions in more ways than one. But more than anything else they give us the experience of generations compressed in a few sentences.

George

Immediately after the Bangalore campaign, George Fernandes went directly to Bombay to consult his doctor. His stiff upper lip extended to his not mentioning a word to us about a painful problem he had been suffering throughout the campaign. It was something to do with his rear end, and he shared it with us colleagues only after making arrangements for surgery at Breach Candy Hospital in Bombay. He had doctors and nurses fussing over him while he underwent considerable pain. My family agreed that I should go for three days to cheer him up as he sounded weak and miserable on the phone. I surprised him by walking into the hospital room and spent three nights sitting in an uncomfortable wooden chair beside his bed making jokes and carrying on some irrelevant chatter to take his mind off the pain. He insisted later that the nurses swore he was remarkably better after my visit but was hurt that no one from his immediate family visited him from Delhi. When he wanted me to visit again, I refused, saying my son had exams and I had my weekly bazaar at Hanuman Mandir to run. He was healing and therefore grumbling whenever he telephoned. I suggested that he come to Delhi and stay in bed at his home, and slave-drive his colleagues from a reclining position.

I sent him two notes with a friend, both displaying the quirkiness of our friendship despite my respect and regard for his experience and seniority. One was a poem, the kind I often concocted spontaneously to wake my daughter in the mornings, or help my son remember a part of his homework:

Are you lying like a whale washed up on shore, looking balefully at the world?

Am signing off for the day,
Got to be on my way,
Please don't sit and sigh,

The days will soon go by,
Many would love to share your fate,
*In having fair hands to irrigate,**
Don't waste your time in empty curses,
Smile and chat to all the nurses.

The People's Relief Committee constituted for relief work on 5 November 1984, was headed by Former Chief Justice of India, M. Hidayatullah, while George Fernandes was its secretary. I was its executive secretary and Chimanbhai Patel, the treasurer. We had collected almost forty lakh rupees from various leaders including chief minister of Andhra Pradesh N.T. Rama Rao and many Sikhs from abroad. Justice (Retd) R.S. Narula and journalist-writer Khushwant Singh were also a part of it and regularly guided us.

The second note to George Fernandes (when he went back to the Bombay hospital for a follow-up), was informally written on the People's Relief Committee letterhead to report on the Committee's activities. I adopted a formal tone for the sake of offering some relief in the form of humour during those difficult times.

Dear Sir, I enclose photographs of 21st February of distributing relief at Guru Harkishan Public School. Shri George Mathew and I were the VIPs of the occasion after which we left on a motorbike (not very VIP-ish!). We also had a meeting with Shri Khushwant Singh yesterday regarding various rehabilitation matters, at the end of which Sh. KS gave me a big K-I-S-S for my efforts. Good reward!

Jaya

Our work received publicity abroad although we had no idea how. There were no television channels and none of us wasted time on the media. But the work brought us a clutch of invitations from the UK to attend functions at gurdwaras and Sikh gatherings. They wanted to honour George Sahib and me formally and thank us for all that we had done to save their people in India. We accepted the invitation. In London, we spent some taxing evenings in homes where elderly parents were extremely worried about

---

*The nurses 'irrigated' his inner passages as part of the healing treatment.

their sons talking rashly about Khalistan* and wanted us to dissuade them. We did so, challenging point by point their Cockney-accented arguments, over many evenings till they fell silent.

When we returned to India, Rajiv Gandhi began speaking against 'a former Janata Minister' who was engaging with the Khalistanis abroad and had addressed extremists in the gurdwaras there. I recall George Fernandes's response in public meetings in Mumbai and even in Balaghat in Madhya Pradesh: 'Imagine the likes of him talking to me on patriotism while making his wife retain her Italian citizenship for over ten years to have a place to run away to!' The citizenship issue has been raised by thousands of people including George Fernandes, the Rashtriya Swayamsevak Sangh (RSS), and it also features in my writings. This is one issue for which I have not heard a Congressperson provide any answer, let alone a satisfactory one.

He was mighty pleased with Rajiv Gandhi's repeated public references to his visit to the UK, saying that Rajiv Gandhi had fallen into his trap and become his *pracharak* (or propagator) now, ensuring coverage and pictures and even some supportive editorials. George Fernandes loved a political fight; in fact, any public challenge. He almost welcomed the idea of going to jail and being beaten up and often wistfully said in his later years that I had learned a lot but he was still waiting for me to be jailed as part of a struggle against injustice. I would retort that these days it doesn't work that way. People are accused, falsely or otherwise, of money-related crimes and not as a part of their struggle for the sake of national duty or justice. Most are jailed for corruption by their political opponents who happen to be in power at that time. But speaking of jails, a correspondence between George Fernandes and me comes to mind at this point.

He had collectively spent more than five years in jail for launching struggles against injustice of various sorts and once wrote to me contemplatively about women in jail. This was in the late eighties when he was in Bhagalpur jail in the course of the fight against the unfair election practices carried out by his opponents.

> *This morning I thought of you going through prison life of your own. Prison—never mind what we say—is no fun. Of course, when you have 263 persons with you, it is easy to pass time. Books, papers and so on also keep company. But it's no fun. You are away from your loved ones.*

*The Khalistan movement was a Sikh movement that called for a separate country for Sikhs.

> *You are away from the many things you think you ought to do and which are your priority. I have often felt the urge to send you to jail for a while. I hope it never, ever becomes necessary. What I would want you to do is to get associated with a prison visiting group and see the insides of a prison, particularly a women's prison. I think a woman in a men's prison would be the object of so much curiosity and subjected to such obscene remarks that I would never want you to step in anywhere near to a men's prison. I remember* [that a well connected] *girl was once visiting Tihar when I was there.... I was told she would be visiting the maximum security yard in which I was lodged. She did not. Later I was told she was subjected to the most vulgar abuse possible, and there is nothing one can do about it—not even the jail official. First, you are among criminals; second, they don't get women in prison and are therefore sex-starved. Third, the good looking and well dressed women in any case bring out the worst in such people.*

I was able to send a note back reporting about the Banka campaign, and added,

> *It was very amusing to see you wishing to send me to jail and then deciding—no—it's very bad for women! I'm quite indifferent—if I go I won't bother about men's remarks, it will only confirm how detestable they can be in certain situations, and I'll ignore it. And I will not be bothered about the physical discomfort—I'll only feel impatient to get out and carry on doing whatever work I was doing. I will enjoy the opportunity to have time to read and write! I'm sure I won't like it but I won't care.*

Almost thirty years after this exchange, as the *Tehelka* case foisted on me in 2006 drags on till date, I have often thought that if they had found a way of sending me to jail they could have done it long ago. It is more tedious to make over 150 trips to five different court rooms facing nine different judges for eleven years with nothing moving towards a conclusion. Of course being incarcerated after a pertinent struggle lends one a badge of honour, but in this case, the attempt was to dishonour me and George Fernandes by showing us as corrupt politicians engaging with defence dealers. However, that story is for later.

I was never pampered either by my parents, my husband or my political mentors. Even if I had occasionally wished for it, it never happened. If I grumbled about having to do something I did not like doing, George Fernandes would sharply say, 'Well, being in a political party is always only a voluntary exercise. And no one makes a bed of roses for anyone else.' He was indirectly telling me I could take it or leave it. I went into political activity with my eyes wide open, fired by idealism, expectations of teamwork and collective activity for a greater good. The example of George Fernandes's single-minded pursuit of justice and his thrill in being part of a political battle, which he thought was justified, was example enough. I admired his fearlessness, integrity, and astute mind. The cherry on the cake was his deep humanity and love for books and animals. He could not have removed my rose-coloured glasses more sharply than when he once wrote,

> *Public life has been defined as the most demanding mistress. Forget the chauvinism or sexism involved in the statement; the fact is it is the most demanding work. You have now some personal experiences of it—the latest being Farash Bazar. And at the end of it all, when you sit down to write the balance sheet, you have generally nothing in hand, because public memory is fickle and short.*

The balance sheet was too far off in the horizon for me to bother about. But I do know that while I did not expect a bed of roses, I did not anticipate that active party politics for me would eventually become a bed of thorns—rather, a glass cage full of scorpions.

From 1985, I became more visible on trade union platforms with the idea of linking the organized factory workers with the unorganized rural producers in the areas of farm produce, crafts and textiles. I became the voice for the craftspersons among hardnosed bargainers for higher wages and bonuses which the poor rural producer could not ask for. The idea was to persuade workers like railway men, taxi drivers, auto-rickshaw drivers, and municipal school and hospital workers to adopt handlooms for uniforms, albeit in polyester-cotton mix for solidarity of the working classes. This also ensured that displaced rural workers did not migrate to cities for better earnings while willing to take up their jobs for less pay.

It was a fascinating experiment and I found myself addressing thousands of workers. They were all part of the unions George Fernandes had founded and headed. A company was to be set up to facilitate the production and supply of such textiles to city workers. We registered the company and collected a lakh of rupees from various unions. A distressed groundnut farmer came from Karimnagar begging for a loan just for two months till his crop was ready. The money went to him from the company. We never saw it or him again. So that was the end of that.

~

George Fernandes's ability to make a speech was an impossible act to follow. I did not get over the fear of speaking publicly in his presence for at least a decade. Much later I learned for myself that if you really know what you are talking about and have a passionate belief in what you are saying, any pitch, tone, voice and manner is good enough to get across to people in the right way. Some bombastic speakers are all noise and no content. Timid only happens if you aren't sure of what you are saying. Reading out speeches was an absolute no-no, and sounding soft and sweet without confidence and assurance would have bored the audience. Despite my age (then 43 and a mother of two), my pleasure when someone liked my speech, was quite childlike. I feel silly now, but I am sure everyone of any vintage and experience likes to be appreciated. My note during this time to George Sahib goes like this:

> *I'd been invited by Madhu Kishwar (Manushi) for a function to honour the family of a Hindu who had died protecting Sikhs in Nov'. Longowal* came. I was asked to speak as well. I wasn't at all nervous of speaking and afterwards people came up and said how well and sensibly (!) I spoke, and would I address the women's wing of the Sikh Forum. One chap Siddu, said, 'I have heard a lot about you and all the good work you did for relief, and I have been writing about you too, but I thought you were a boy.' That was hilarious! Longowal also specially thanked me. Gosh!*

The snide whispers of course began soon enough. While I blissfully never noticed the fact that I was a woman among a phalanx of male leaders and workers, being unselfconscious about such things all my life, for them I was a mere 'woman' and nothing else. George Fernandes once reported that a

*President of the Akali Dal during Punjab insurgency in the 1980s, Harchand Singh Longowal was assassinated in 1985 at a Sherpur village gurdwara.

A late-1930 portrait of my grandfather
Sir Vasudeva Rajah of Kollengode by Amrita Shergil.

My mother (left) with Begum Ghiasuddin, or Aunty Apa,
as I called her, in the only photograph I have of hers. (New Delhi, India, 1945)

With my father, K.K. Chettur
(New Delhi, India, 1946)

In ceremonial Japanese clothes with my mother Meenakshi Chettur (Tokyo, Japan, 1951)

In rural Saurashtra costume as part of a Government of India-sponsored fashion show. (New Delhi, India, 1957)

At a dance rehearsal of a chorus line before
our graduation event at Smith College.
(Northampton, Massachusetts, USA, 1963)

Celebrating Graduation Day at Smith College with our house mother, Ms Stillwagon.
(Northampton, Massachusetts, USA, 1963)

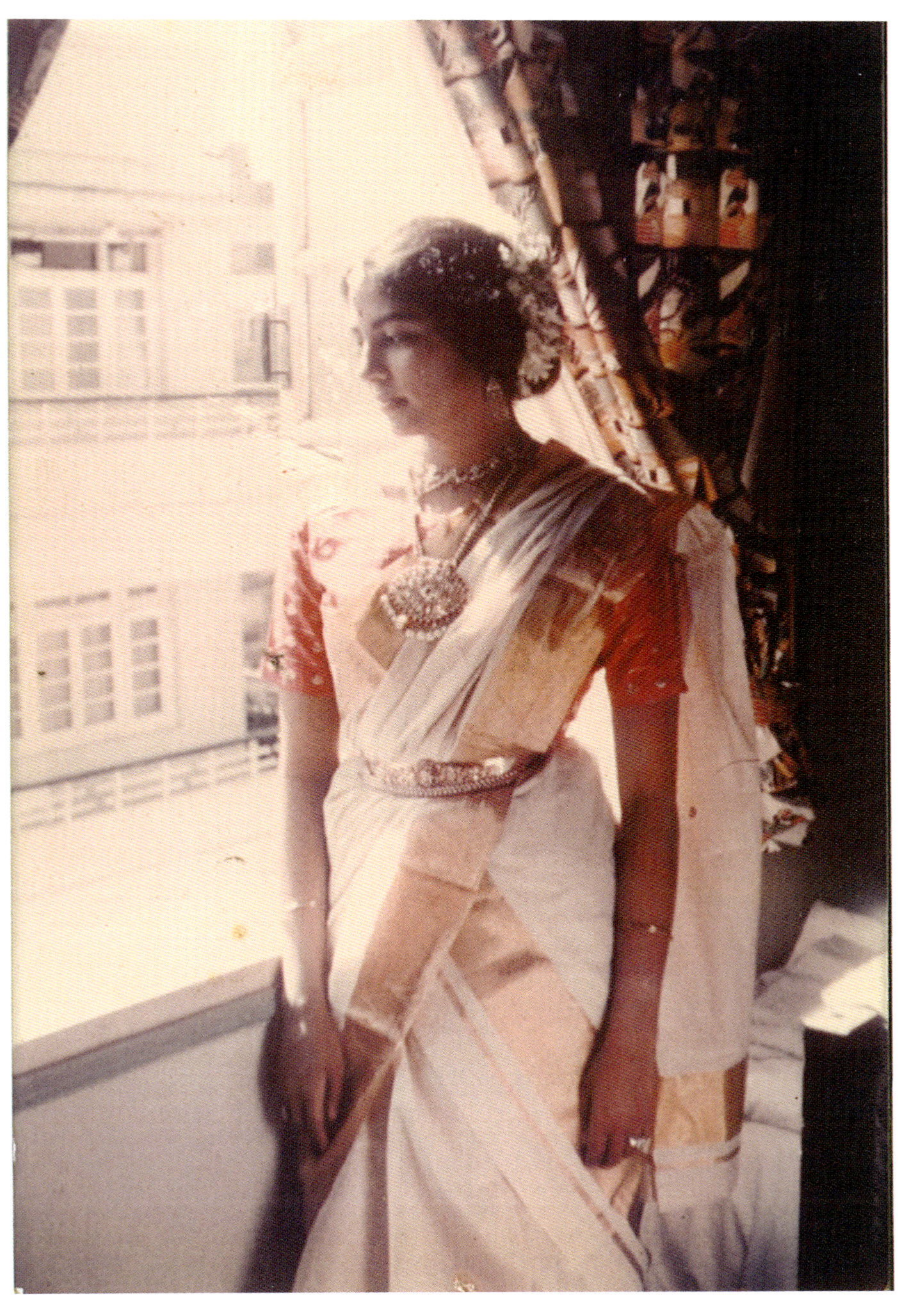

Ready for a small ceremony in traditional Kerala attire on the morning of my wedding.
(Bombay, India, 1965)

At my wedding reception—seated beside Ashok Jaitly, and surrounded by aunts, my niece and nephew from Kollengode. (Bombay, India, 1965)

George Fernandes and me drinking milk at a village on the way to Patna from Muzaffarpur on polling day, during the Lok Sabha elections of 1980.

In conversation with George Fernandes when the car had broken down while returning from Muzaffarpur to Patna—on polling day, during the Lok Sabha elections of 1980.

Explaining embroidery ideas to women. (Kutch, Gujarat, India, 1982)

Distributing relief kits to the 1984-riot victims. (New Delhi, India, early 1985)

Visiting our family home in Kollengode, Kerala,
sometime in the early nineties

With George Fernandes for a conference on Tibet, and meetings with
Japanese socialists and university students. (Kyoto, Japan, mid-nineties)

At the inauguration of the crafts bazaar arranged by the Dastkari Haat Samiti, on behalf of Delhi Tourism and the Ministry of Textiles, to announce the forthcoming Dilli Haat. (New Delhi, India, 1992)

At my son Akshay's wedding with his bride Isabelle Faure Jaitly (in the white paper gown), my daughter Aditi and former husband Ashok. (Fecamp, Normandy, France, 1998)

The cover of *The Week*, in its issue dated 17 April 1994, carried this photograph of me protesting near Parliament against the government's impending economic policies.
Photo courtesy: Arvind Jain, The Week

At an air force event with Defence Minister George Fernandes, Air Marshal Krishnaswamy (to his left), former MP Ajay Singh (extreme left), and George Sahib's official assistant, Ashok Subramaniam (to my right). (Rajasthan, India, 1999)

With well-known Hollywood actor, Richard Gere—also a staunch Buddhist and a supporter of Tibet—during one of his visits to India. (New Delhi, India, 2000)

At daughter Aditi's wedding with former cricketer Ajay Jadeja, at Kashmir House; here seen (from the left) with son Akshay, former husband Ashok, and my daughter-in-law, Isabelle (standing beside me). (New Delhi, India, 2001)

At a protest rally against the Taliban attack on women and the Bamiyan Buddha statues in Afghanistan, with George Fernandes, other Samata Party members and Tibetan activists on International Women's Day. (New Delhi, India, 2001)

Displaying the crafts maps made by the Dastkari Haat Samiti to Prime Minister Atal Bihari Vajpayee (immediately to my left) and Finance Minister Yashwant Sinha (to my left and in front of me). (New Delhi, India, 2002)

With daughter Aditi at the *annaprasham* ceremony of grandson Aiman at the Guruvayur Temple. (Kerala, India, 2003)

Former President of India Dr A.P.J. Abdul Kalam (to my extreme right) releasing my book titled *Vishvakarma's Children*, along with eminent classical dancer Leela Samson (centre). (New Delhi, India, 2001)

Celebrating Holi at the L.K. Advani-residence, with Mrs Yashwant Sinha, George Fernandes (centre) and others. (New Delhi, India, 2003)

Addressing anganwadi workers and helpers from across the country who regularly demanded regularization of their work at children's day care centres. (New Delhi, India, 2005)

Celebrating the Dastkari Haat Samiti's twentieth anniversary.
George Fernandes is seated to my far left. (New Delhi, India, 2006)

With George Fernandes during his ayurvedic treatment at the Kalari Kovilakam that was refurbished as a health spa. (Kollengode, Kerala, India, 2006)

At the Dalai Lama's residence with the Dalai Lama (to my left), George Fernandes (centre), Ajay Singh (to George Sahib's left) and his wife Shiromani. (Dharamshala, India, 2009)

Being greeted by Governor Naval Kishore Sharma and Narendra Modi, after the latter took oath as Chief Minister of Gujarat for the third time. (Ahmedabad, India, 2007)

Photo courtesy: PTI

Showing the late Boutros Boutros-Ghali, former Secretary-General of the United Nations, the Akshara exhibition at UNESCO headquarters. (Paris, France, 2013)

Greeting L.K. Advani on his wedding anniversary. (New Delhi, India, 2014)

With Ashok, Akshay and Aditi at the wedding of Ashok's step-daughter from his second marriage. Ashok Jaitly was ailing and passed away a few weeks later.
(New Delhi, India, 2015)

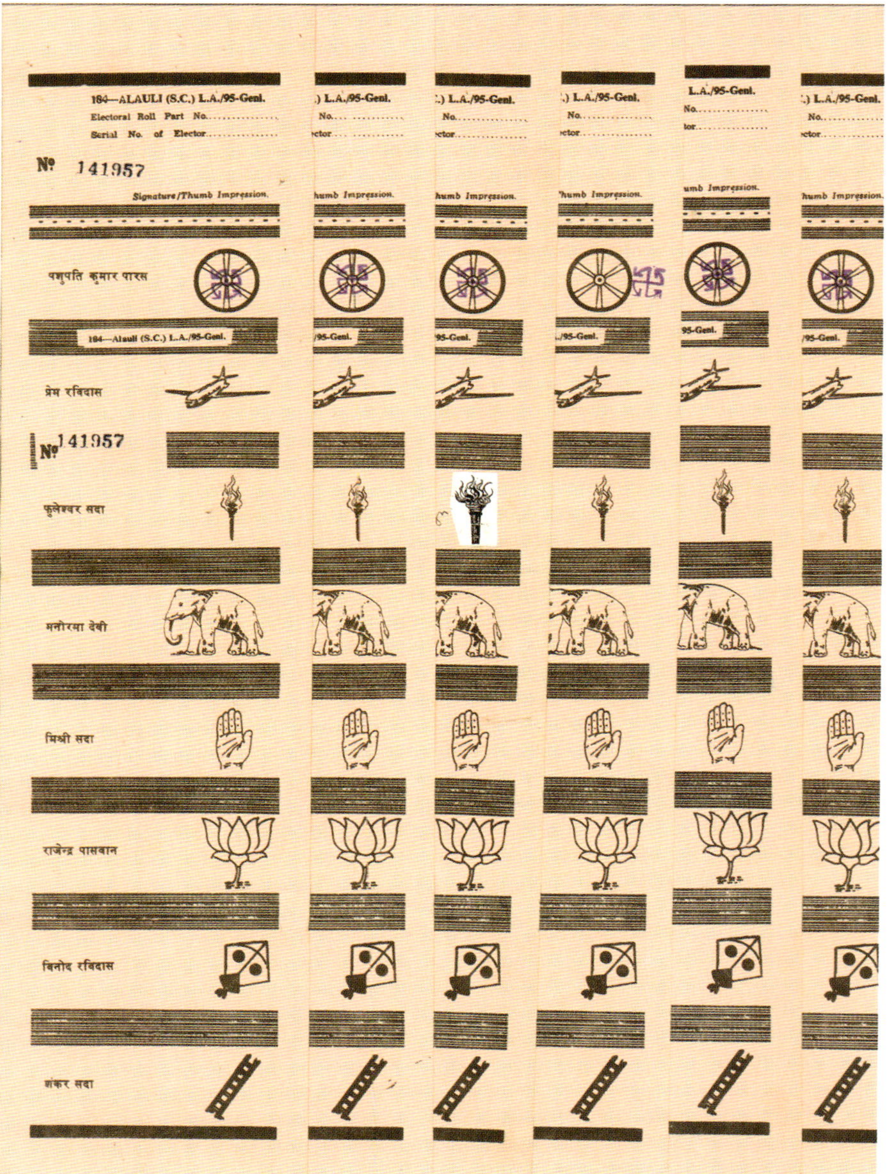

Representative of election malpractices in Bihar during the 1990s—scans of systematically pre-stamped ballot papers that were brought to the notice of the Election Commission of India. The press was destroyed in a mysterious fire.

Indian Express

Jaya Jaitley's charge against PM

Express News Service

New Delhi, Nov 28: Ms Jaya Jaitley, who was appointed chairman of the National Institute of Design in Ahmedabad by the National Front Government and whose chairmanship was terminated in one of the first decisions taken by the Chandra Shekhar Government in its review of the previous Government's actions, has regretted the termination as something which had "politicised the institution and the post".

In a letter to the Prime Minister, copies of which were released to the Press, Ms Jaitley whose appointment raised a controversy, said that though she had 20 years' experience in the field of design and marketing and had worked to bring technological benefits to the downtrodden crafts people, she had not sought any favour or post from the National Front Government. But, she said, an "undignified and orchestrated" controversy on the subject had been launced in a section of the Press against her.

She had been charged with criticising the institute.

Ms Jaitley regretted that her line of thinking was not appreciated by those in "ivory tower" establishments who were comfortable with only the "captains of large industry or status quo administrators".

She also accused the Prime Minister of succumbing to the dictates of the elitist rulers behind the scenes.

Times of India 22-6-2000

Jadeja fixes a good match

NEW DELHI: Cricket star Ajay Jadeja has married Aditi Jaitly, the daughter of Samata Party president Jaya Jaitly, in a secret wedding.

The couple is currently in London, indiaabroad.com reported, quoting a close friend of Jadeja at the ITC golf course, the cricketer's favourite hangout. "Jadeja confessed that he has married Aditi," the friend said, adding that the cricketer did not want to go public with the news yet, as he wanted to make his film debut first.

According to sources, Jadeja has signed a film with leading lady Sonali Bendre and they were supposed to start shooting this month. The producer, however, wanted to wait a while because of the recent slump in Bollywood which has been hit by a string of box-office disasters.

"Jadeja thinks that news of the wedding will affect the publicity for his debut film as well as his own star status," commented the friend.

The friend added, "Jadeja said that if the film does not happen till November, then they will tell the whole world that they are married, at a big party." *(IANS)*

'Jaya Jaitley's charge against PM',
The Indian Express, 28 November 1990

'Jadeja fixes a good match',
The Times of India, 22 June 2000

A cartoon of me in a newspaper advertisement for a particular brand of bread. It conveyed, albeit wrongly, that being Dilli Haat's boss, I could decide what bread should be sold there. (*The Indian Express*, 4 December 2000)

Why Jaya didn't make it to RS list

HT Political Bureau
New Delhi, August 28

DID THE government change its mind on nominating former Samata Party president Jaya Jaitly to the Rajya Sabha? BJP circles believe so. The list of nominations to the Upper House, which was released on Thursday, left one vacancy.

Prime Minister A.B. Vajpayee, who had met BJP leaders on Sunday to finalise the list of nominees, called on President A.P.J. Abdul Kalam on Tuesday. It was not clear whether the subject of nominations was discussed during his meeting with Kalam.

Reports about Jaitly's name being under consideration kicked up a controversy as she, besides being an active politician, was under investigation by the Phukan Commission looking into the Tehelka tapes.

The government was reportedly under pressure from the Samata to nominate Jaitly, a close associate of Defence Minister George Fernandes. On the night of August 25, a top government source told the *Hindustan Times* that her name was on the confirmed list along four others: actress Hema Malini, RBI Governor Bimal Jalan, journalist Chandan Mitra and former wrestler Dara Singh.

All four have made it to the Upper House, with three others, ISRO Chief K Kasturirangan, Hindi scholar Vidya Niwas Mishra and social worker Narayan Singh. But not Jaitly.

On the face of it, the government chose not to fill the vacancy to avoid friction within the NDA. But the speculation now is that the berth might eventually go to a sitting Congress member who also holds a Constitutional position. This member, due to retire in July 2004, has drawn closer to the BJP in recent months.

The RS seats had fallen vacant after the retirement of eight nominated members: Shabana Azmi, Raja Rammana, Kuldip Nayyar, Dr Selvie Das, Mrinal Sen, C Narayana Reddy, Harmohan Yadav and K S Duggal.

Jaya Jaitly
Missing out

'Why Jaya didn't make it to RS list', *Hindustan Times*, 28 August 2003

C/30 Sujan Singh Park,
24th November, 2002

Dear Justice Venkataswami,

It is extremely regrettable that the opposition parties have chosen to denigrate the judiciary and bring a halt to the work that has taken considerable time and effort over the past twenty months.

Even though I have often felt that the Honorable Commission was not sympathetic to my genuine and just requests, especially for the forensic examination of tapes, fresh transcribing of transcripts and order of witnesses, I always respected your intention to be fair and get to the truth.

I am really sorry that you have had to go through the agony of the recent events brought about by the opposition and certain other vested interests. We are used to such attacks as public people but they did not have the right to denigrate members of the judiciary.

Please accept my regards and respects,

Yours sincerely,

Jaya Jaitly

A letter expressing my regret and sympathy over Justice Venkataswami's resigning from heading the Inquiry Commission, 24 November 2002

Justice K.Venkataswami

611, BEL Guest House,
Padam Bahadur Mal Block,
New Delhi – 110 049.

Dt.27th November, 2002.

Dear and respected Ms.Jaya Jaitly,

I acknowledge receipt of your letter dated 24th November 2002. I thank you sincerely for the sentiments expressed in the said letter.

Wishing you all well,

Please accept my regards and respects.

Yours sincerely,

(K.VENKATASWAMI).

To

Ms. Jaya Jaitly,
C/30, Sujan Singh Park,
New Delhi.

Venkataswami,)
)
)

To
Ms.Jaya Jaitly,
C/30, Sujan Singh Park,
New Delhi.

Justice Venkataswami's short and kind response to my letter, 27 November 2002

No. 114/CP/NAC/2004 64

SONIA GANDHI
CHAIRPERSON
NATIONAL ADVISORY COUNCIL

10, JANPATH
NEW DELHI - 110 001
PHONE - 23012686, 23014481
FAX - 23018651

September 25, 2004
27

Dear Shri Chidambaram,

I am enclosing a copy of a letter written to me by Directors of First Global regarding alleged harassment by some of the agencies under the Finance Ministry. I have been informed that this matter has already been discussed in a high-level meeting and certain corrective measures have been agreed to. I would like you to look into these issues on priority in order to ensure that no unfair and unjust treatment is meted out to the petitioners.

With good wishes,

Yours sincerely,

Sonia Gandhi

Shri P Chidambaram
Minister of Finance
North Block
New Delhi

urgent

Sonia Gandhi's letter to P. Chidambaram requesting that petitioners First Global not be meted out any 'unfair and unjust treatment', September 2004

FIRST GLOBAL

2, Crescent Chambers,
4th Floor, Tamarind Lane, Fort
Bombay - 400 001.
Tel : 00-91-22-2265 [illegible]
Fax : 00-91-22-2265 [illegible]
E-Mail : firstglobal@vsnl.com

20th September, 2004

Smt. Sonia Gandhi
Chairperson,
United Progressive Alliance,
New Delhi.

<u>Sub.: Our continued harassment by Govt. Agencies</u>

Respected Madam,

As you are aware, under the previous BJP-regime, various government agencies like the Income Tax, Enforcement Directorate, SEBI etc, had been used by the then government to ruthlessly persecute us, by initiating multiple frivolous cases and proceedings.

We regret to inform you that even till today, our harassment continues, albeit in a more covert and surreptitious manner. In fact, these authorities have refused to withdraw/ modify their orders/ actions against us even when judicial/ quasi-judicial authorities have given them an option to do so. We detail some of this below:

- We still cannot travel abroad freely, because of the Income Tax Dept's patently absurd restriction on this Fundamental Right of ours. We have managed to get only limited relief from the Bombay High Court on this count – and even though the Hon'ble High Court had given the IT department an option to withdraw their order, they have not done that. The Income Tax Dept cooked up absolutely ridiculous tax proceedings against us, and using these fabricated charges continues to deny us our Rights and Liberties. We can only feel a deep sense of regret that we have been one of India's largest individual tax-payers. If this is the treatment meted out by the IT Dept to large tax-payers like us, is it any wonder that the average Indian feels it futile to be tax compliant, when harassment by authorities is virtually a certainty, and the redressal against such harassment practically non-existent.

- Just about ten days back, the Income Tax Dept has attached all our businesses. Even during the days of the BJP-rule, when the venom in the govt agencies was far higher, this did not happen. Essentially, the IT Dept wishes to take away our businesses too, after having taken away all our other assets, and having virtually bankrupted us. We fail to understand what purpose virtually killing us is going to serve, and that too, now, when such a move was not considered necessary even at the height of the BJP's terror regime.

- <u>As is clear, the objective of the IT Dept continues to be to not let us travel freely so that we can't earn our livelihood abroad, while at the same time, by</u>

auctioning off our companies here, not let us earn our livelihood in India. Respected Madam, what are we to do?

- SEBI also continues to oppose our appeal for restarting our Indian businesses, even though the Hon'ble JPC has held that there was no evidence against us and even though the Securities Appellate Tribunal specifically asked SEBI, *"Can't you review your own order?"*

- Not only that SEBI has also continued to delay the hearing on our appeal by asking for adjournment on the ground that they needed to bring in a senior lawyer to oppose our appeal.

- The Enforcement Directorate (ED) till date has not returned our legitimate funds that they illegally seized, nor have they returned our computers. We have written multiple times to them, all in vain.

Respected Madam, we have no recourse left, but to write to you for redressal. We have neither the will, nor the resources to gain relief through expensive and lengthy legal battles. The reliefs we are asking for all within the domain of the respective department/ agencies' powers to redress in no time at all. We are not asking for court proceedings to be stopped. We are only asking for what is well within the powers of these agencies, to be redressed. We just want the harassment to stop and our legitimate reliefs granted without having to litigate meaninglessly for years.

Warm Regards,

(Devina Mehra) (Shankar Sharma)
Director Director

Letter from directors of First Global to UPA Chairperson Sonia Gandhi requesting for a redressal of the constant 'harassment' by government agencies, September 2004

GEORGE FERNANDES

Phone : 66 83 73
6/105 Kaushalya Park
Hauz Khas
New Delhi 110016

Bhagalpur
Feb 4. 85
'86

Hello, The student meet was mammoth by any standards. Spoke for over 90 mins, though the public address system was horrid. Autograph signing took another 45 mins.

Very poor preparations for the conference. They are all a bunch of nincompoops, scoundrels and frauds here, with the usual honourable exceptions, of course. They wrote out a budget of Rs. 24,200. Got promises for Rs. 1,200. Collected half that amount. What does one do with these people? What movement can you lead with them? I want to say 'to hell with it all' and get out from their chaos once and for all time. Yet, one has to fight, because those poor people down there need a voice & strength which you can provide them.

I'm expecting a big turnout for the conference, even if our fellows should be fighting their caste battles here and are not ready to receive them. Let's hope I'll have something positive to report tomorrow by this time (3.10 pm).

Please send my mail including CMIE documents & other papers with Vinod to Patna. And plan the Bhag trip in any way you wish. And don't forget to have the ragi every morning – and the 'golis'!

Keep well & smiling.

Love

[illegible]

A letter written by George Fernandes to me during the election campaign in Bhagalpur. This is one of the numerous letters we wrote to each other over the period of 1985 to 1989.

George Fernandes
MEMBER OF PARLIAMENT
(LOK SABHA)

3 Krishna Menon Marg
New Delhi - 110 011.
Tel: 23017172

4th December 2004

To,

The Speaker
Lok Sabha
New Delhi.

Sir,

Section 4 of the Commission of Inquiry Act 1952 makes it mandatory for the Government to lay before each House of Parliament the report if any, of the Commission of Inquiry made by the Commission under sub-section (1) together with the memorandum of the action taken thereon, within a period of six months of the submission of the report by the Commission to the Government.

The Phukan Commission submitted its report more than six months ago and Justice Phukan had made a statement to that effect. It is surprising that the Government has chosen to breach a mandatory law by keeping the report away from Parliament.

May I request you as the guardian of the authority of Parliament, to direct the Government to make the report available to Parliament without any further delay, as required by the law.

With regards

Yours sincerely,

George Fernandes

Recd. on 6/12/04 at 1130 hrs.
6/12/04

George Fernandes's request to the Lok Sabha Speaker to table the Justice Phukan Inquiry Commission report, December 2004 close colleague in the Hind Mazdoor Kisan Panchayat Federation told him that the stalwarts were resentful; first, because I was seen as his protégée but more importantly because I was a woman. He tried to reassure me saying he didn't really believe the report but even if it were true, I was doing pioneering work in the crafts and handloom sector and 'these fellows are clueless about this area of work'. He never believed in wasting time on such petty-mindedness and just loaded me with more work, saying 'work never killed anyone'.

So there I was, juggling my time between Sikh relief work, Janata Party activities with socialist women stalwarts like Pramila Dandavate and Mrinal Gore, seeing that George Sahib's office ran smoothly at Hauz Khas, and handling the paperwork while he was away. I also continued with the Gujarat handicrafts development work at the Emporium and in Gujarat, and simultaneously managed the usual household shopping, and the children's homework, while attending to someone with flu or dengue, taking Sannu's dog with a loose tummy to the vet if both George Sahib and Leila were away, entertaining visitors at home, caring for my mother and her establishment, and a host of other small things that crop up as unnoticed 'errands' a woman has to do. But of course, if I chose to be a part of politics in the midst of all the quotidian errands, it was entirely my choice.

~

The Janata Party had a major camp at Yercaud in Tamil Nadu, where ideologies, policies, and organizational issues were discussed threadbare for two days. Sadly, it was the only one of its kind in my thirty years of political activity to follow. Senior politicians and political thinkers sat on the floor in groups of ten to twelve, discussing various subjects till late in the evening. Chandra Shekhar, Ramakrishna Hegde, Biju Patnaik, George Fernandes, Eza Sezhiyan, Syed Shahabuddin, Madhu Dandavate, Surendra Mohan, Rabi Ray, Pramila Dandavate, were just a few names in the democratic socialist pantheon of that time. Many of us were a decade or so younger and fairly inexperienced in the hard-nosed practicalities of politics or even tough struggles and jail time. Despite that, the easy informal air of the seniors, coupled with serious, intense discussions on issues and programmes relating to industrial policies, handlooms, the Shah Bano judgement* and Muslim attitudes, alliances, coalitions, women's reservations, and caste injustice, were energizing because we were encouraged to share views which were taken seriously. We even discussed Party workers needing to abjure alcohol, and basic commitments and rules to be observed by active members of the Party. I found it healthy, democratic and non-hierarchical with no pompous speeches or condescension towards women like me. Luckily, I found I had already earned respect among the individuals present for my handicraft development, fight for handlooms and Sikh relief work.

Despite George Fernandes's warning that it would not be a bed of roses, it seemed like a reasonable start to me.

~

It was particularly satisfying that senior leaders in the Party camp at Yercaud had spoken firmly of the ills of alcohol, an issue that I have always supported. My intense dislike towards the consumption of alcohol started with seeing an alcoholic uncle in my childhood; he was lovable when sober but left family members in dread every time he went out as it was usually rickshaw-pullers who brought him back passed out cold from the roadside. As kids, we would not understand what was wrong but it was ominous in the evenings when he was around. Though later, while as a doting grandfather he spent all his time with his grandchildren, and had given up the addiction, he had by then ruined his life and several relationships. In fact, I have seen what happens at close quarters when alcohol takes over. I could never understand why people needed the fortification of a glass in their hands to be 'sociable', relaxed or uninhibited when a self-confident, innately pleasant and open-hearted person could be all of these things without this harmful crutch. I would be irritated at social evenings where the men drank till they became repetitive and boring while thinking no one was wiser than them. As I became more involved in political life, I gave up accompanying Ashok to

---

*The Shah Bano case involved a sixty-two-year-old woman from Indore asking that her husband, who had divorced her, pay her a monthly maintenance sum. While the Supreme Court ruled in her favour, the ruling was perceived to be against Islam. The Congress, owing to the pressures of an election year, sided with the Muslim orthodoxy's dismissal of the woman's right to have access to the maintenance amount and responsibility of the spouse, and came up with the Muslim Women Act of 1986 which gave Muslim women the right to a maintenance sum for only three months after divorce.

such parties and found myself in a few anti-liquor movements.

Nowadays, with rape being such a front-page issue, I cannot understand why people miss those little printed words '4-year-old raped by uncle *under the influence of alcohol*'. At TV studio discussions, whenever I mention this aspect among the many that cause rape, it is glossed over quickly. When I asked off camera why this happens, a frank young anchor said, 'Ma'am, have a look at all the cars parked outside this building after 9 pm. All media men are drinking in their cars'. I was particularly irritated when a group of friends who happened to be strong feminists called me over for a social evening and offered me a whisky as I entered. I jokingly replied, 'No thanks, I am a Gandhian'. The slightly derisive response to this was, 'We hope not in other matters'—implying celibacy. I never thought feminism meant drinking and smoking like men who do this at the peril of ill-health, just as I never believed that successful women politicians must imitate the corrupt, muscle power and other dominating ways that men adopt to get ahead. Entire villages in far-flung rural areas in many states have sunk into a quagmire of poverty and even prostitution because of alcohol, and every other woman working as domestic helps in cities has an abusive, drunken husband. No one wants to address these issues and count the numbers because states also survive on the revenue from excise on alcohol. Mahatma Gandhi once called to shame any ruling establishment that wanted its people inebriated in order to provide them development. Other than some momentary, false and illusionary pleasure, I have never understood what people get out of clinging to the glass in their hand so tenaciously.

I realized the disconnect between India's rural women and menfolk of all kinds on the issue of alcohol when I went to Dharampur (Himachal Pradesh) and then by the Kalka Mail to Jagjit Nagar (Kasauli, Himachal Pradesh) on the narrow gauge toy train in the late eighties. The world turned pleasant and quaint with sunshine, and the flowers hanging from pots overhead at the station were delightful. The mountain air was fresh. I was reminded of Kashmir and being among the hills for so many years. Still, I hated the cold and much preferred the sea the love for which was ingrained in me as a Malayali. On the train, I read Dr Lohia's talks on morality, women and true equality to get my thoughts stirred for the event to which I was heading. It made me feel I had read him long before I actually did—all those seemingly radical thoughts and 'progressive' attitudes had always simmered below my seemingly well-adjusted conservative surface but I had never had the courage or confidence to voice them.

A young man had been asked to fetch me, 'the great Chief Guest', at Kalka. Hence instead of continuing on this lovable little train, I sat on the back of his motorbike travelling up the hills for 40 kilometres till we reached a huge gathering of women from all the Mahila Mandals in the area. They had secretly organized an anti-liquor event under the garb of a *mela* (fair). They were to prepare a memorandum for the chief minister demanding that liquor shops should no longer be given licenses in the area. They were fed up of men coming from Chandigarh to get drunk in the local bars, creating a bad impression among their children as they tottered out vomiting and lying passed out in their fields, or harassing school-going girls in buses. Even the village men came home drunk every day. They were desperate to speak out but were suppressed by the men in their homes and village. Wrinkled old women, young women dressed in the best finery for the pretend *mela*, many standing before an audience for the first time, nearly all illiterate—spoke passionately to an audience of two thousand women who applauded as they made each point. I spoke last, when I warmed to the mood and felt touched by their pleasure at the fact that a woman from Kerala had come so far to listen to and share their problems. I spoke about how women's seemingly domestic problems were actually related to society and development—larger issues that faced the country. We had to be equal participants in all public activity and make our voice heard. We had to take men along and make them understand our views so that there is peace at home. The petition finally said 'no decision by the panchayat on use of land for licenced bars, liquor shops and such like should take place without 50% of the participants being women'. I spent the crisp, cold, very bright and sunny day chatting to all the *pahari* women (women from the mountains), feeling sorry to get back to a dusty, chaotic life in Delhi so soon.

On the way back in the train, while discussing Dr Lohia in a note to George Sahib, I wrote:

> *This whole matter of women finding their voices and strength only works when they are economically independent, right? Which means the next step for any woman is to say to the man, 'I don't like such and such', or 'Don't drink' or, 'If you dominate and harass me I shall leave' and*

to be able to carry out the threat. Men won't suddenly change their ways and will not appreciate women asserting their independent view, which means many homes will have to break before the next batch of men are trained through personal needs or social pressures to act fairly and equally. In the meantime can there be in one lifetime both partners genuinely transforming? I think not.

I may have been subconsciously voicing a situation closer to home.

Khushwant Singh and I once had an interesting conversation about alcohol. I lived in the same compound in Sujan Singh Park as he did. One evening, I thought I would enquire about him since he had known me from the time I was a teenager. Once, reviewing my book on the crafts of Jammu, Kashmir and Ladakh, he had written I was a tomboy in my teens when his son and other school friends used to chase me but I never gave them any encouragement. Hardly relevant to the book, but anyway, typical of Khushwant. We chatted about the People's Relief Camp Committee's work for the rehabilitation of the displaced Sikhs, apart from books and drinking. I confessed I didn't like drinking nor thought it did any good to others. He revealed his tendency to get amorous though not offensive when drunk. He felt it was necessary to be uninhibited at times. I said it was undignified to be uninhibited under the influence of alcohol; moreover, one didn't necessarily need alcohol to be uninhibited. He said he did not believe I allowed myself such liberties!

∽

After a deeply troubling time since Indira Gandhi ordered military action in the Golden Temple, her sad assassination and the torture inflicted on the Sikhs in 1984, Giani Zail Singh was almost abandoned. In the late eighties, George Fernandes would visit him and occasionally take me along. Sometimes, the former President of India would send word for me to visit. Perhaps he knew of my relief work in 1984. I wrote a note to George Fernandes after one such visit in the extreme heat of August:

Poor Giani—his air-conditioner is very noisy, his phone is dead and his cook doesn't know how to make lassi. He said it was difficult to manage on an allowance of Rs 11,000 for his office work. I am told by credible people that the Congress is spreading the story he sent you abroad to poke about on Bofors!

George Fernandes was instrumental in Zail Singh's allowance being raised. Also, the contentious Indian Post Office (Amendment) Bill (1986), subsequently prepared by the Rajiv Gandhi government, was finally withdrawn by V.P. Singh in 1990. The bill, which would have authorized the government to censor personal mails, had earlier been returned unsigned by both Zail Singh and R. Venkataraman. Zail Singh remained a loyal friend to us. He defied the Rajiv Gandhi government in August 1989 by attending the inauguration of our International Convention on Tibet and Peace in South Asia. He had not replied to our invitation, but on the day of the event all the newspapers had headlines that the former President had been advised by the government not to attend it. 'Ha! What wonderful publicity we have today! Now our programme is already a success,' I remember exclaiming to George Sahib when I reached his place early and showed him the newspapers.

Giani Zail Singh arrived at the venue just fifteen minutes after a call came from his office informing us that he was on his way. He stated significantly in his opening speech that democracy is kept alive in countries by its people and not by its governments. It was a big day for me as the secretary and main organizer of the convention. It was also a big 'coming out' occasion for me to be part of an internationally publicized event, annoying our own Congress government and the Chinese, and befriending well-known figures like Petra Kelly and Gert Bastian of the Greens movement in Germany and others from the USA, Russia, Australia, Nepal and other countries. I got busy arranging for safety pins for the paper name badges (names handwritten by my daughter in calligraphy-style sitting in bed early morning), to mobilizing student-volunteers from the Jawaharlal Nehru University (JNU), coordinating speakers with Professor Mantosh Sondhi, a great Tibet supporter, making all the arrangements at Constitution Club, and organizing accommodation and transport for everybody. It was a superhuman effort which made me ready to take on the organization of any function after that, be it weddings, handloom conventions, huge crafts bazaars and, of course, elections. The Tibetans, who have always relied on the support from socialists from the time of Dr Rajendra Prasad and Jayaprakash Narayan, were overjoyed at the sudden boost of voices supporting their cause, as India had remained silent on their problems even while being courteous and hospitable to the Dalai Lama. The wide publicity that our convention received, carried across the world by Petra Kelly and others, had motivated many other countries to hold conferences. Since many socialists managed to enter Parliament through that secret meeting between George Fernandes, Mulayam Singh and Ajit Singh to counter Devi Lal at my tiny apartment, a Parliamentarians' Committee on Tibet consisting of these socialist members and MPs from other parties was initiated with a conference at the Hamdard Auditorium in Delhi. Till then, it had been an uphill struggle for His Holiness. Three months later, he received the Nobel Peace Prize in 1989.

My children had learned to take all these activities—certainly unusual among IAS wives belonging to upper-class families, and with two children—in their stride. But I never stopped to think whether I was doing anything out of the way. When Aditi and I travelled to Ladakh with photographer Kamal Sahai for my book on the crafts of the state, the airport at Leh became a trouble spot. Flights had been cancelled every day, hotels were overbooked as a result, and there was pandemonium with passengers shouting about missed connections and no place to stay. The airstrip was being repaired and pilots were refusing to fly outside a very short time slot. The Governor had ordered a special flight earlier to evacuate some people but the logjam began again. The Indian Airlines offered no seating place, food, solace or solution. I was agitated and demanded the airport manager arrange lunch and request the Governor for another flight. When he prevaricated, I booked a call to the Governor and made the request myself, also leading the passengers to a gherao of the airport manager so that he could not leave his room. Lo and behold, in an hour another flight had been arranged, we all got packed lunches, a heart patient got a stretcher and medical attention, and as we climbed up the steps to the aircraft, I got a cheer from all the passengers. Aditi stood amazed at her mother, although I am sure it must have been a little embarrassing for a fourteen-year-old.

The latter part of the eighties and most of the nineties were full of agitations of one kind or another. There were big demonstrations at Parliament Street and Jantar Mantar. I appeared on the cover of *The Week* holding up a placard against signing the General Agreement on Tariffs and Trade (GATT) accord. I wrote fierce articles in *The Economic Times* hammering Arthur Dunkel, who led the GATT campaign, for suggesting the paisley design on his tie could be patented, bringing benefit to the craftsperson who designed it. Economics, politics and India's community culture all seem to come together in my argument against patenting designs individually.

~

In February 1986, George Fernandes was the convener of countrywide demonstrations against Rajiv Gandhi in which all opposition parties and senior leaders including H.N. Bahuguna, Madhu Dandavate, Atal Bihari Vajpayee, Samar Mukerjee and V.K. Malhotra in Delhi participated. The turnout of the better organized, cadre-based parties like the BJP and CPM (Communist Party of India [Marxist]) were the largest even though the Janata Party was the convening entity. We were all taken to the Mandir Marg police station where we were kept for three hours. The leaders used the time to make fiery speeches. It was one of the few demonstrations of a genuinely joint opposition that went far beyond everyone's expectations.

At the last moment, the trade unions pressed George Fernandes to be in Bombay for their show, so I reported all that happened to him in detail, ending with:

> *The newspapers said 8000 to 9000 persons were arrested, but the police station announced the exact number as 13,800 persons, including 750 women, which included all of us. As Aditi says, 'Mummy, if you hadn't gone would they have said 749 women?' She obviously believes the police ensures accuracy.*

Outside of these united efforts which gave some feeling of joy, inside the Janata Party—as Rajiv Gandhi's popularity could be seen evaporating because of the failure of the Rajiv-Longowal Accord and the Indo-Sri Lanka Peace Accord*—a sense of discord and murkiness reigned. Biju Patnaik did not let the socialists in Orissa raise their heads, and was

*The Rajiv-Longowal Accord also known as the Punjab Accord was signed between Rajiv Gandhi and Harcharan Singh Longowal in 1985, wherein against the acceptance of the Akali Dal's demands, the Akali Dal had agreed to stop their agitation. This drew the wrath of several Sikh leaders and politicians. Some of the clauses in the agreement weren't fulfilled eventually. In 1987, Rajiv Gandhi and Sri Lankan President J.R. Jayewardene signed the Indo-Sri Lanka Peace Accord in Colombo. With the aim of resolving the Sri Lankan Civil War, Colombo was to relinquish power to the provinces, the Sri Lankan troops were to withdraw and the Tamil rebels were to surrender their arms to the Indian Peace-Keeping Force or IPKF. However, the Tamil groups, especially the Liberation Tigers of Tamil Eelam (LTTE) did not keep to their word. Violence ensued.

frustrated with Chandra Shekhar 'over everything and nothing' as George Fernandes wrote. Pramila Dandavate did not want Maneka Gandhi taken into the Party as the Emergency had not been forgotten. However, Ramakrishna Hegde firmly insisted upon it, leading to Surendra Mohan being furious with everyone. H.D. Deve Gowda and Abdul Nazir Sab in Karnataka had their own list of complaints about each other. All big ex-Congress style leaders wanted a big 'wave' to appear to win rather than use their diminishing strength of money and muscle. George Fernandes spent his time rushing between workers' meetings, strikes and bandhs all over the country, handling the politics in Bihar with Karpoori Thakur, and mollifying sulking colleagues in different states. Often, I became the messenger back and forth as everyone believed that I had no vested interests of my own. I was too junior and harmless.

Occasionally, after a rough afternoon with an angry Chandra Shekhar who repeatedly referred to him as the 'militant socialist *neta*', George Fernandes would grumble and mutter under his breath about the pointlessness of doing all this. All these manipulations and manoeuvres pointed to the forthcoming meet at Parandwadi in Maharashtra in the mid-nineties where Chandra Shekhar, Biju Patnaik and Ramakrishna Hegde were all wanting to be elected president but not really coming out and saying so. Dummies and distractions were put up along the way. Generally, George Fernandes became the scapegoat and I complained about why he always had to play the midwife to nurse someone else's ambitions. His biggest and constant frustration was one that was common to most socialist groups and parties with weak organizational structures: Leaders were so consumed with their own importance that everything revolved around their egos and whoever hung around them. There was no commitment to a solid ideology or long-term loyalty to the organization. Everyone wanted to be a leader. Nobody was content as a worker. His colleagues also complained that George Fernandes ran around too much to assuage other people's anxieties. Of course, many of them didn't add that he was not nursing theirs, although they expressed it to me till my very last day in active party politics! It wasn't the best environment to encourage a newly converted political worker like me but hope and idealism were the occasionally elusive props to lean on.

Meanwhile, Chandra Shekhar liked the leather shoulder bag I carried to a meeting with him. I told him it was handmade by rural artisans in

Rajasthan. He asked me to get a thousand bags made for the main delegates for the Parandwadi Party Convention where he was hoping to be Party president. I was thrilled that my involvement with politics was benefitting our rural people and got them made in record time at a hundred rupees each, while being bedridden in the midst of a bad bout of jaundice. The bill came to one hundred thousand rupees apart from packing and transportation, which was a big amount in the nineties. Imagine my shock when I realized he expected me to gift these to the Party. No one was going to pay me. Greatly annoyed and realizing my financial plight, George Fernandes persuaded the Bombay trade unions to make the contribution on my behalf to pay the artisans. I learnt a lesson on how parties function. There always has to be a donor for public work no matter how much personal money may have been available.

~

The Bofors scandal exploded out of Sweden during the late eighties. George Fernandes made two trips to Sweden to meet officials and journalists closely connected with the Bofors revelations by the Swedish newspaper *Expressen* like Per Wendel, and Indian journalist Chitra Subramaniam, and socialist colleagues in Europe who facilitated many inroads into the system. Swedish social democratic politician Olof Palme had supported him during the Emergency, and Bernt Carlsson, who was appointed the United Nations Commissioner for Namibia in 1987, had been an old friend. At one time, he shared an apartment with Ram Jethmalani who was on the same Bofors trail, and shared many funny stories of how the landlady/hostess tried to seduce them both!

Meanwhile, I would lecture George Sahib by telling him he should not hobnob with people like Arun Nehru, who was by now out of the Congress party and by V.P. Singh's side on the Bofors bandwagon, but take to the streets and build a people's movement instead. V.P. Singh joined hands with Chaudhary Devi Lal, and as more big names came on their cavalcade, Rajiv Gandhi struggled, giving speeches in his lawns about destabilizing forces in the country. Then I would laugh at my temerity to lecture George Sahib because there was no way his political instincts would keep him away from a situation developing in a way that would displace the Congress leadership.

There was more heartburning and agitation in the minds of leaders composing the different groups that were attempting to merge against the Congress. Deals, disgruntlements and celebrations happened simultaneously when the Janata Party, Charan Singh's Lok Dal, Sharad Pawar's Congress (Socialist) and V.P. Singh's Jan Morcha merged after a million tussles and confabulations. When the Janata Party came into being after the Emergency, Jayaprakash Narayan committed the mistake of not insisting on an election for its leader. He nominated Morarji Desai instead of creating a situation where the legitimate concerns of Jagjivan Ram, Chaudhury Charan Singh and others could have been addressed democratically. When the Janata Dal finally came into being, the seeds of its fall were also clearly built in. The worst was the very first formal occasion of electing the prime minister. The rest, as they say, is history.

In 1989, V.P. Singh needed the support of several parties that merged to form the Janata Dal but never formed a team of close, trusted colleagues. Files were locked in a cupboard in his bedroom. If something required urgent signature, the key to the cupboard was in the pocket of the loose white pyjamas he was wearing. On the day V.P. Singh was expected to be elected as leader of the Party in the Central Hall of Parliament, Chandra Shekhar had almost come to terms with the fact that he may not be the contender but that he could win the position in a fair election. However, V.P. Singh proposed the name of Devi Lal to divert Chandra Shekhar. Devi Lal, in turn, as part of what seemed like a deal between them, passed the crown back to V.P. Singh who then declared Devi Lal the deputy prime minister. George Fernandes had worked hard and long to prime V.P. Singh to lead the combine that would defeat Rajiv Gandhi after the Bofors scandal with ideological material, and getting others in place and taking a back seat in every power-packed situation. He constantly said, reworking an old phrase, 'If there wasn't a V.P. Singh, we would have had to invent one'. He knew his flaws well, and believed anyone, including himself, was more deserving, but he was always the loyal soldier, formulating strategies by reading the tea leaves realistically for a larger political goal.

I was sitting with George Fernandes in his office awaiting the commonly expected developments to be announced when the Devi Lal-V.P. Singh manoeuvre took place. He was stunned, as was everyone else. Without a second thought he telephoned Chandra Shekhar, sharing his shock and disgust at the way things had unfolded. We knew this was a thoroughly miserable start to a new 'clean' era. The end came soon enough through the tumultuous events that led to the announcement of the Mandal Commission recommendations. This too was decided surreptitiously without the prime minister consulting or confiding in the BJP and the communist parties, who were the main outside support to his minority government. Ironically, he had done this not because of firmly held ideological beliefs about the upliftment of the backward classes, but to checkmate Devi Lal's own soaring ambitions.

14

ELECTIONS
The Highest University of Politics

MY HOME FRONT IN THE early eighties was not all that pleasant. Some of my in-laws thought anyone going into politics in those days was bound to join the crooks and criminals. Close friends from childhood were all from upper-class backgrounds; they thought I was going down the drain for hobnobbing with a rabble-rousing trade unionist, who never combed his hair, washed his clothes and was rumoured to drink half a bottle of rum every evening just because his name was 'Fernandes'. Some independent journalists wrote that when George Fernandes was Minister for Industries in the Janata government he took a flight to Mumbai every weekend to be with different women. It was hinted through rumours that he had sunk so low in politics that he had only Sampa Das* and Jaya Jaitly as advisers. Sampa was a Bengali friend who worked in the Indian Airlines and was devoted to George Sahib. She faithfully cooked hilsa (fish) curry for him to carry when he was passing through Calcutta. The thing is, no one understood the logic or reality of men and women being equally devoted to him. Men would jump off a cliff or be ready to go to jail if he so ordered. Eventually, even my set of friends and acquaintances began to be wary of me and often took a dig at politics, politicians and political parties just to get under my skin or maybe to feel superior. I was so pathetic at asserting myself that I would 'hmm-ha', smile vaguely and pretend I hadn't noticed the pinpricks.

Stupidly, I would feel miserable and cry when I recounted these unpleasant incidents to George Sahib, who barely had time to listen or comment except once, after he had gone to a dinner at Arun Shourie's place where many socialites were present. I must have become the subject of

*Sampa Das was formerly Samata Party president in West Bengal.

some conversation there in my absence, because his next note to me said:

> *They are getting jealous of you, that you are carving something out of your own. But more than that, it seems to me they are worried that one of their crowd is moving away from them. The Establishment, all over the world, gets upset when one of theirs turns 'traitor'. So don't worry over the effete elite and their views about you or your work.*

Despite my own well-pedigreed background, I did always have an aversion to elitism, and that snobbish intellectualism that substituted action. People who wrote feature articles analysing and opining always seemed to believe they had a better grip on reality than those in the trenches lining the dusty, bumpy road of politics.

I used to suffer from sharp sneezing attacks and headaches from the piercing smell of *beedi* smoke or perspiring armpits from polyester shirting in public buses. It happened with ladies' perfumes as well. I saw this as a metaphor for my crossing over from a comparatively genteel life and refined background to all things that came from the street. Doing this in the company of the most radical anti-establishment person around was unusual for everyone, including myself. My mother used to remind me that her grandmother, the grand Dhatri Maharani of Kollengode, was just as perverse. She fought the British while wearing her large golden globe-shaped earrings and multiple necklaces, arranged for martial arts classes secretly and grew medicinal plants, both against British regulations, and 'never wore a blouse, except when Englishmen came to visit'. It was a disappointment to my diamond-earring-loving mother that I only wore cheap, thirty-rupee, silver earrings picked up in the Bhuj bazaar, with a tribal *hansli*, a necklace, worth fifteen rupees bought from a roadside haat by a forest in Orissa. From someone she hoped would play the piano, wear her hair short and speak immaculate French, she was now worried whether my participation in trade union and political demonstrations would land me in jail. Being a mother, her concern was only for my safety. Hence she was happy with my argument that if I didn't wear a gold chain no one would snatch it. As for my anti-establishment activities, she'd say: 'Well, if you are in the company of George, I know you will be safe'. Little did she know how he loved to court trouble, had survived many attacks on his life, enjoyed sojourns in jail and was always ready for the next political fight.

Journalist Shekhar Gupta once wrote that George Fernandes had visited him for an interview at *The Indian Express* office as defence minister. In response to Shekhar warning him that he had a bad cold and cough and would not shake hands, he had apparently held his hand out and said cheerfully, 'Don't worry Shekhar, I am not pedigreed.' When I read this story some years later, I found George Sahib's description of himself spot on, and realized that I had unconsciously de-pedigreed myself to a large extent as well. Sampa Das called it 'de-glamourized', but that didn't fit me since I never attempted to be glamourous. In the socialist world of political activity, it would be positively incongruous, unlike many ladies in Parliament today who are hardly ever without *zari*-bordered saris and visit beauty parlours regularly.

Stepping out of this fairly genteel world into the midst of election campaigns was a big step. These are arenas where any committed party worker can afford to think of nothing but to work for the victory of the candidate. No sleep, no food, no questions asked, just slog from 6 am till midnight, whatever the job. Activists and politicians who demand reservations for women without any experience of actually slogging it out in a party organization only display their distaste for mingling with the good, bad and the ugly. That is real life.

~

My first election experience was at Muzaffarpur in Bihar, in 1980, where I was, in reality, a mere observer who made herself slightly useful. George, the Giant Killer of 1977, was fighting the Lok Sabha elections, this time with his back to the wall against upper-caste dons who held sway with their guns and bombs, preventing the Other Backward Class (OBCs) and Scheduled Castes (SCs) from approaching the polling booths. Having heard a lot about this politician through the experiences of Ashok, he encouraged me to see things for myself and suggested I spend a couple of days there to get a first-hand experience of what happens. I set off for Patna and was helped by parents of a bureaucrat friend to get on the boat to cross the Ganga. It was almost midnight in a chilly January. George Sahib had sent his colleagues to fetch me at the other bank. I could barely see them holding up lanterns through the fog. We reached a local supporter's residence around 1 am. But just as I reached, the lights in the room Leila Fernandes and a friend were using, were turned off. The hosts were planning to have me share their room. A little embarrassed at this unexpected, unwelcoming reception, they ushered me in the dark to another room and told me to quietly crawl under the mosquito net. Exhausted, I crept in and slept at the very edge of the bed as it seemed there was someone else in it too. In the morning, I discovered I had shared the bed with four other family members—women and children. We all woke up in the morning looking at each other in surprise. The house was semi-complete. There was no separate space for bathing. Brush your teeth at the hand pump and bathe in a small empty storeroom with no drainage, or on the rooftop, I was told by the lady of the house. I chose the latter. As I stood looking over the rooftops of Muzaffarpur amid the cold open air, I hoped no one could see me.

For two days, I was assigned to be part of a team of women who went from house to house in the railway colony and other poor working class areas, telling people to vote for George Fernandes and teaching them how to stamp and fold a ballot paper lengthwise in half and then over, to fit in the ballot box. George Fernandes's famous speech defending the Janata government and then leaving it, was raw. It was no longer an easy time for the man who had the second highest vote in history just two years ago. Newspapers accused him of distributing motorcycles and blankets; the Left parties said he had been a corrupt Minister of Industries. I campaigned faithfully with full knowledge that none of this was true since Ashok had spent every waking hour with him and would not have remained loyal if any such thing had happened. In fact, at a dinner one evening, a businessman, not knowing who he was, boasted he had personally handed over money to George Fernandes. Ashok called him to the Ministry the next morning and asked if he was prepared to say this in front of the minister. The man ran away!

George Fernandes won by a margin of only 30,000 odd votes. It was a huge drop. I came back to Delhi where curious friends at evening dinners were waiting to hear a blow-by-blow account of this unusual activity as if I had been to some nether world and had come back unscathed.

~

By the time the next campaign experience came along, it was 1984. I was already a changed person. George Fernandes was asked by Chandra Shekhar to fight from Bangalore North as Karpoori Thakur was non-committal about supporting him in Muzaffarpur. I felt it was a mistake to leave the constituents that loved him but he too was unsure about Karpoori at that time, and after much doubt, chose Bangalore as being 'safer'. Ramakrishna Hegde assured George Fernandes he would have his men provide all the ground support. It was to be an easy ride. To the latter's horror he found voters actually asking who he was and the promised ground support evaporated without a trace when money was not adequately provided. C.K. Jaffer Sharief, his opponent from the Congress, had a good hold locally and a well-organized team. Fired up and committed to taking an open stand against the Congress, I stayed at George Fernandes's home with his mother and brothers for ten days, helping workers with slips, posters, leaflets and other Party material. In the evenings, we went in large groups to campaign door to door or address public meetings all over Bangalore North. I began to understand Kannada, especially words that were repeatedly used in political addresses like '*sullu*' for lies and '*prajaprabutva nashagolisu avaru*' for 'destroying democracy', etc. However, my timid speeches about the state of politics then had to be in Hindi to whoever in the audience could understand the language. I spoke about various issues like the ongoing problems in Kashmir and my recent experiences in Delhi to persuade voters not to vote for the opponents. On hindsight, I doubt if it resonated at all. Bangalore's Hindi was very odd. On the eve of elections, I remember a heavily built Muslim woman, a political enthusiast who was part of the women's team coming to me and asking for a hefty sum of money: '*Paisa dena, stamping karko vote dalna*,' she assured me under her breath, thumping a closed fist over the palm of her other hand. Once I understood she was demanding funds to stamp ballot papers in bulk, I was taken aback.

George Fernandes was defeated by a margin of about 40,000 votes for lack of ground support and the wave that swept over the country in favour of Rajiv Gandhi after his mother's assassination. This woman remained convinced that the loss was because I didn't let her stamp extra ballot papers. She was disappointed in me as a woman, she said.

~

By 1985, the Party leaders who were in opposition were becoming increasingly wary of George Fernandes raising multiple issues outside the Parliament. If he created too much noise outside, they feared being exposed of inaction. It was best not to let him remain an 'outsider'. They wanted him to fight the by-election from Banka in Bihar. For all his love for struggle, he too felt like a fish out of water when he did not have Parliament as a platform to hammer his opponents with incisive speeches, telling statistics, and a challenging audience. I was cautious, as usual. I wrote:

> *As far as I can gauge, the situation isn't as it must appear to you … if the BJP doesn't withdraw there is nothing in the Lok Dal withdrawal … I don't view it as just a good challenging fight (which you love) and barge ahead believing that everyone means what he says at face value … all these BJP, LD, JP types saying you must go ahead. I don't trust a single one of them. They can lead you a-dance as they did in Karnataka, swearing to support and stabbing you from behind. As for the 'people', we all know how they are broken down by fear, money, etc.… Everyone stands to gain by your victory and only you stand to lose if you are defeated in a three-way fight. Think coolly (Gosh, how can I be advising you!). I am taking courage because all your close colleagues here including Vinod* [Vinod Prasad Singh] *agree … I know you will say the answer to everyone is to 'fight' but when, where, how is important. Now it should be a fight to win and not your famous 'failure is the other side of success' phrase.*

As usual, he did not take my advice.

I was put on the task of seeking Lok Dal support from Chaudhary Devi Lal, and money from Prakash Singh Badal who was never contactable as his mother was very sick at the PGI, and other small contributors apart from the Bombay unions who were providing the money for banners, posters and leaflets along with teams to work on the ground. The election agent was Yashwant Sinha who later became Union Finance Minister. A lot of coordination between him, the Party office and the workers in Banka had to be done. Jyoti Basu in Calcutta first promised a helicopter and then his secretary called to say that it was out of order. I had to frantically arrange for a helicopter for Hegde to campaign for a day for George Fernandes since Hegde refused to travel any other way because of back trouble. Chandra Shekhar finally managed a Vayudoot. On my way to meeting Hegde at the Delhi airport to ensure he travelled to Banka to campaign, since they could all change their minds at the eleventh hour, I met M.J. Akbar, our old friend who was then a Congress MP. We had always been friends and yet Akbar was sarcastic about George Sahib and our efforts. I wrote to George Sahib that it was a most unpleasant experience since Akbar often spent time with him and had even contributed a small amount for other elections. However, at this time he was playing the role of a politician opposed to us.

I took Shiraz Sidhwa, my journalist friend, and accompanied Hegde on his day's campaign to Banka in this tiny plane. It was odd to see a pathetic Bihar Police guard of honour in place to receive Hegde at the helipad. It was completely incongruous. I also had to tackle Biju Patnaik for material help in between his 'Humpfs' every now and then, Syed Shahabuddin, a senior Party leader, proving extremely difficult to manage with his many tantrums, apart from trying to organize a PUCL (People's Union for Civil Liberties) team to go as observers to ensure the election was free and fair. In between, I would run to Madhu Limaye who had some advice to pass on regularly to George Fernandes who got thrown into Bhagalpur jail for a few days owing to having arranged a satyagraha amidst it all! It was a lot of learning at one go.

I would receive an occasional note from George Sahib through some travelling colleague, to one of which I replied:

> *I was happy to receive your note but not too happy at the extent of violence you hint at—because there is a limit in terms of money and muscle power we can muster to counter that. Our weapons are based on hope and idealism, honest effort and solid guts—let's see how far that takes us—guns apart! Was chasing the Lok Dal chaps for a couple of days—lots of hemming and hawing and going around in circles but the papers today say they have declared support. I guess they couldn't avoid it finally although Ajay Singh conveyed that Karpoori was stuck in a complicated situation since they were supporting BJP elsewhere and were getting their support too.*
>
> *The media is quite excited about the' 'thrilling' contest. 'Fiery', 'redoubtable', 'colourful' GF is giving everyone some fun. Not much sympathy for Chandrashekhar Singh* [the Congress opponent] *anyway. The Election Commission letter is good.... Publicize it there and I've asked Party Office to send out a press note on it here.*
>
> *Zaidi, a party secretary, has promised to get Chaudhury's appeal signed, printed and sent with Sharad Yadav. I'll keep breathing down his neck from here.*

I strongly believed backstage work was as important. The candidate is the actor in a play but he cannot function without all the stage hands putting everything he needs in position. I helped many Party leaders get elected through myriad efforts like badgering the Election Commission to prevent booth capture, to seeing the posters were printed and dispatched properly, to finding men and materials for their support. I expected that in return, the victorious candidates whom I had worked for, would raise issues in Parliament on matters that concerned my areas of work involving artisans and weavers. I honestly believed one didn't necessarily have to only be a member of Parliament to be politically active or relevant. Of course, one learns that the job is a thankless one. Men believe it to be a matter of right to be served according to their wishes, but isn't one taught to be selfless in politics? Most times I have been fully satisfied with this approach, but in later years, I have to admit to occasionally wishing I could be in Parliament too, primarily to raise issues concerning policies for India's traditional arts and crafts. That is because my Party leaders, other than George Fernandes, showed scant interest in this sector. The attending trappings like a good salary, accommodation travel and other perks that came with being a MP, did not attract me. They were never a part of my lifestyle, and were equally shunned by my political mentor.

Coming back to polling day, Madhu Dandavate, Swaraj Kaushal, Sushma Swaraj's husband who had been a socialist activist in his youth, Jaipal Reddy, who later joined the Congress, and others, kept phoning for news. Mobile phones were a long way away from being created. No one could get through the landline most of the time. Booking 'lightning calls' at three times the rate had become standard procedure since nothing else worked. The mischief was revealed the next day.

For everyone in our team it was obvious that the Banka elections were massively rigged, and of course, George Fernandes lost by around 20,000 votes to Congress's Chandrashekhar Singh. Surendra Mohan and other senior socialists were locked up at police stations and scores of vehicles impounded, leaving the voters stranded on the roadside. Teenagers were put into voting lines, local policemen were dressed in kurta pyjamas to cast bogus votes. People said it was common knowledge that Rajiv Gandhi had set up a whole house as a control room to ensure every seat could be lost except this one. Yashwant Sinha sent hundreds of complaints to the Election Commission. I sat up nights receiving calls of impending danger which I faxed to the Election Commission. Nothing happened. The media published lengthy, detailed stories with photographs of booth capture and rigging which were openly assisted by the District Magistrate and Superintendent of Police.

Meanwhile, the stress knocked my back out of shape. I spent three weeks flat on my back on a hard bed at home compiling press reports of the rigging which went into a booklet called *The Press in Banka* where I wrote a long diatribe saying election rigging of this nature by the state was undemocratic and how the media was finally telling it like it was. The booklet was widely distributed, but that was that.

Then, Chandrashekar Singh passed away suddenly, and his widow Manorama Singh stood for election. George Fernandes opposed her but the story and the result were the same. Some colleagues were so angry that we decided to hold a demonstration against Bindeshwari Dubey, the then chief minister of Bihar. As he attended a function at Pragati Maidan in Delhi one evening, Dr Sunilam, a young socialist activist, Vinod Prasad Singh, a veteran socialist and close comrade of George Fernandes, some other Party workers and I arrived at the scene. As the chief minister was leaving we raised *murdabad** slogans and threw eggs at him. Mine got him on the back of his shoulder. We ran out and no one chased us. Looking back, it was silly and childish but it gave us a lot of momentary pleasure. I told my children I had carried warm socks in my handbag just in case we were arrested and had to spend a cold night in jail. They didn't bat an eyelid; they had got used to my crazy ways.

Apart from elections and handicrafts development work, there were sudden interludes from a different world which were thrilling. Just after the Banka elections, I had met Günter Grass, the famous German novelist, in Calcutta and invited him to visit George Sahib in Delhi. I thought it would be a fascinating interaction as I had admired his books greatly. He came to George Fernandes's small Hauz Khas apartment for tea with his wife Ute. We talked for a few hours about life, politics, literature and many other things as if we were old friends. Later, there was an exhibition of Günter Grass's etchings at Max Mueller Bhavan. I went there to see if I could meet him again. As soon as he saw me, he left his conversation with three Germans and took me to a corner of the room to tell me how

---

**Murdabad* translates to 'death to or upon'

happy he had been to meet George Fernandes and how important it had been to know he was a socialist who had been through the Emergency, jail, electoral defeats, and was still very much fighting. Then he said something I found significant and perceptive: 'You must make sure he uses his energies by deciding what is important. He must not try to do a hundred things at once. He must not let people misuse him.'

After that, I took my children to see a film adaptation of his novel *The Tin Drum* (1959) at the IIC to get them acquainted with Grass's work. I was happy that my love for good literature had not been erased by the grittiness of electoral politics.

Once the Bofors scandal* erupted in the latter part of the eighties, things went downhill for Rajiv Gandhi. The rise of V.P. Singh created conditions in 1989 for the formation of the National Front. Yashwant Sinha and I were given desks at the Janata Party office to handle the logistics of the election. We had to manage a variety of people with tact, like one short-statured, goatee-bearded man in a three-piece suit who came repeatedly carrying a briefcase and visiting cards saying he was a world-renowned traveller who had visited 148 countries for which he deserved an election ticket. Suman Sahai of the Gene Campaign wanted to fight from Muzaffarpur since she had studied in Germany and her in-laws were from Muzaffarpur. I faced some angry youth from Bihar who shouted at me asking what business I had to be at the Party office, and tried to forcefully gain entry. Once, a young socialist activist from Kanpur camped at George Sahib's office at Hauz Khas, standing on his head in a yoga pose all morning, refusing to leave till he got a ticket to fight the elections. He did not get a ticket but he did get high fever and had to be sent to the doctor. Others jumped all over the hoods of cars carrying leaders to Parliamentary Board meetings. I often had to drive George Sahib out from meetings with him hiding in the backseat muttering, 'wretched head hunters. They have not done a moment's work!'

---

*Spanning over the 1980s and 1990s, and coming to the fore during the time V.P. Singh was defence minister, the Bofors (Bofors being the Swedish arms manufacturer) scandal involved Indian National Congress politicians, and officials from Indian and Swedish governments receiving kickbacks or illegal payoffs from an arms deal in Sweden. This also saw the then Prime Minister Rajiv Gandhi being implicated in a major way at the time.

George Fernandes was the eternal peacemaker and persuader among miffed leaders with big egos and those expecting important party positions in what was hoped to be a new dispensation at last. He kept retreating from any designation he was assigned, to hand it over to Reoti Raman Singh and other colleagues of Mulayam Singh Yadav who needed to be mollified. Devi Lal, as Chairman of the Parliamentary Board, did not even allow George Fernandes to sit in their meetings and humiliated him by making him sit outside. During the same period, prominent women leaders like Pramila Dandavate were insulted by being told they couldn't get tickets because they were city women with short hair. I often had to play chauffeur, driving people from one meeting to another while sitting outside uninvolved in the heavy but utterly ridiculous politicking, bickering and tussling that went on for people lobbying to have their cronies given tickets. Each thought if more of their people were elected they could pitch for the top spot. Since George Fernandes was totally sidelined because of the vaulting ambitions of others, he found it difficult to get his loyal stalwarts from the socialist movement tickets to fight the elections.

George Fernandes joined forces with Ajit Singh and Mulayam Singh (the latter having common socialist associates) to accommodate in his people through the other two who were on the Parliamentary Board. I was living in a tiny flat with my daughter in Sarvapriya Vihar at that time. I was asked to host these confabulations so that they could carry out their discussions in utmost secrecy. For two long days, they negotiated and fought, cooped up in my living room, arguing for or against some name or the other. Mulayam Singh would get annoyed and often attempt to walk out, but each time he did that my faulty door handle would stick and he would struggle to open it. At these times, the other two would manage to persuade him to cool down and return to the negotiating table. The success of this strategy was that Devi Lal and Chandra Shekhar were none the wiser, and many deserving and impeccable socialists like Mohan Singh, Harshavardhan Singh, Bhabani Shankar Hota and Gopal Pacherwal entered Parliament through these other channels. Just to keep the negotiations going till they ended cordially, my daughter and I kept making tea and snacks for them, pretending not to notice whenever the door jammed.

Fine politicians like the late Dinesh Goswami from Assam, and veteran socialists like Madhu Dandavate, Rabi Ray, who later became Speaker in the newly elected government, Surendra Mohan, the thinker and academician among the socialists, well-meaning persons from the labour movement and NGOs, and I, were assigned to work together to create a policy document for the National Front on issues like the right to work, reservations for the backward classes, and policies on agriculture and education among others. Someone in the group from the NGO sector once sarcastically asked whether politicians actually worked in order for us to have the right to demand the right to work. No one was amused. There always seemed to be a dividing line between political parties and NGOs who call themselves members of 'civil' society. Politicians grumbled, asking if that meant they were 'uncivil'. The socialists, in particular, believed in the importance of the right to work and remembered the Antyodaya scheme, which had earlier provided food for work, and other such programmes initiated under the Janata government. Jobs and employment were always a major concern. It was later transformed into a national programme called the National Rural Employment Guarantee Act (NREGA). This caused another set of problems like leakage of funds under the United Progressive Alliance (UPA) regime, and continues till today with major attempts at plugging the leaks now under the NDA-II government.

~

The mood in the country was building up against Rajiv Gandhi on the Bofors matter and V.P. Singh's meetings were a star attraction. George Fernandes was successfully managing to get the BJP and the Left parties to support the National Front formation. He had regular talks with his friends in the BJP and RSS as well as with Indrajit Gupta and others from the Left in Delhi. He was bringing them around to support from the outside under certain well-defined conditions. The Election Commission announced it was introducing electronic voting machines in one hundred odd constituencies. I found it significant as these were where the Congress expected to lose but needed to win to reach a majority. I came across a lengthy, detailed, well-researched article on electronic voting fraud in the *New Yorker* and how it was possible to programme the chip to vote as instructed in a pre-determined pattern. I also found it odd that these were not being introduced in urban centres among educated voters for trial but in out-of-the-way places.

I found an expert in digital matters who was also convinced it was possible and that for this very reason the system was not in use in many sophisticated democracies. The two of us worked hard and put together a convincing presentation on how electronic voting machines could be pre-programmed to produce a dishonest result, and how the number of machines and places where they planned to be introduced corresponded with the seats Congress needed to win. I requested the top Party leadership to allow us to show this to them and the press. A huge contingent of seventy journalists arrived at the press conference called by Devi Lal and V.P. Singh at Haryana Bhavan, where we were asked to make our presentation. Of course, it was all speculation, but backed with evidence and an actual demonstration of how a vote could be rigged.

The publicity that followed was huge. The use of the machines was cancelled. They reappeared in a modified form only a couple of years later when all political parties were called to the Election Commission to satisfy themselves of the functions of its specially developed machines. The National Front leadership were mighty pleased with their achievement at discrediting the ruling Party and sowing suspicion at that stage. I faded quietly into the distance. The excitement over my efforts to save over a hundred seats from fraud was satisfaction enough. Also, it was a pre-election effort and not like the crybabies of the present day who blame the electronic voting machines (EVMs) when they lose badly. But I did wonder if my being a man would have afforded my efforts a more effective recognition within the Party.

The ensuing 1989 general elections saw violence in Rajiv Gandhi's constituency, Amethi. Even the Gandhi family's old friend Pupul Jayakar protested and signed a letter to be sent to the President of India. We went to complain to the Chief Election Commissioner R. Peri Sastri. We were shocked to find him literally shaking with nervousness.

Each involvement with elections till the Election Commission got strong from within as an autonomous body, was a struggle against booth capture, violence, polling agents being driven away, vote contractors promising to organize bulk votes and disappearing into the night, finding caches of home-made bombs, and the blocking of poorer castes from reaching polling booths. Thugs employed by candidates went in procession on motor cycles behind the upper-caste candidates swearing to anoint their foreheads with the blood of our candidates. Nobody stopped them. This was Bihar till a new Election Commissioner, T.N. Seshan, came along and created interminable, phased polling, calibrated movements of security forces, and teams of observers who were generally kept marooned in their guest houses, by a clever Lalu Prasad Yadav who was the Chief Minister. These were the bad lands of Bihar and as it appeared to me, here, election fraud was allowed in the name of social justice.

~

Lalu Prasad Yadav's casteist leanings shown by the favouring of only his community, and information about his rampant corruption kept rising to the surface. V.P. Singh had given prime place to three leaders as faces of his Mandal movement: Lalu Prasad Yadav, Ram Vilas Paswan and Sharad Yadav. The latter had declared at a socialist conference in Madhya Pradesh that he had been a socialist all his life, but now he was a Yadav. This shocked many of the older clan who knew Lohia's slogan was the abolition of caste through positive discrimination, inter-caste marriages and other means. He had also warned that beneficiaries of this process should not adopt the feudal, corrupt ways of the upper castes. The reverse seemed to be happening now. Most had invested in gold, properties, dynastic ways and an air of arrogance they had fought against earlier.

After the fall of the V.P. Singh and Chandra Shekhar governments, in quick succession, Congress Prime Minister P.V. Narasimha Rao had signed all the pacts leading to a globalized economy which to us seemed like the domination of corporate global rule. George Fernandes had taken on the fight against India signing the World Trade Organization (WTO) agreement leading to globalization. He believed it would harm India for generations to come. He campaigned with leaders of state governments like J. Jayalalithaa (Tamil Nadu) and Biju Patnaik (Orissa) with a team of scientists, economic and agricultural experts to explain how federal structures and the country's sovereignty would be eroded by global corporates. When he went to Patna, Lalu received them dressed in a lungi and vest, sans his underwear, and with his feet up on the coffee table. Considering he had been the humble youth leader who would bring tea and make loudspeaker announcements for stalwarts like George Fernandes and Madhu Limaye during the Janata Party movement, George Fernandes felt thoroughly humiliated. The team was evicted from the Patna state guest house the following morning. Meanwhile, Lalu went around campaigning on the platform of anti-WTO telling the public that under the new regime, large seedless tomatoes would be produced. When these were cut, cow dung would pour out. He made a mockery of the movement. Why? Because these Mandal icons felt that George Fernandes and his team, which comprised of naxalites, Marxists, socialists, the RSS and activists like Medha Patkar, were a deliberate anti-Mandal diversion in which economic sovereignty was being highlighted and the caste factor was being deliberately sidelined.

In mid-1994, Nitish Kumar approached George Fernandes at a trade union conference in Dhanbad asking him to take steps to break away from Lalu's grip and the Janata Dal. His Kurmi caste was being marginalized. Documents had surfaced proving corruption in the purchase and sale of fodder by Lalu Prasad's Bihar government. George Fernandes went to V.P. Singh asking how we could fight the Bofors corruption if our own house was tainted. V.P. Singh refused to listen. Fourteen members of the Janata Dal headed by George Fernandes, including Rabi Ray, Nitish Kumar, Harikishore Singh and others, covering four states, as required to be declared a national party, broke away and formed the Janata Dal (G) and began a process that ended into the formation of the Samata Party in late 1994. Many of us second-rung Party activists were part of it. We filled the Talkatora Stadium at its formation conference. I was nominated general secretary of the Party on the suggestion of Harikishore Singh, a senior socialist Parliamentarian from Bihar.

The Samata Party went into the 1995 Assembly elections in Bihar fighting all the seats on its own. While Nitish Kumar travelled in helicopters, George Fernandes, as president of the newly formed Party, travelled in an old Ambassador car on Bihar's legendary roads which Lalu had promised to make as smooth as film actor Hema Malini's cheeks, but forgot to do so. Meanwhile, a case was filed in the Supreme Court with clinching evidence of the fodder scam. I organized demonstrations everywhere including at Jantar Mantar in Delhi, dressing up two-wheeler scooters as cows. We were called 'a small but feisty party' by the media as these demonstrations always had something eye-catching about them.

The 1995 Assembly election in Bihar against Lalu Yadav was a complete washout since the opposition was not united. It was hell for me handling the organizational end with the usual booth capturing, non-deployment of central forces and those pre-stamped ballot papers. When we asked the Left parties to become our ally in the fight against Lalu Yadav, their cynical reply was, 'Win the elections, and then we will join you'.

The Samata Party got an ignominious seven seats out of the 300 plus that it fought for. Nitish Kumar wanted to resign his MLA seat and keep his Parliamentary one despite strong advice and pleas from all of us immediately after. We sat in the fading evening light at 3, Krishna Menon Marg, discussing this and many other important issues for the future of the Party. George Sahib pleaded most strongly, refusing to permit Nitish Kumar to resign, saying he needed to be stationed in Bihar to fight and build the Party on the ground as its true leader and that being in Parliament was not good enough to capture the hearts of the people of Bihar. In the middle of the discussion, Nitish Kumar suddenly got up and went inside the house. We thought he had gone to the washroom. When he came back he said he had telephoned the press and announced he had resigned his Bihar Assembly seat. He presented our shocked group with a fait accompli. That was probably the first sign of his self-serving ways. I angrily asked how he could defy authority and well-meant advice in this underhand manner. He remained silent, smiling slightly, but he may not have ever forgiven me. After all, I guess, how could a woman speak to him like that? George Sahib was shocked and upset, and relapsed into an angry silence.

In my office drawer, I still keep a wad of pre-stamped ballot papers from Bihar (see photo section). They had been obtained by one of our Party workers and reached me soon enough. They were stamped serially in exactly the same place, positioned just left of the wheel symbol of the Janata Dal (then headed by Lalu Yadav, the chief minister of Bihar). Section 144 was in place on Parliament Street near the Election Commission of India. We could not go in a procession to protest and bring this to the notice of the public. It was too important to keep to a closed door meeting. I made poster-sized cloth banners in protest against the Bihar government and distributed them to our Samata Party activists who kept them folded in their pockets. We walked in twos and threes till we reached the gates of the Election Commission where we whipped out the banners and raised slogans. The media loved it. We discussed the issue at length with the grave Election Commissioners and presented our evidence. They promised to enquire. The very next day news came that the printing press which had brought out these ballot papers had burned down in a mysterious fire which was ignored by the state fire department till a nearby army establishment saw it and raised an alarm. The evidence was thus destroyed and District Magistrate Raj Bala Varma, who was said to be a favourite of the chief minister, was not only promoted but was often seen in close attendance to Rabri Devi when she became the chief minister during the time her husband Lalu Yadav was convicted of corruption.

All these incidents sank after minor short-term storms. 'Social Justice' and 'Secularism' were justifications for such atrocities to be condoned by the elite media and their aligned parties. These activities kept us busy and in the public eye in the capital of India but made no difference in Bihar which was in the grip of state and caste factors. Since I led all such agitations it did not make me popular among the 'liberal' brigade of the Left and Congress. It didn't bother me in the least.

~

In the general elections of 1996, the Samata Party formed an alliance with the BJP. George Fernandes argued that the Samata Party needed to do so for its very survival. Secondly, post the Babri Masjid demolition*, George Fernandes did not believe in making the Party untouchable, even as we would fight extreme communal activities. He said joining hands would moderate any extremist thinking, Hindu or any other, since 'Mandir' as religious consolidation was merely a counter to 'Mandal' which was seen as caste dividing Hindu society. Also, had we not remained a strong separate entity, it was possible that votes from the Kurmi and other backward castes would shift to the BJP, decimating us in the process. There was also a rumour that Nitish Kumar was considering joining the BJP. George Fernandes was lying in Jaslok Hospital in Bombay; he had to be operated for the second time following a head injury he received from fainting in the bath while washing clothes, weakened as he was from a bout of viral fever. It was during this time that an invitation came for him to attend a major *adiveshan* (conference) the BJP was holding in Bombay; L.K. Advani, its topmost leader, was addressing it. George Fernandes asked Nitish

*On 6 December 1992, the Babri Masjid, a sixth-century mosque, was destroyed by hundreds of *kar sevaks* in Ayodhya. They did so upon the claim that the mosque had been built on land that was considered to be Lord Rama's birthplace. Soon after the demolition, disastrous Hindu-Muslim riots across the country ensued in which thousands died. (See http://indianexpress.com/article/india/babri-masjid-demolition-timeline-ayodhya-ram-mandir-advani-uma-bharti-mm-joshi-supreme-court-4619160/)

Kumar to go in his place. I suggested accompanying him to dispel media speculation that Nitish Kumar was one step away from joining the BJP. George Fernandes too felt this was a good idea. Advani was very effective in dispelling notions that the BJP was a Hindu-only party. He told the huge crowd that everyone was free to follow any religion or God they wished as long as they accepted they were Indian citizens from a common ancient civilization. We saw no problem with that.

The alliance in the ensuing election saw no campaigning on the Ram Mandir, Article 370 or any other contentious issue. There were no slogans of *Jai Sri Ram* that had filled the air a few years earlier. It was purely about the condition of Bihar. As usual, I was active behind the scenes. The result of the Bihar alliance was that we succeeded in ensuring that Lalu Yadav had fewer seats than H.D. Deve Gowda in the Janata Dal combine enabling Gowda to be the prime minister. When he later stepped down in favour of I.K. Gujral, the latter telephoned me to seek George Fernandes's and my support to be the prime minister. He had a good relationship with us, having attended our then-seen-as-maverick international conferences of Tibet and Burma when many others had stayed away.

We were happy that our election strategy had saved the Party (we had six members in Parliament including Nitish Kumar) and saved the country from having Lalu Yadav as prime minister. Of course, all those who attacked Lalu Yadav's corruption daily attacked us too for giving legitimacy to the BJP, thus terming us 'communal'. It was called 'an ideological betrayal'. They did not understand that for people like us, political decisions and strategies were towards the far more important goal of defeating the Congress and keeping Lalu out too. However, no ideologies were compromised. They also never acknowledged that neither Party ever committed a communal act during its alliance in Bihar.

~

For many years before the 1998 general elections, I had been writing articles such as 'Why Sonia Should Say No' (1991) and 'The Bahu's Inheritance' (1999) both in *The Indian Express*, about why Sonia Gandhi should not be a claimant to the high seat of politics. However, as the 1998 general elections came into view, so did she, with her children in tow. Sitaram Kesri, the Congress president, had been miserably shunted off into oblivion and she proclaimed she was now up front for the country and her family. Around the same time, television channels burst on to the scene with 24×7 news. Every Party had a spokesperson. The Congress and BJP had press conferences every afternoon where journalists took issues from one party to another. The Samata Party was prominent as it was headed by George Fernandes who had stitched the NDA together, assuring a thoroughly possible outcome of a Congress defeat. However, being in a coalition with the BJP meant fighting a smaller number of seats. But the Bihar leaders of the Samata Party had not moved with the times. None realized that television now gave Party views and people huge visibility and carried the Party message far beyond the crowds at public meetings. Every candidate was only interested in the particular constituency and the state, and not television bytes. Television was an indulgence they felt was unimportant. As a result, off they all went to Bihar leaving me looking behind my shoulder to see who our spokesperson was supposed to be. Nobody cared and nobody designated me as one either. Seeing the media descend every day to hear what we had to say vis-à-vis the Congress, I faced the cameras and fixed our press meet time half an hour before the others so that we laid out the agenda for the day. I questioned dynastic issues concerning Sonia Gandhi and also raised doubts over her competence. I defended Om Prakash Chautala when the Election Commission prevented him from voting as chief minister by banning him from entering the state on polling day. I fielded queries about the tiresome communal/secular debate and whatever else came up of relevance on a particular day. Soon, I came to be seen as an effective spokesperson of the Samata Party, apart from being its general secretary, yet officially remained un-designated by its leadership till the very end.

In the Party, nobody watched television as they were in the field in Bihar, and nobody cared even though the rest of the country noticed. I too had not realized that I had achieved a wide national presence just by speaking into a microphone, participating in television debates and, of course handling all press conferences and the affairs at the Party office. This was when I often sat with Narendra Modi, who was then General Secretary of the BJP, to discuss election trends and results at television studios. We were fairly well-coordinated in our responses although we never had any prior consultations. He was generally quiet and serious, and very respectful when I joined a panel to give our comments. He was not given to small talk which was a pleasant change from useless banter that many men adopt with women in television studios. We were in tandem as alliance partners so there were obviously no differences of opinion.

Certain states fade from people's minds, unless they are politically important for a short while. They are in news with regard to issues like elections, violent agitations or when ruling governments are toppled through overnight defections. We don't realize how much we alienate them in this callous process. Manipur comes into this category. The Samata Party had become fairly prominent in Manipur thanks to decades of interest shown by its socialist leaders. George Fernandes was a particular favourite among people there as he travelled in these parts often and Dr Lohia had always raised the importance of paying attention to India's Northeast—borders, its people and their aspirations, I too went to Manipur often, and spent many hours with the feisty Meira Paibi who carried flaming torches at night to keep drunks, drug users and violent groups away from their villages; I would often also visit the over four hundred-year-old all-women's Ima market where they sold vegetables and local handlooms. I have attended weddings and funerals, addressed Party meetings and election rallies in far-off places like Moreh, Churachandpur and even Longpi in the Ukhrul district where women practise a unique technique of walking around the potter's wheel to turn the black-coloured pot instead of rotating the wheel.

During the Assembly elections of 2001, when James Lyngdoh from Meghalaya was in the Election Commission, militancy had risen to new heights. There were at least twenty-seven ethnic outfits dominating some area or the other. Our Party president, Radhabinod Koijam, forwarded me four letters he had received typed on formal letterheads from four different militant bodies, duly signed, demanding a down payment of twenty and thirty lakh rupees for them to leave our candidates alone to campaign during an election. I led a delegation to the Election Commission.

'Mr Lyngdoh, sir, you are the body that has to ensure free and fair elections. Please take strict action against those making these threats and demands,' I said, presuming he would respond on the basis of this first hand evidence.

'Oh! Is Manipur a part of India?' he said with his eyebrows raised and a half-smile on his face. I could understand the pain behind what he said.

I am sure he acted on this complaint behind the scenes to the best of his ability, but nothing changed.

~

In the middle of all this I was made Party president in January 2000. I had no illusions. It was a cynical decision taken just to solve a technical problem created by the Election Commission. The Party leaders had fought on the common Janata Dal symbol so the Commission decreed that anyone fighting on one symbol could not be an office bearer of another Party. So George Sahib had to step down as president. I was a convenient stop gap recommended by Bashist Narain Singh, MP from Bihar, and the decision was unanimously approved by everyone else. As usual, George Sahib sat silently throughout. My mother was at that time on her death bed when I was called at 2 am for an emergency meeting where this decision was taken. A couple of days later, I was called from the hospital again in the middle of the afternoon to be part of a press conference with BJP chief L.K. Advani and JD(U) chief Sharad Yadav to announce that the three parties had come to a seat sharing arrangement. My mother was fading fast, but I had to leave her.

As the press conference got over, the hospital telephoned to inform me that my mother had passed away. It was a most bizarre and ironic experience receiving congratulations and condolences at the very same time in the week that followed. I needed personal time to process my feelings on the loss of a parent, which was quite different from my father's untimely death when I was thirteen. I had to be at home meeting those who came to condole, like Farooq Abdullah, sundry friends, Tibetans with prayer scarves, domestic workers and others from the poorer sections of society whom my mother was always helping. Kashmiri carpet vendors who were our neighbours laid out all their new carpets on the floor during the small memorial meeting at home. Then, I had to put on another hat and face and go to the Party office and George Fernandes's home to meet hundreds of Party workers and favour-seekers. Sadly, Nitish Kumar who was always particular that people visit or enquire when his relatives were in hospital, did not find a moment to condole or even speak about my mother's demise to me later. Sharad Yadav apologized for missing the condolence meeting. Digvijay Singh, a minister from our Party, and George Fernandes, helped me with some formalities. I had to borrow money to put a notice of her demise in the newspapers. My former husband (Ashok and I had separated by then) was ill in Jammu and my son was travelling in Europe on his way back to India from the UK; thus Aditi and I had to manage everything on our own. There was hardly any time to grieve or mourn and one could not celebrate the so-called honour of being made president of my Party.

~

As Party president, I had tried to have a decisive say in the allotment of tickets at our meetings of the Parliamentary Board. Most often the men would speak so loudly they drowned out my voice, ignoring the fact that I had already started speaking. It was annoying and frustrating. I have read later that this attribute of overriding others' voices is a common characteristic among men and a part of a subconscious power play on their part. In such serious meetings I was regularly asked whether I would serve tea to them or someone would comment on how nice I looked. This was not a request or comment they would direct to a male counterpart. Whenever a good woman-aspirant's name for a ticket would come up I would support her vociferously to be told no by other members there, saying it would be a losing seat. I would insist that a woman had to be given the opportunity to contest even if she was going to lose the same way a man would lose a seat that was impossible to win. I once had to fight to send extra funds to a woman candidate in Bihar whose election was delayed by a week because of floods. No one wanted her to have the funds required to cover the costs of those extra days.

Our general secretary, Shambhu Sharan Srivastava, and I worked together to bring out a monthly newsletter in Hindi and English on behalf of the Party at the cost of two rupees each. It contained news of Party activities across the country and issues of importance like resolutions taken at the Population Council of India and political matters relevant at the time. I requested Party presidents of each state to pay. The most anyone had to pay was four hundred rupees for two hundred copies. Yet, Raghunath Jha, then Party president in Bihar, who later fought with Nitish Kumar and left to join Lalu Yadav's Rashtriya Janata Dal (RJD), and most others, never did. I never found out if anyone read them. Only Betty D'Souza, MP and always a good friend at my side, and the Party presidents of Lakshadweep and Andhra Pradesh bothered to do so. I realized that the days of writing, reading and Party publications were coming to an end as far as the politicians of our Party were concerned. I really was the odd one out, not counting George Fernandes who never stopped engaging with the written word.

I knew George Fernandes was on my side in all these efforts but he would keep silent and let me fight my own battles. He was a cruel but excellent teacher who loved throwing me among the scorpions even when he felt sad when I lost.

~

When the NDA lost the elections in 2004, the media and politicians from opposing parties cited their own reasons according to whatever suited them. For some, it was the over-exaggerated India Shining campaign, while for others it was the *Tehelka* exposé (which was disproved when Mamata Banerjee walked out of the NDA on this issue but lost the West Bengal Assembly elections the very next month). Some said it was the 'genocide' of Muslims in Gujarat in 2002. Placed at the heart of things, I believed it was not really any of the above. Being out of the election fray, I had a different vantage point. I was getting dismayed at seeing the arrogance of the BJP growing at the cost of its allies. It was also a mistake to have the elections before time without having consulted the allies. It had an alliance with our Samata Party in Bihar but did not continue with it in Jharkhand. It dropped Om Prakash Chautala in Haryana at the last moment and hitched on to Bansi Lal. It wanted to shed the alliance with the Dravida Munnetra Kazhagam (DMK) and tried to leave the unpleasant task to George Fernandes who thought the DMK was keen to continue it but was not being placated. The BJP began to announce it would win a majority on its own. I was disappointed, as in contrast I could see the Congress stitching up alliances. I wrote a note to Sudheendra Kulkarni at the PMO laying all this out. Of course, my comments were too insignificant for anyone to notice or be responded to although many of our Party workers in the field agreed with me and gave me daily feedback to reinforce my views.

By the time the 2009 elections came around, I had quit the JD(U) which had swallowed up the Samata Party, much against my wishes. I believed we had initiated the battle in Bihar against Lalu Yadav. The JD(U) was a latecomer, having been with Lalu Yadav till then. I also knew we were the larger and better-organized Party. We had put in a lot of effort to create the Samata Party, its symbol and its strong presence in the public eye. Suddenly, it was all getting washed away. We also felt uneasy that Nitish Kumar was happy to sacrifice the name and personality of the Party built by him and George Fernandes from scratch to embrace his old caste-ally Sharad Yadav. This, despite the fact that Yadav had not contributed much to national politics for years and had at that time no presence in Bihar. I assumed that Nitish probably felt comfortable having a Party colleague he could dominate and manipulate according to his wishes.

In 2003, I decided that neither I nor the newly merged Party needed each other anymore. I was left alone facing the *Tehelka* fallout—from Enquiry Commissions to the vindictiveness of UPA's 'caged parrot', to the CBI foisting FIRs, charge sheets and court hearings on me. Meanwhile, I remained devoted to my vast number of craftspersons and their needs and I derived a lot of strength working with them. Sometimes I would bury myself in guiding the choice of colours an artisan could use in a work just to escape the ugliness around me. In the 2009 general elections, I was compelled to be involved in handling an ailing George Fernandes's solitary, ill-advised and quixotic fight-cum-horror story in Muzaffarpur. It was my last experience at election involvement. By then, I had learned everything there was to know about the face and underbelly of electoral politics in India.

15

NATIONAL POLITICS AND DIPLOMACY

Instincts in Action

I WISH THE TITLE OF THIS chapter could have been a little longer, for instance, 'How I prevented a diplomatic embarrassment in China' or something on those lines—the way American books sometimes are titled. There's the famous *How to Make Friends and Influence People* by Dale Carnegie, and one titled *I'd Tell You that I Love You, but then I'd Have to Kill You* by Ally Carter. When I was searching for examples of long titles, I came across two that could have been good inspirations for the title of this book: *Smashed, Squashed, Splattered, Chewed, Chunked and Spewed* written by an ordained pastor named Lance Carbuncle, but maybe I would have sounded too defeated—which I am not. Another title I would have loved to appropriate was *The Girl who Circumnavigated Fairyland in a Ship of Her Own Making* by Catherynne M. Valente, but maybe making it *The Lady Who Circumnavigated the Land of Politics and Found Herself in a Soup of Her Own Making*. Anyway, I will stop musing.

The Samata Party was crucial to the formation of the first NDA government headed by Atal Bihari Vajpayee in 1998. (Vajpayee's earlier stint in 1996 had lasted only thirteen days because only the Akali Dal was prepared to join the government.) Perhaps not realizing what Indian politics was all about, Sonia Gandhi had clearly over-committed with her statement outside Rashtrapati Bhavan stating that the Congress had 272 members supporting them with 'more coming'. When George Fernandes and I had gone to visit I.K. Gujral in 2008 to invite him to a big event in Bangalore, we had a heart-to-heart chat over tea. He told us that Sonia Gandhi had visited him at that time and naively blurted out, 'I want to become the prime minister. How do I do it?' Gujral told us he was highly amused and gently explained to her that things didn't happen that way and that she had to approach the matter in a completely different manner.

In his autobiography *Matters of Discretion* (2011), he speaks of the same occasion and reveals that he told her that she should not trust Harkishen Singh Surjeet of the CPM who was ultimately keen on backing Jyoti Basu.*

This little titbit was never known nor spoken of publicly, and subsequently her 'sacrifice' and 'renunciation' of the prime ministerial post in 2004 were extolled across the world. This enabled people to forget the ambitiousness of the hasty '272' claim.

I contributed in a small way in Congress's not being able to make 272. Jyoti Basu, despite being a willing candidate from the opposition side, faced opposition from within his own party, while Sonia Gandhi was in a determined mood to head the government with everyone else tagging on from wherever they could be brought in. Mulayam Singh was holding out. His Party meeting to decide on this issue was scheduled for the next morning around 8 am. The previous evening, there was a dinner function at Samata Party's leader, Digvijay Singh's residence. On this hot April night, Chandra Shekhar and George Fernandes were also present. I was on tenterhooks about the Congress numbers and found myself far away from a partying mood. I was annoyed that our senior leaders were not being proactive about preventing what I saw as an impending disaster for the entire nation and casually socializing instead. I grumbled in George Fernandes's ear that they had no business to be standing at a dinner party instead of attempting to ensure Mulayam Singh did not support the Congress. I asked him and Chandra Shekhar why they could not put some pressure on Mulayam Singh at this crucial time. They huddled in a corner for a while, and it was decided that Chandra Shekhar would telephone Mulayam Singh the same night. We all went our different ways, but I was so worried that I reached 3, Krishna Menon Marg at 7 am the next morning to find out what had happened in the night. Apparently, Mulayam Singh had gone underground and was not reachable even to Chandra Shekhar. It seemed ominous. George Fernandes phoned Mohan Singh, a loyal friend and by then a senior member of the Samajwadi Party. He was going into the meeting and promised to call back with the news as soon as a decision was taken. He strongly shared our views on the subject and promised to express them forcefully at their meeting. I was on edge. Around forty-five minutes later, he telephoned to give us the crucial news:

---

*See Gujral's *Matters of Discretion: An Autobiography*, New Delhi: Hay House Inc., 2011, p. 335.

they had decided not to support the Congress. Apparently, Mulayam had made himself unavailable in order to avoid calls from Harkishen Singh Surjeet that had come all night. I was relieved, not realizing that Sonia Gandhi would eventually be the ultimate power center in the upcoming UPA era.

~

When country went into elections in 1998, the group that formed the first NDA had learned a lesson: they had to come together with a clear programme and team. The National Agenda for Governance (NAG) was formulated steering clear of 'contentious' issues like Article 370, Ram Temple/Babri Masjid, and the Uniform Civil Code. The plan had pretty much worked for us and the BJP at the level of Bihar, so a larger national view touching on all aspects of governance was not hard to formulate and adopt. George Fernandes became NAG's secular face although he never subscribed to such designations, as he reassured all other parties who were hesitant the first time around to come on board.

As usual, George Fernandes did not want to join the government. He always felt constrained and wanted to be among the people, fighting for justice wherever needed. There was much work to do, he always muttered. Since I had a tough time when he was in power, this position was fine for me, but his close friend Jaswant Singh later came over on behalf of the prime minister and pleaded, even shedding tears, saying they all thought the government would not have the credibility it required if he were not in it. Vajpayee had threatened to go to the President and tell him they would not form the government. All this succeeded. George Fernandes had no option but to succumb since he had worked so hard towards creating a viable non-Congress option.

Vajpayee had planned to give Ramakrishna Hegde the Defence portfolio but he offered George Fernandes a choice between Defence and the Human Resource Development Ministry. About the latter, he confided in me that it had nothing of worth to handle as education was a state subject and there were only few central educational institutions like central universities, and the IITs and IIMs, to handle. This did not interest him much. The next morning I telephoned him really early as some thoughts had come to me at 5 am. I came straight out with it: 'You know, I seem to get my brightest thoughts at the crack of dawn. Today I woke up and my first thought was why don't you consider accepting Defence?'

George Sahib said, 'What will I do among those stiff-uniformed fellows with so much saluting and Sir-ing?'

I shared my view that this was a minor part of the job at hand, and that here was an opportunity to reformulate India's security policies vis-a-vis Burma, Tibet and China. We had known for long that the Foreign Ministry's line of thinking had favoured Nehru's position on remaining soft and on the backfoot, and the Left had never considered India's interests on such matters. It had kept us weak and subservient in terms of our own strategic interests. I reminded George Sahib that our Party had even held two important international conferences on Tibet and on the restoration of democracy in Burma for India's strategic interests apart from needing democracy in our neighbourhood. One of these had been held more recently at Mavlankar Hall which former prime ministers like I.K. Gujral, Deve Gowda and others had attended and lent their support to. These were strong concerns of the Samata Party. 'Here is your chance to hear the Defence and armed forces' viewpoints, which has till now been subsumed. You can give their voice some space for consideration in our policies,' I argued.

As a Party of socialists, we had argued at many conferences that it was important for India that Tibet remained a buffer and zone of peace, and that as long as China strengthened the hands of the ruling generals in Myanmar, India would be at a strategic disadvantage in our Northeastern states. Serving and retired armed personnel had engaged with us discreetly at these conferences and we knew that they wished to express their views on national security more freely before the political class and had never been given a fair opportunity. (At a reception at the Taj Mansingh Hotel soon after the government was formed, a young Foreign Ministry official joined our conversation and soon began to boast about how the old China policy may be sought to be changed by the new incumbent but that he wasn't worried because the Ministry would soon set him right! It was amusing that he was so confident. I remained silent as I did not want to introduce myself and spoil his mood.)

'Hmmm,' George Sahib responded on the telephone in a distant, non-committal sort of way. I didn't, however, detect a negative or dismissive tone in the response. I was silently pleased that my advice had been considered worthwhile when he did agree with me later in the day and took on the job with a passion and vigour that was typical of George Fernandes.

Little did I realize that while Vajpayee and the NDA were happy with his being part of the government, I was going to be attacked later by the scorpions in full force till I actually quit party politics, discreetly, but in disgust.

~

Around ten days after coming to power in 1998, the NDA government conducted the Pokhran nuclear tests. Pakistan, too, demonstrated its nuclear capabilities to the world soon after. It was widely believed they had China's support in the process.

A few days later, Karan Thapar had the now famous television interview with George Fernandes in which he said China was 'Potential Threat No. 1' in answer to a question about whether China was Enemy No. 1. George Fernandes had very clearly and deliberately answered, 'No. Potential Threat No. 1'. This created a major furore amongst the opposition, particularly the extremely voluble communists and the Congress who were seen as having played footsie with China from a position of disadvantage for years. George Fernandes was repeatedly attacked for saying he had called China 'Enemy No. 1' which he had not, but the media was happy to play the opposition's take on this for years even after repeated corrections and clarifications from the Party and Karan Thapar himself.

Manoj Joshi, a senior and more balanced journalist, wrote a perceptive article in *India Today* of 18 May 1998 titled 'George in the China Shop'.* The article begins thus:

> In sabre-rattling on China, George Fernandes *succeeded in shifting India's* security concerns to where defence specialists, and indeed the Ministry of Defence's own annual reports, have been saying they ought to be—somewhere between Islamabad and Beijing.

This echoed what I had conveyed to George Fernandes that morning on the phone when he was reluctant to accept the Defence portfolio. I felt that my political perception was not so far off the mark.

~

*See http://indiatoday.intoday.in/story/china-is-the-potential-threat-no.-1-says-george-fernandes/1/264241.html

By 2003, China was keen to invite Prime Minister Vajpayee to visit. They believed they needed to overcome George Fernandes's years of hostility and reservations first. The Chinese Ambassador made a few courtesy calls at his Raksha Bhavan office, where a tapestry reminding the world of the horrors of Hiroshima hung on the wall above the visitor's sofa area. These culminated in an invitation for George Fernandes to visit China to pave the way for Vajpayee's visit. Their invitation was very warm and generous. They offered him an aircraft to visit any part of China the Defence Minister wished. Perhaps this meant a visit to Tibet too. He was terribly excited about the visit. It was not surprising, despite his stand towards them vis-a-vis India's strategic interests and his support for Tibet. It was a major historic moment for him in his political journey. He saw this as an immense opportunity for him to personally pave the way for cordial relations between the two countries. I knew he was eventually a highly practical and pragmatic politician. Additionally, he was highly diplomatic and a thorough gentleman in his dealings with other countries.

China was in the throes of the severe acute respiratory syndrome (SARS) epidemic. Everyone was shown wearing masks. George Fernandes carried loads of anti-SARS vaccines among other gifts but chose not to wear a mask. This impressed the people of China. His visit was an eye-opener. He returned to share with us his perception that the two countries shared two goals: overcoming rural poverty and bringing about economic development. He had discussed other commonalities with the Chinese President and the Prime Minister: of corruption, and the immense poverty both still had. While on his visit, he was shown a Buddhist monastery in Beijing where the Prime Minister's wife worshipped regularly; they were telling him they were not godless. He was highly impressed by their efficiency. Also, George Fernandes did not use their aircraft to go anywhere.

Bhartendu Kumar Singh, a research scholar from JNU, sums up (better than I could) the significance of his visit in a paper titled 'George Fernandes and Sino-Indian relations':*

> The recent visit to China by George Fernandes got good media coverage both within and outside India, despite the international focus on Iraq. The reason lay not in his being the first Defence Minister of India to have visited China in a decade, but his being

*See http://www.ipcs.org/article/china/george-fernandes-and-sino-indian-relations-1044.html

> 'George Fernandes'. It is, therefore, interesting to know what makes George Fernandes so important for Sino-Indian relations. Despite being a proclaimed 'socialist,' George Fernandes, in his over five-decade long political career, has associated himself with nearly everything that makes China uncomfortable.... He was very pessimistic of Nehru's friendly overtures towards China, and was very vocal when India surrendered its special privileges in Tibet under the 1954 Treaty. Post-1962, he was even more aggressive towards China. This is documented in his 1966 discussion with a Geneva-based Sinologist, Edgar Snow, author of Red Star Over China. George presented the case for an independent Tibet. This would have taken care of Tibetan's search for national identity and met India's security needs. George continued to speak out for Tibet even after the PSP faded away…
>
> His recent visit has enabled George Fernandes to undertake this image-building exercise. From his speeches and statements during his visit, he wanted to convey that he was 'pragmatic' in his approach. Instead of dwelling on threat perceptions, he talked about China's developmental success, its excellent work culture, and lessons for India. Moreover, the timing of his visit, when China is facing the 'SARS' challenge, earned him the goodwill of his hosts.

Prime Minister Vajpayee finally visited China in July and this was hailed as a historic visit. George Fernandes was only happy to do his bit to facilitate things as much as possible for the country's good.

~

Meanwhile, only a couple of us in the Party know about an extremely tense episode that took place while George Fernandes visited China.

It is hard to tell the time difference between New Delhi and Beijing at this point of time but the Fernandes entourage had just about arrived in China when at midnight, I was woken from my sleep in Delhi by Nitish Kumar asking for George Sahib's contact number there. I asked what had happened. He said it was an urgent Party matter. I gave him his personal assistant Ashok Subramaniam's mobile number. At 6 am, Party General Secretary Shambhu Sharan Srivastava rang me to say Nitish Kumar was desperate to speak to Sahib. He was at war with Raghunath Jha and some senior Parliamentarians from Bihar for challenging him on some irrelevant matter and wanted George Fernandes to immediately dismiss them from the Party. I was astounded. If he managed to make this happen, the consequences were hard to imagine. Shambhu fully agreed with me. I called Ashok in Beijing right away and told him what was happening. He said Nitish had spoken to him at 2.30 am but Sahib had been sleeping and so nothing had been conveyed as yet. By then, George Fernandes had woken up. I told him an ugly internal tussle was going on here which would break the Party. More importantly, it would be a huge embarrassment for the country if the Defence Minister was seen giving priority and attention to petty squabbles back home. I strongly advised against it. George Fernandes didn't indulge in any further discussion. He agreed and suggested I draft a note. He said I should convey it to Ashok. His mind was focussed on China. I hastily scribbled a few words on a sheet of paper by my bedside, called Ashok again, and dictated it to him. I still have that sheet and can quote verbatim:

> *I earnestly request my colleagues in the party to refrain from mutual recriminations and organisational complaints at a time when I am preoccupied with a prestigious and historic visit to China.*
>
> *In China, I am a senior representative of the NDA govt & our country & not just the leader of the Samata Party. Any disharmony or demands on me to attend to party squabbles not only minimizes our fight against Lalu Yadav's misrule but will denigrate our party, and the govt of which it is a part, and the country, in the eyes of the international community.*
>
> *I am sure that my colleagues will not mind exercising some restraint for a few days. Personal complaints and egos could be kept aside till I return—in the interests of party unity and national prestige.*

Ashok did the needful and the visit went on without any further hitch. Nitish Kumar may or may not know about my role in this.

I kept behind the scenes on many such matters as I would have been considered 'out of line' in the larger scheme of things, but my political instincts had developed quite strongly by then, and I often had to deal with such problems which thankfully got nipped in the bud very quietly.

16

CHERCHEZ LA FEMME
A Typical Scorpion's Agenda

SOME POLITICAL PERSONALITIES ENJOYED WHAT is called '*phokat mein prachar*', or free publicity, even if it was negative. Not being prone to performing in public as most politicians are primed to do, I didn't seek it. I was a performer on television as Party spokesperson, but that was by default. I suppose viewers did find me a bit different, as I didn't evade issues, spoke softly, and was more proactive than my appearance indicated. When a handloom sari-wearing woman with a big *bindi* and silver earrings spoke sharp politics in a pretty polite but no less combative manner, curiosity was bound to arise.

The media's natural modality in covering political incidents is to sniff the air for gossip, concoct a theory around it, toss out a story with the pretence of some evidence and wait eagerly for combat and controversy to fly around. And if a woman is a part of the story, that's a 'wow!' Otherwise, their output is boring. The last time I was significantly in the news for controversial nonsense was the time when my appointment to head the NID was cancelled. There were some odd stories about my work in the crafts, and some Party-related reports that didn't attract the interest of spice-seekers, or 'knicker-sniffs' as George Fernandes derisively called those who made it their main vocation to sniff around for any possible smell of dirt.

During the V.P. Singh regime, friends outside the Party told me they had met businessmen at social occasions who gossiped that while Fernandes did not take bribes, his colleague Jaya Jaitly willingly accepted them in the form of gold jewellery. Known socialist colleagues in the Party were worse. Nearly everyone wanted to be on some railway committee or the other to entitle them to free travel. Others wanted their kin to be passed in an exam or cleared in an interview without the requisite marks, insisting that ministers' offices and colleagues in earlier regimes had helped them do so. One of them regularly brought me his cronies demanding I hand out money to them for travel. I would be asked to arrange railway passes for them and others. Friends would request seats for family travel on the minister's quota. I would ask George Fernandes's permission before doing anything of this nature. He would refuse saying that neither was the government a charity establishment nor should his office be used as a travel agency. Of course, I would get the brunt of everyone's anger as they would not dare approach or blame him. George Sahib too was happy to avoid them by using me as a convenient shield.

Eventually, this person, who has remained a non-entity in national politics and should remain so, felt he had enough of my lack of help. He wrote a long letter to Nitish Kumar and some other leaders in the Party under an assumed named with many complaints against me. The most astounding on the list was the accusation that I sent my daughter out to different important politicians' homes to further my interests. It is particularly tragic that when women in public life are to be attacked, people think nothing of dragging their daughters into the mix. No one mentioned it in the Party. It was hard for me to maintain a stoic face and pretend I had no knowledge of it. Later, I even managed to conquer my anger and feel a little superior by helping this particular individual financially when he broke his leg and was helplessly marooned for a while. People imagine women get a lot of benefits by being close to famous men in power. Well, that must be a joke.

Quite soon after George Fernandes took over as defence minister, a strange issue cropped up. The Air Force Wives Welfare Association (AFWWA) occupied defence land at the roundabout near the prime minister's house. This attractive little shopping complex called Santushti is popular among diplomats and the elite. There was apparently some file moving within the Ministry about a proposal to withdraw it from commercial use. Based on sheer gossip, a story came out at the bottom of the front page of *The Indian Express* around this exercise, alleging I was behind it. Apparently, I wanted the defence minister to withdraw the allocation to AFWWA and hand it over to me for another 'Dilli Haat like space' for me to run. Since I had established Dilli Haat, it probably seemed credible that I was now greedy for more space for craftspersons.

George Fernandes was completely puzzled as he had not known of the existence of Santushti, I had never mentioned such a thing, and the file for change of land use had not been put before him. There was obviously some politics and speculative games taking place within the Ministry. Defence wives were seeking an appointment with the minister. Even the environmental activist M.C. Mehta's name came up in the matter. I knew nothing of all this at the time but it must have been presumed by those who didn't want to hand over the space, that a controversy could prevent it. While there was nothing one could do to deny it, such a story was enough to plant a seed in many people's minds that some wrongdoing on my part was entirely possible. Eventually, it was a damp squib because Santushti was never taken away from the AFWWA but the minor *tamasha* or show got me some unwanted *phokat mein prachar.*

A similar story appeared when the Tibetan settlements in Dehradun and Chakrata invited me to accompany George Fernandes on a visit which was more of a social and goodwill visit so that I could go to a Tibetan veteran's noodle-making factory, a children's school and a carpet production establishment. George Sahib was to witness some special acrobatics and physical feats by the border forces which comprised many Tibetans. The whole trip was ridiculously harmless. The Tibetan community has always treated me as a solid comrade-in-arms and would have been shocked that my visit was to be later painted in the press as a trip by a Mata Hari to a spy establishment. Only Left-oriented journalists could have cooked up that gem.

The excitable gossip mongers' chase had more to offer. Towards mid-August 1998, my son Akshay was to get married in France to a French girl, which needed a *certificat de celibat* to legally ensure he was not married to anyone else. He was working in Japan and had to go directly to France but the certificate had to be obtained from the Ministry of External Affairs (MEA) in India. An official from the MEA, working in the Ministry of Defence, was kind enough to oblige in the absence of my son, since everyone knew he was not already married. This was enough for the news to spread in scorpion circles that a wedding was in the offing.

My son, who is now a corporate lawyer, bought economy tickets for me and his sister. His father paid for his own. We all set off for Paris and Normandy with presents worth exactly eight thousand rupees bought from Cottage Industries Emporium for the entire, very large, French family. My daughter and I wore our old Kanjeevaram saris with no zari on them.

We didn't wish to look like Christmas trees at the wedding, as Indians are usually, perhaps, perceived to appear. My daughter-in-law confided in me when we reached her home that she had got herself a wedding dress made of fine white paper. Her mother had spent something like €5000 on it mainly because of the designer's fee. After all, it was only paper. She was worried I would disapprove. Instead, I loved the idea. The eccentricity and quirkiness of it was just up my street. Or so I thought. Soon enough, a news piece titled 'Jaya Jaitly's daughter-in-law was wearing a wedding dress costing half a million dollars' appeared on the Internet, which was still an unfamiliar medium for us. Not only that, but George Fernandes received an anonymous letter at his desk in Delhi saying that I had taken a bribe of fifty lakh rupees to be spent on my son's wedding in France. What could anybody do but ignore it?

The Indian version of Akshay's wedding followed, Kerala style, with minimum expense under a tree at Kashmir House at the end of December 1998. There was a modest reception inside where Aditi offered a Bharatnatyam performance for the guests on a small stage prepared for the purpose. No pandal, no fat contractors, no exchange of voluminous gifts, just lunch and fun in the winter sun. No fanfare, no press, only a large contingent of French in-laws, who enjoyed *henna* on their hands, glass bangles, gajra (flowers) in their hair, Indian attire, and trips to Agra in the heavy fog.

But, and there always is a 'but'; George Sahib, then the Defence Minister, had dismissed Admiral Vishnu Bhagwat, head of the Indian Navy, the same day as the wedding. Since he was pre-occupied with all this, he barely stepped in to greet the couple for a moment. A huge controversy unfolded in many phases. This included Ms Jayalalithaa, supremo politician of Tamil Nadu, using the sacking as an excuse to topple the first NDA government. It was a strange situation where I couldn't figure out when a person was a friend and when a foe and went back to being a friend again—but, I digress.

The repercussions, however, landed on me like an unexpected tonne of bricks and spun into an uninvited battle between two completely unconnected women instead of a clash between a cabinet minister and the seniormost naval officer in his Ministry. It had something to do with his obstructing decisions and wishes of the minister and somewhere compromising security matters. The details are probably well-documented in the ministry and elsewhere. Mrs Niloufer Bhagwat jumped into the battle by choosing me as a target to defend her husband, as his lawyer. It started with an accusation that the defence minister always insisted I should be invited to every social function of the defence brass. She made cheap allegations about my character not realizing that irrespective of whether I was Mother Teresa or Monica Lewinsky, it had no connection with her husband's situation. Madhu Trehan did an interview with Mrs Bhagwat, which appeared in *Hindustan Times* on 10 January 1999, where instead of answering the questions, she made some unconnected remarks about me. I protested to the *Hindustan Times*, asking how they could publish such indecent remarks. They published my letter on 18 January and responded with an apology stating:

> The comment was retained as it showed the personal and petty level to which the dispute between the admiral and the minister was descending. The interviewer's next question was aimed to show that Mrs Bhagwat was straying and not replying to what she asked. However, we understand Ms Jaitly's anguish, and apologise for any offence caused.—Editor

Mrs Bhagwat did not stop her tirade. She spoke with many voices; of a wife, and as a politician, by drawing attention to herself as half-Muslim being victimized by a communal government for having participated in the Sri Krishna Commission of Inquiry into the Bombay riots. She attacked us, as his lawyer, in an unconnected case against a Sikh naval officer, accusing the NDA and the Akali Dal of favouring Sikhs and thereby exposing their communal attitudes. She then implied George Sahib was favouring a Christian when Admiral Sushil Kumar, who was appointed in Bhagwat's place, turned out to be a Christian by sheer coincidence. She fell silent on that soon enough. It happened in a very funny way. A reporter even asked Admiral Sushil Kumar why he had dropped his surname, Isaac. Till then even the defence minister had no clue as to his religious identity which surely is of no concern when assessing a person's seniority and competence. Her next accusation was that 'all naval appointments were bought and sold'. She accused George Fernandes and his associates of being 'temperamentally low' because they followed Jayaprakash Narayan who had supposedly asked the armed forces to revolt. She further declared her husband's sacking as 'worse than the Emergency'. The media, as is its wont, played her up and complimented Bhagwat for his graceful restraint.

I took my role seriously as a representative and de facto spokesperson to defend the NDA and its politics as well as governance. I refused to be painted as some shady mistress attached behind the scenes to the coat strings of a 'nasty' defence minister of 'low character'. My article titled 'Wife, Lawyer, Politician or Mouthpiece?' appeared on 4 February 1999 in *The Pioneer* in response to her diatribes, always spiced by snipes at me. She fell silent after that, but Vishnu Bhagwat soon donned a politician's hat and landed on election campaign platforms organized by the CPI in Nalanda, haranguing George Fernandes at every opportunity. Nothing worked in their favour. They faded from sight, the opposition dropped them and the media moved on.

~

All the accusations made by Mrs Bhagwat became the checklist of allegations *Tehelka* built into their elaborately planned sting called Operation West End, aimed at bringing George Fernandes and the NDA government down. In that, *Tehelka* finds a character who supposedly tells them all about corruption in defence matters because he lives near the naval barracks in Bombay. The purchase of missiles or ships, and the Barak deal issue dragged in A.P.J. Abdul Kalam and George Fernandes. They made any unsuspecting character a defence dealer crawling out of nowhere, one of whom was supposed to have claimed that I got two per cent on each file that was signed, or that I was the 'suitcase' woman of the defence minister. All the usual innuendoes of me being a second wife, companion, live-in partner, and co-conspirator in corruption were seeds planted in *Tehelka's* flowerpot by the verbal onslaught Mrs Bhagwat had let loose. As usual, it was *cherchez la femme*, the very French, very sexist expression that indicates a woman is the indispensable ingredient that leads to every great man's achievements or downfall.

To be fair, however, there was an added non-sexist dimension here. When Mulayam Singh Yadav was defence minister, Amar Singh was his party's general secretary. It was widely rumoured, with no evidence to prove it, that he was the go-to man to 'facilitate' decisions. Delhi abounds with such defamatory allegations to which I no longer pay attention. Theirs was not a party ever short of money as was the Samata Party which could often not pay its monthly telephone bills of four thousand rupees at the Party office. People cannot be faulted for automatically presuming the next incumbent and the general secretary followed the same alleged system. Rajeev Shukla, now cricket honcho and Congress party loyalist, was then an independent member of the Rajya Sabha, hoping to be made a junior minister in the NDA. Anyone wanting such things arrived at the Fernandes house to lobby. If he was busy, they found me. One day, he struck a conversation with me starting like this:

'Jayaji, you and George are among the most popular and in-demand people in Delhi to meet.'

'Why so?' I asked.

'Do you know that people are willing to pay twenty lakh rupees to have a cup of tea with you?'

'Good God, whatever for?'

'Well, if they want to show they are close to the person who is close to the minister, it gives them an advantage outside among defence commission agents. They will show they have spent half an hour in this house having tea with you. It cuts the competition. Even if you don't help them, it helps them,' Rajeev very kindly explained. The whole procedure seemed an elaborate sham enacted between aspiring defence dealers.

That is how I heard about this sordid world of defence deals and commissions and realized Delhi was teeming with people who turn into serpents and scorpions at the sound of money. Having been uncomprehending of the world of business, negotiations, percentages and murkiness, I blanked out and remained oblivious to such things, not bothering to engage my mind with such unpleasant talk. I soon realized that many defunct old socialists, Party workers, perfumed ladies in chiffons, young smart alecks and an assorted range of people kept asking for time to meet me. I politely met the political characters I knew but froze when the topic of their conversation veered towards some 'file' that had been cleared but 'just needed George Sahib's signature'. This is it, I thought. Even offering tea had become dangerous. Not a single person's request was either forwarded to or mentioned to George Fernandes at any time. Anyone in the Ministry would swear to that. In fact, they did, when officers were later asked formally in the Inquiry Commission and court, they confirmed I had never made any request or engaged with the Ministry at any time. Occasionally, if I happened to meet George Sahib, I would mention the names of colleagues who seemed to be turning into sharks circling the premises hoping to make money from 'a cup of tea'. He would growl and avoid them like the plague. This created a batch of disgruntled 'friends'. The real dealers or commission agents as they are called in polite circles, were well hidden, I presumed.

I must correct myself. One did emerge.

Soon after the Pokhran nuclear missile test, India was in the doghouse among certain countries. George Fernandes started wooing Japan through his old socialist friends there. While counting friends there were many discussions on who would reach out to India-friendly groups in the US Congress and Senate. I received a call from a foreigner who gave his name as Christian Michel. He said he wanted to meet the minister to assist in ways to lobby with these groups in the US. He gave Naresh Chandra, the then India's Ambassador in the US, as a reference to his credentials. I said I would pass the message on. George Fernandes rang Naresh Chandra in Washington DC. He sounded slightly uncertain but did affirm that he knew him. Presuming it was a strictly diplomatic strategy to be discussed, George Fernandes decided to make me the sounding board till he could figure out what was going on. I agreed to meet Michel and he suggested the IIC lounge as the meeting venue. When I met him, he had a badge saying PRESS, and a magazine on some advanced aircraft stuff—*Dassault*, I think—on the coffee table. He patted both and said, 'This is for cover.'

Eek, I thought to myself, what is this cloak-and-dagger operation?

'Cover?' I ventured, curiously.

He came out with a long tale on how he had been an informant for years, and claimed to have helped Prime Minister P.V. Narasimha Rao keep tabs on Sonia Gandhi whenever she visited London. He opened up one of those electronic diaries that fancy people had those days, to show me times, dates, places and people he had met in London. He may have been fabricating all this in trying to establish his credibility. I was disinterested in this information and didn't utter a word. I was trying to see what he was getting at.

Michel then tried to educate me on all the real defence dealers who operated in India and the bureaucrats they had in their pockets. He mentioned the Choudhury brothers and a former Admiral. (I had never heard of them at that time but their names cropped up in conversations later in the *Tehelka* tapes. Significantly, *Tehelka* never went to their homes or offices because its stories consisted of sham dealers, agents, companies and offers. But I get ahead and need to rewind.)

Michel then blatantly offered me the opportunity to make a huge pile of money for the Party. I guessed it was positioned as a quid pro quo for some favour to *Dassault*.

I said, 'We do not do such things.'

'How will you run your Party?' he asked, slightly condescendingly.

I got a little riled at that. 'I would rather beg in the streets,' I replied.

I kept my cool in front of so many people in the IIC lounge but beat a hasty retreat, reporting the entire story to George Fernandes the same evening. He told me to write it out in a letter in full detail and send it to the Defence Secretary. I did so the next day. Neither did I get any acknowledgement nor am I aware if any action followed. George Fernandes had too much on his plate to keep any of this in his mind as the Kargil War soon followed.

Michel managed to get my home number after that and called half a dozen times to revive the conversation, but I refused to meet him or discuss anything.

When the *Tehelka* allegations struck in mid-March 2001, with all its immediate repercussions, I received a fax from Michel, saying: 'Dear Mrs Jaitly, I am so sorry about what has happened. I warned you about them. Sincerely, Michel.' The fax remained in my files for a long time, till it faded, as fax papers did then.

The next time the name Michel appeared it was in the AgustaWestland helicopter deal* in which the Congress was accused of shady dealings. Christian Michel and Guido Haschke were the middlemen named by the court in Milan.** Was this the son, or the same man? I have no idea, nor do I want to know.

*'AgustaWestland: CBI, ED mount aggressive hunt for Christian Michel', 11 December, 2016
Read more at: http://economictimes.indiatimes.com/articleshow/52017280.cms?utm_source=contentofinterest&utm_medium=text&utm_campaign=cppst

**See http://www.thehindu.com/opinion/interview/I-am-victim-of-quotpolitical-conspiracyquot-says-alleged-VVIP-chopper-middleman/article14262539.ece; and http://economictimes.indiatimes.com/news/defence/vvip-chopper-scam-christian-michel-the-man-who-flew-away-with-rs-330-crore/articleshow/52001253.cms

17

GOOD AND BAD MATCH-FIXING

Tehelka Sting I

CONSPIRACIES AGAINST PEOPLE PERCEIVED TO be in 'power' are meticulously planned and have a carefully orchestrated process. The perpetrators are efficient, stealthy, networked and rich. It is easy to go after unsuspecting innocents and paint them as criminals. With ample help from a blood-thirsty media, a gullible and inflammable public and the cynical adage that 'politics is not about fact, it is about perception', they always have an advantage.

On 22 June 2000, George Fernandes, Digvijay Singh and I were on a morning flight to Rajkot to attend a state Samata Party conference. *The Times of India* was at hand. On the very front page was a small column headed, 'Jadeja fixes a good match'. It stated categorically that 'cricket star Ajay Jadeja has married Aditi Jaitly, the daughter of Samata Party president Jaya Jaitly, in a secret wedding' (see photo section). A 'close friend from the ITC golf course' is quoted as saying, 'Jadeja confessed that he has married Aditi' with additional information about him keeping it a secret because he planned to make a film with Sonali Bendre and it would 'affect his star status'. We were stunned. My daughter was in London for a dance performance. Ajay was there for a match, I think, and of course they had been classmates at Sardar Patel Vidyalaya and good friends since the age of eleven, but they had been extremely careful not to flaunt their friendship in an age where a celebrity's personal life is front-page material for voyeurs. Family respect and propriety within honest, liberal attitudes were values we brought up our children with. For a very brief second, I was hurt that my daughter would get married behind my back. I was instantly ashamed of losing faith in her openness, but if I had momentarily faltered, why would the media and public not believe it? I called Aditi in London as soon as we landed in Rajkot, where the media obviously made our poor Samata

Party conference secondary to this.

Aditi had just woken up when I told her what *The Times of India* said. She burst out laughing and said, 'Ma, it's so ridiculous you should throw the newspaper in the dustbin.' Ajay and Aditi were both quite used to gossip being written about Ajay and did not give it a second thought.

Looking back, observe again the headline of this news report: 'Jadeja fixes a good match'. Just consider this: the match-fixing controversy created by *Tehelka's* supposed exposé of crooked cricket players had hit the headlines in May 2000. It had invaded the cricket landscape entirely. The marriage headline popped up exactly a month later, connecting the reader to the 'bad' cricket match-fix. Ajay was then a very popular and successful cricket player who could have eventually headed the Indian team. He was lauded by veteran cricketers like Sunil Gavaskar, Geoffrey Boycott and Ian Chappell, among others. He always scored well or won the matches he played in by coming in when the team was doing badly and turned it around with his talent and cheery demeanour. Sceptics could check the statistics for those years.

Exactly a month later in July, the doorbell rang at 8 am at my very modest Khirki Village home, built as a make-shift extended one-room, one-floor space. It was all I could afford after selling some old wedding silver and cashing in my Gujarat Emporium Provident Fund. Either the trade union-owned Maruti car which I drove or Ajay Jadeja's lent-by-Sahara Lancer car, or the vegetable-seller's hand cart, occupied my garage. The neighbouring *paan* (or betel leaf) vendor, extremely embarrassed, would occasionally agree to have morning tea at my dining table—that's how 'local' and grounded I was. By the way, at the time I was president of the Samata Party, an important ally of the government. The context needs a reminder.

Aditi and I were alone at home. We went to the door, accompanied by my two very amiable dogs—Eva, a German Shepherd, and Pepper, a black Labrador. A man with two policemen carrying rifles asked me rather harshly to open the door. Through the wire netting, I asked who they were and what they wanted. They first kept asking me to open the door. I repeated my response.

The man said, 'Income Tax office.'

I laughed. 'If you have any tax queries you could meet my Chartered Accountant.'

He replied with a grim face, 'Open the door and tie up your dogs.'

'They are very friendly and won't do anything. But what do you want?'

The official indicated to the policemen to aim their rifles at our dogs and shoot them.

I flared up and asked what right they had to behave like this with my dogs.

'Isn't this Ajay Jadeja's house?' they asked, a bit surprised at my not being submissive enough.

'No, I am Jaya Jaitly, president of the Samata Party and this is my house,' I said, a bit surprised at their question but only slightly curious, unsuspecting of what was coming.

The fellow's eyes opened wide, and he called someone on his mobile. In a few seconds, another man arrived, apologized politely that he was late, and requested that I opened the door just to answer a few questions. I did so without tying up the dogs and strongly objected to such aggressive behaviour towards pet animals who were wagging their tails and hadn't even barked. The dogs that divided their time between my home at night and George Fernandes's premises in the day were 'political'. They welcomed people, crowds and joined some *dharnas** too. They had instinctively learned not to offend visitors.

It turned out to be a not very funny comedy of errors. The senior, a more decently behaved person, phoned his boss and described how he had discovered it was Jaya Jaitly's house. He was instructed to ask me to fill a questionnaire. Their intended raid plan was abandoned but they asked to look around. They asked me why some men's underwear was lying around. (Answer: They are my son's. He occasionally comes here to bathe and change after playing golf along with Ajay.) They asked whose car was in the garage with the golf clubs in it. (Answer: Ajay's. He leaves it here for my daughter to use when he is away. He is currently in London. It belongs to his employer. It is old.) I asked if I should open my cupboards and if there was anything more they wanted to examine. Highly embarrassed, the officer telephoned his boss again and said in Hindi, 'Sir, there is nothing here but wooden objects.' I found that funny but kept a serious face. We had a wooden armchair, a dining table, a chest of drawers, beds and a couple of unlocked cupboards. The only valuable item was a sixty-year-old

*Non-violent forms of protest that usually involve going without food or water

camphor chest belonging to my parents. It was just wood to them. There was nothing more than clay artefacts, handloom, and sadly, no gilded fittings or staff. In their eyes, this must have been unbelievably sparse for a Party president. My son called at one point but I did not mention what was going on. There seemed no need to agitate him.

I proceeded to 3, Krishna Menon Marg to prepare for the release of crafts maps at the India Habitat Centre the same evening. Aditi went to Ajay's tiny rented office space to look after his correspondence as he was not well-versed in English at that time. She usually handled his correspondence and minor paperwork every now and then. I decided to treat it as one more day of the normal rubbish of politics and did not worry that she would be alone. Late in the evening, when I met Aditi again she reported the raid on Ajay's office after she had reached there. It had gone on for hours. The officials found cash worth seventeen hundred rupees only. They ordered snacks and tea, and the petty cash was used to pay for the order. When they listed the cash among the goods found, Aditi had to object, arguing they had spent it all so it was no longer there. I do not know if it was finally added or not. They took away the computer, laptop, and a bunch of bank deposit slips, which they offered to leave behind if she paid a bribe of fifty thousand rupees. She is a spunky child, so she replied that bank deposits proved money was legitimately deposited in the bank and thus accounted for, so they were doing her no favour. She added she would need to call Ajay in London and ask his permission to write them a cheque since they could see there was no cash. They left.

We learned from an honest tax officer later that it was wholly illegitimate to do that as tax officials are given allowance for food and contingencies. The same officer also told Ajay during the examination of bank accounts that were ten years old, including stubs for travel for cricket matches while he was still in school, that his 'to-be mother-in-law' had never been on the list to be raided. Either they foolishly thought the house actually belonged to Ajay, or my name was added informally as part of some conspiracy to draw me into the picture. It was hard to imagine why they would risk raiding the house of a Party president of an important ally of the government unless there was a reason to defame me or else, more likely, it was simply the usual case of one wing of the government not knowing what the other was doing.

George Fernandes was in Sierra Leone or some such far-off place at that time. He called in the afternoon to check on things here as he routinely did. I mentioned casually that the tax authorities had come to my home but that he need not worry about me. Later in the day, some local pharmaceutical factory owners from Lucknow came to me with a representation that needed to be brought to the prime minister's attention. Lucknow was his Parliamentary constituency. I called N.K. Singh, an old acquaintance from college days, then in the PMO, and passed the visitors on to him. I did not mention anything about the incidents in the morning; I was no alarmist who would run to the PMO to sort out something that seemed like a containable situation. I was astounded that a handicraft-devotee, leading a non-glitzy, simple lifestyle, and president of an allied party in government should be the target of such actions. I was also angry at the petty corruption of the tax officials. Still, I thought it best not to embarrass the government and did not ruffle the waters anywhere as I was not personally affected and these matters weren't known publicly.

What followed though was a series of trash dumps and tragedies. The following day, the front page of one of the foremost newspapers of the country, *The Hindu*, had a story saying raids on the cricketer's had led the authorities to Jaya Jaitly's farmhouse. Reports appeared in other sections of the print media overnight that I had 'made calls', 'pulled strings' and abused officials. I recall a small snippet in *The Indian Express* reporting no money was found but some secret defence papers were. I decided to meet Finance Minister Yashwant Sinha, my old colleague from Janata Dal times.

I recounted the whole story of the demand for food and bribes. I specifically said this was for his ears only as I had no objection to them landing up at my home, or any enquiry made against anyone since we do not indulge in malpractice, but that he should find a way of reigning in the corrupt elements in his tax department. Strangely, the fact of my visit reached the media, most likely through one of the staff. This, in turn, set off another spate of stories from me protesting to the finance minister and prime minister, to Ajay Jadeja owning my house as *benami* property, to that he had a house in Cyprus. (Poor fellow had never heard of Cyprus since he only played cricket and didn't study much at school. One prominent weekly magazine said he earned Rs 8 crore—an impossible amount in the year 2000; this was before the days of auctions and huge endorsements). Every day, the media released more lies about Ajay, with some additional spice about me. He was said to have relatives holding his property in Dubai because someone found a cousin called Jai Jadeja living there. They said the bookies' diaries had 'AJ' written in them. None of these allegations amounted to anything eventually as it was not possible for them to produce evidence where none existed. I was inextricably tangled into the loop and began to be referred to in the media as the future mother-in-law of a tainted cricketer before any investigation had even taken place.

As a political figure and Party president, I had to separate fact from fiction. So I held a press conference where the Samata Party always held them, at the verandah of 3, Krishna Menon Marg. I also requested Sports Minister S.S. Dhindsa and Minister of State for Finance, Dhananjay Kumar, at the press conference not to allow the atmosphere to be vitiated by false reports. Dhindsa was quoted in a lengthy, rather unpleasant *India Today* story ('Mother of all rows', 7 August 2000) as saying: 'Jaitly tried to threaten IT officials visiting her place.' The storm was carried further by *The Week* ('Sack them', 6 August 2000), and *Outlook* ('Mums's not the Word', 7 August 2000). *The Times of India* had a front page headline 'Jaitly bats for Jadeja' which tried to report my press conference in a balanced way. Earlier, *Punjab Kesari* (27 July 2000) had a story titled '*Jadeja ki hamdard Jaya ka chutkaaraa jaldi nahin*' (Jadeja's sympathizer Jaya not to be let off so soon). US President Donald Trump's 'alternative facts' of 2017 are nothing compared to what was being churned out almost every day in those days. The story said five bags full of currency notes were in the boot of the car found in my home. These imaginary notes were linked to me as Samata Party president, and me to George Fernandes, the defence minister. They deduced that this was the reason why the thief (me) was scolding the policemen (the income tax authorities).

It is easy for anyone to see where the story was going.

Many more lengthy and negative articles appeared in regional languages. Each questioned my credentials, my audacity to speak out and my 'interference'. They openly implied a hand in corrupt practices. The issue of *India Today* that carried the article 'Mother of all rows' also carried an article by Tavleen Singh titled 'Tabs on the Taxman', cautioning against allowing tax officials from becoming bounty hunters. She was the only one who got a part of the point.

Nitish Kumar, our Party colleague, and always holier-than-thou, publicly questioned my interest in cricket, saying socialists and Dr Ram Manohar Lohia did not believe in such sports. When I rang to ask him why he said this, his answer was a smooth segue, 'Jayaji, my hair has become white because of the media.' It was obvious he was sidestepping the issue to avoid admitting he did not approve of me defending Ajay. I left it at that.

After the story of tax officials coming to my house and my purported behaviour, our honourable Parliamentarians didn't leave me alone. The opposition raised the issue in Parliament, including the incident of my dogs, who promptly became famous. Reformed dacoit-turned-MP Phoolan Devi of the Samajwadi Party, jumped in my defence and diverted the discussion. She came straight to me at 3, Krishna Menon Marg right after that and told me the whole story: '*Hum mahilaon ko ek doosre ka saath dena chahiye. Main jaanti hoon aap kaisi sadhaaran mahila hain. Maine unko rok di!*' (We women must support each other. I know what a simple kind of person you are. I stopped them), she said, in great excitement. She was bold all right. And I was very grateful. When Phoolan Devi was shot dead in 2001 at her residence, I was the first one to reach her house after the news broke.

Kapil Dev, who also suffered indignities at the hands of the tax people, said in an interview to *The Times of India* on 30 December 2001, that he was 'heartbroken' by what happened to Ajay who was his special protégée. Significantly, he said, 'It probably never occurred to Ajay that certain relationships could prove to be derogatory to his career.' He didn't realize the words could also mean being close to me could have harmed Ajay's life.

In the early days that *Tehelka* and Aniruddha Bahal came out with the match-fixing story, we were thoroughly confused on many counts. Bahal had befriended Ajay and dropped in at his house now and then. They had no discussion even remotely on the subject of match-fixing. Suddenly, he was accusing Ajay of being a crook and harming India's standing in sports. Friends and family scrambled to deal with the atrocious lies that hit the headlines on a daily basis. We gathered plenty of evidence that clearly showed the loopholes and hollowness of the stories. By then, Parliamentarians had jumped into the act. Kirti Azad, former Indian cricketer and politician, and others began demanding an enquiry. It got referred to the CBI and the BCCI, when there was no definition of what constituted 'match fixing,' nor any laws framed around it.

Matters went into a huge spin leading to a five-year ban on Ajay which meant an end to his upward-moving career, and his one and only passion in life—cricket. I will not go into the intricate details of the wheels within wheels of what went on subsequently, starting with *Tehelka*'s highly questionable and spurious match-fixing story in which they used Manoj Prabhakar, a disgruntled cricketer, to damage the reputations and careers of certain top players; the lies told in the CBI report; the many loose ends in their argument; the injustice of the process that followed; and the many machinations that brought the government and BCCI's politics to common meeting points. Fictitious bookie personas were created and false accusations of easily refutable kinds made by the CBI. A friend reported that a cousin had been shaken down by the CBI in Bombay and accused of being a bookie until he paid 25 lakhs to be let off. Such stories were utterly useless to me without evidence. An insider friend in the CBI, not involved with the case, told me that the cricket investigation was being headed by a protégée and protector of an influential political leader from Bihar.

The CBI came up with more gems that could be easily demolished by easily available evidence. But the unstoppable battle tank rolled on. There was no time for us to gather responses on one thing when something else popped up. At that point what could anyone say? We are a strong family with a very close bond between each one of us. Equally strong is our sense of values that are intolerant of deceit and dishonesty. The attack on all of us made us even more determined to stand tall and fight, looking everyone in the eye.

During harrowing moments, I would ask George Sahib, 'Why is this nonsense never-ending?' His answer was, 'Never-ending, maybe, but never bending.' He was much more interested in cricket than I was, and although he never watched television, he was up on all the scores of matches being played. There was nothing he could do to help in this case, and none of us asked him to be involved in any way.

The story ended with Ajay challenging the ban in the Delhi High Court and being exonerated fully in January 2003. Such victories never make the headlines, and it was too late to retrieve his cricketing career in India's national team. In fact, one of the saddest moments in my life was seeing Ajay sitting silently the evening of the day the ban was announced, his eyes brimming with tears. He has always been a smiling and ebullient booster of spirits within his team, at home, with schoolchildren or on television. His open-hearted generosity of spirit makes him a friend of eunuchs, rickshaw peddlers, golf caddies and taxi drivers. That is why the memory of that day is even more poignant and my heart crumbles whenever I remember it.

Ajay has recovered from this huge hit with tremendous grace, courage and goodwill towards the world by deciding to put it all completely behind him forever and move on. It is not for anyone to speculate or re-open now the whys and hows of this tragedy, both for an individual, a family, and India's cricketing honour. Besides, the intricate and mind-boggling details of what happened at each step and at many levels are a part of Ajay Jadeja's own story to tell, if ever he wishes to. It is not for me or anyone else to intrude anymore, and it appears in this book only insofar as it directly encroached on my life and work.

Next, *Tehelka* aimed at the Ministry of Defence in which the NDA government was their prime target with George Fernandes as the intended prey. It became clear to me much later that the *Tehelka* journalists were a bunch of mercenaries posing as investigative journalists who were selling themselves to the highest bidder. They chose a subject that would catch the imagination of the public and turned it upside down, claiming to fight corruption. The thing was that the world of corrupt people cannot be changed by people who use dishonest means, so they eventually had no effect on anything except that they ruined a bunch of innocent lives.

This episode was clearly a conspiracy that cast a huge shadow on my political credentials, character and family. But at the time when all of this was happening, there was not a moment to analyse what was really going on or even if there were dots to connect. It is only in hindsight that the links begin to appear, by which time it is too late. The way by then had already been paved for the subsequent phase of the devilry that *Tehelka* was to unleash. The *Tehelka* journalists' next hit followed a year later in March 2001, exactly two weeks before Ajay and Aditi were, in reality, to be married. Ironic timing again.

18

'WHY SHOULD THE TALIBAN NOT SHOOT YOU?'

Tehelka Sting II

IS THE TITLE A TAD overdramatic? Not really, if this was to be compared to another question I was asked over a social media chat that took place in a 'chat room' organized by the newly arrived online world. The other question? 'For how much do you sell your daughter?' The year? 2001, soon after my role as president of the Samata Party had been ratified in a Party conference in Mysore in January 2001, and my daughter Aditi's wedding had been fixed to be held on 28 March 2001. The occasion? I was being asked questions across every kind of media after *Tehelka* (of the match-fixing fame) had exploded a fresh bomb called Operation West End, in which I, among others, was shown supposedly engaging in conspiracy and corruption with arms dealers in the presence of crooks, middlemen and army officers at the residence of Defence Minister George Fernandes. I came up against a cruel mix of a gullible public, misogynists who hate women in politics, a gleeful opposition, the entire sensation-seeking-lynch-mob-oriented media, the usual scandal mongers et al. For them, what could be more 'atrocious, anti-national, immoral' and wonderful material for attack, than a woman heading a Party supposedly caught in an act of corruption within a story of 'how the security of the country was being compromised by greedy politicians'. Worth being interrogated and asked to account for such deeds, if not shot rightaway I would say, had the incident presented by *Tehelka*, reflected an iota of truth.

I can afford to sound flippant now. The raw edges have been smoothened, the tears hovering behind my eyelids have dried up, the fierce anger at such perfidy is under control and the utter bewilderment of how such allegations could have been made against me have been overcome by the political challenge and daily practicalities of dealing with it. But I am jumping ahead.

∽

It was a quiet afternoon on 15 March 2001. I was in a tiny room in a back lane of Kalkaji in South Delhi, cocooned with Jaswinder, the typesetter, who was helping me design the invitation card for Aditi's wedding on the computer. It was a small-sized, single-colour printing job on handmade paper. Nothing ostentatious. Ashok Subramaniam, George Fernandes's private secretary, called me saying, 'Ma'am, there's supposedly a huge revelation taking place at a press conference at Imperial Hotel about you and others doing defence deals. You had better come to Sahib's office immediately.'

It sounded so outlandish that as usual I laughed out loud, asking, 'What great revelation? Has someone gone crazy?'

'They claim to have tapes which they are showing. Please come, wherever you are.'

I reached Raksha Bhavan to find George Fernandes sitting completely still with his forehead wrinkled. He said Parliament was apparently in an uproar because Priya Ranjan Dasmunshi had rushed in saying '*Gaiyee! Gaiyee! Sarkar gaiyee*!' (Gone! Gone! The government is gone!)

The tapes were being aired on the television screen in the room. George Fernandes never watched television and was not doing so now. His mind was ticking with whether any security areas were breached, who these people were, and readying for a meeting of his officials to get to the bottom of what was going on. I watched some blurry images of me at a desk talking to unseen people. The claim was I was meeting some representatives of an arms company called West End International, along with a certain General Murgai and others I had never heard of. Aniruddha Bahal's (the one who had befriended Ajay for the cricket sting) commentary was a seedy story about how everyone in the Ministry of Defence, from the Minister to the underlings, were all corrupt to the hilt.

'I am going to the prime minister to resign,' George Sahib said.

I could see what was happening and exploded with anger at what was being perpetrated in the name of investigative journalism—constructing sensational fiction out of innocent conversations filmed in a completely different context in which people were victims of blatant entrapment.

Or else, the whole presentation was a huge mistake that would be soon clarified. I did not have to tell George Sahib that I had never engaged in a situation as was being alleged. He knew me too well to even ask. I argued that he should not resign just because people were presenting some nonsense. They are crooks. Catch them, find out how they did all this, was my advice. However, events soon spun out of control.

Rumours were spread that they had many more tapes which compromised even the prime minister. Press and television vans were chasing us everywhere, pushing us over in the melee. The tapes were shown repeatedly, and meaningless conversations took place accompanied by ugly interpretations. In some scenes, the BJP President Bangaru Laxman was being shown accepting a hundred thousand rupees as a donation for the Party. You could see the currency notes. He indulges in a conversation with them about defence matters. He resigned from his post. For some years after that, his face became a symbol of corruption in Indian politics.

For four days, George Fernandes insisted on resigning while L.K. Advani and Jaswant Singh advised against it. The media was all over us while George Sahib spent most of his time with his officials at Raksha Bhavan. Party colleagues had come in from across the country to express their solidarity. Sudheendra Kulkarni from the PMO, other friends like R.V. Pandit (who was, apart from being a lifelong friend of Vajpayee and L.K. Advani's, the former publisher of Imprint and producer of the well-known film *Maachis*) and my children—all spent long evenings at 3, Krishna Menon Marg discussing what could be done. Pandit and I went to Ram Jethmalani who, along with his juniors, prepared a petition to the Supreme Court requesting it to stay the airing of all the tapes on various television channels till their authenticity was established. The Supreme Court merely said they would take it up later, which of course was of no use, since the tapes were aired on fourteen Zee TV channels soon after. L.K. Advani was saddened by George Fernandes's insistence to resign. He too was accused of corruption in the Home Ministry, but strangely *Tehelka* withdrew that story a couple of days later. They preferred to focus entirely on the defence deal story.

Mamata Banerjee, always self-righteous, promptly jumped off the NDA ship, which the Congress thought was sinking. It is another matter that she did this to benefit in the forthcoming Assembly elections in West Bengal where the Left parties put up posters asking the public, 'If she could not remain loyal to the NDA, how can you trust her?' She lost the elections, subsequently returned to the NDA and settled in again. It was however, just for a while, since her sense of secularism seemed to waver in accordance with the electoral benefits she would get.

Pramod Mahajan and a couple of younger ministers met the prime minister pressing him to let go of the defence minister to deflect accusations against him and save the government from more resignations by other parties and diminishing the strength of the NDA. Obviously, the whole exercise was meant to destabilize the government by hitting at Fernandes, its prime pillar. The prime minister finally gave in and agreed to let George Fernandes resign although there was no intention of leaving the NDA.

In the meanwhile, Nitish Kumar and other members of our Party approached George Sahib for my resignation as Party president. They were all in his sitting room, while George Fernandes came to me separately to convey their views and told me to address them directly. I was still vociferous that having done no wrong and having been fraudulently represented, I found no reason to resign particularly when no Party member could ever accuse me of corruption. I faced a room of grim-faced, silent men like Nitish Kumar, Prabhunath Singh and Digvijay Singh. I told them that it was a time for them to show solidarity with a woman who had served the Party loyally and honestly since the very beginning without asking for anything in return. Surely it wasn't the time to leave me by the wayside to fend for myself among the crowds baying for my blood. I argued some more. No one responded. After some minutes of silence, I got up and walked out of the room. I did not resign.

Political opponents always ask for your resignation at the slightest opportunity. They like to convey that if you don't resign, you are guilty. But when you do resign, it is treated as an admission of guilt, although it is dressed in a moral cloak to save the face of the so-called offender. You are treated as guilty till proven innocent, the process of which may take decades. The idea of this is to get a person out of the way somehow, irrespective of the lack of evidence, logic, reason or likelihood, irrespective of the person's lifelong reputation of having maintained their integrity. While being president of the Party did not matter to me, I did not want to get into this tangled trap of appearing guilty irrespective of whether I was or not. I also did not believe in false moral posturing. George Fernandes felt he had to accept responsibility as the person heading the Defence

Ministry, irrespective of what the truth was.

The following day, Jaswant Singh brought the prime minister's message to the Defence Minister, accepting his resignation. George Fernandes was only too eager to oblige. The Opposition had prevented him from speaking on behalf of his Ministry in the Parliament. This was an atrocious tactic of the opposition since they were preventing an elected person responsible for securing India's borders from discharging his duty towards the people of India. It has been their habit to obstruct the truth rather than arrive at it through a people's democratic platform. He was deeply troubled about how the morale of the troops would be affected by such stories about their leaders. This was what affected him the most at all times. Since he was prevented from speaking in the Parliament, he put in his resignation and headed straight for Doordarshan where he made a lengthy statement on the issue and allegations by *Tehelka*, assuring the country that nothing had been compromised. He was even attacked for using a government television channel for this purpose.

Neither did George Fernandes say anything separately to me, nor did he try to defend me in public. I respected him for that. It was not his job to defend anything but the country and its borders, and the morale of the men who fought to protect the countrymen. Our friend Ajay Singh, who was Minister of State for Railways during the National Front government, would visit often over the years. He would engage George Fernandes in conversation about what was going on around us. He told me many years later that he never forgot a remark George Sahib made during one such time. He had looked sad, apparently, and said, 'You know, Ajay, our country has a long way to go to get used to accepting an independent, intelligent woman in politics.'

Apart from the message of the prime minister accepting George Fernandes's resignation, Jaswant Singh conveyed that Vajpayee had also wanted me to resign from the post of president of the Samata Party since the BJP president, Bangaru Laxman, had resigned. I found it very odd that the request for my resignation should come from the leader of another Party, howsoever senior and important he may be. The actions of a Party organization and its members should be guided by the decisions of its own leadership. Moralists and others may have criticized my stance, but I firmly believed that if one is not guilty and the tapes gave no evidence of my taking money, other than grainy images and a suggestive defamatory commentary of an event that was not what it was made out to be, I should not have to bow before anyone's accusations. Obviously, once George Fernandes, as my Party leader resigned, I could not possibly stay on. I followed the prime minister's instructions. However, it has always rankled me that it seemed as if I was thrown to the winds by some members of my own Party perhaps working through the prime minister. They could not be the people to decide anything in my Party, but they probably knew George Fernandes would not go against the prime minister's wishes while they ran the risk of him defending me within the Party. Anyway, my departure suited the purpose of some of my Party colleagues of removing an independent woman whom they could not manipulate from a position of authority.

In a show of solidarity, our three other ministers, namely Nitish Kumar, Digvijay Singh and Srinivasa Prasad, resigned too. It was a pretty little charade that lasted precisely two weeks. They hung around George Fernandes coyly hinting they wanted their ministerial positions back. He told me this under his breath in irritation since he knew their ambition and need to cling to a chair, but he also knew the government felt shaky without Samata Party representation in the cabinet. He spoke to the prime minister who readily took them back and all was well in the trio's world again. They knew George Fernandes was indispensable whether he was in government or not, and I didn't count at all. Since then, none of our Party's senior leaders have ever telephoned to ask how I was coping with the Commission of Inquiry and later, the courts. No one offered legal or financial help except our lone female member, Betty D' Souza, who occasionally gave me personal cheques for 25000 rupees. She has remained a constant friend.

All the feminists inside and outside political parties made scathing comments against me. Other than Vandana Shiva, no well-known activist or friend stood by me publicly. I realized good people remained silent while the political ones attacked. Brinda Karat of the CPI(M) met me in a television studio many years later. She apologized for not standing by me, giving discipline of 'the Party line' as the reason. I responded by saying that it didn't matter as I was, by then, used to fighting my battles alone.

I went to every television studio that invited me for a discussion. I believed I had nothing to be ashamed of and I needed a forum to give my side of the story. Soon after the story broke, CPI(M) leader and former Lok Sabha Speaker Somnath Chatterjee growled in NDTV's 'We the People': 'Seeing is believing'. I argued that firstly, the tapes weren't showing me do anything wrong, and secondly, tapes can be doctored easily with the help of modern technology. I explained how as a public person I had to meet even unknown visitors and couldn't just say 'go to hell' without hearing them out. For six months or more, the 'go to hell' part, said rather gently and conversationally within a long sentence, was extracted and played over and over as a 'promo' for the channel. I became a fallen star.

For the record, I need to describe what seems to be the goings on in those tapes—without the intentionally damning commentary by one of the three *Tehelka* 'heroes'. The problem with recounting such an event which had no significance or consequence in my work day, is that it was supposed to have happened in December 2000. Since I could not recall this visit by some peripheral characters even four months later in March 2001 (when it was aired), I have had to rely only on what the *Tehelka* tapes show. Also, since the matter is now sub judice, I will only recount what I presume happened from what is visible on the tapes:

Three people have entered George Fernandes's Parliament-allotted residence at 3, Krishna Menon Marg. It was a house with no gates or guards ever since George Sahib had them removed a few years earlier. On the tapes, there is a scene of the house taken in daylight while the other scenes are all in the dark of the evening. There is some coming and going of people, while some are seated talking among themselves. The wrapping and rustling of paper is shown on the grainy film while some whispering goes on. They enter the room where I worked as I am shown speaking on the phone to someone who wants help to become a member of the India Habitat Centre. My large room always had people coming in and out to use the common computer or photocopier, or to just sit and wait for me to speak to them. The persons engaging in conversation with me are never seen on screen in my presence. The visuals contain no surreptitious activity by me, nor any intrigue or conspiratorial double entendres. I am generally sociable with anyone, including complete strangers, if I do not suspect ill-intent. Perhaps it's foolish and naive to be like that in political life but we are all taught to offer even strangers a glass of water as an expression of decent human gesture. One person is partially introduced as a manufacturer of electronics. After a bit of useless conversation it is mentioned that they want to give something for the Party. I just say 'Oh'. Again, the conversation meanders until a voice interrupts the conversation saying, 'Can I give it to madam?' As a Party donation is always welcome,

I ask them to 'send it to Srinivas Prasad, our minister, who is arranging a party conference'. I neither discuss it nor receive it. The voice says 'okay, okay, okay' and shifts to talking about difficulties his company is facing in getting a response to some request in the Defence Ministry. What follows is a boring back and forth between them and me in which I am guiding them to follow the procedures of approaching the concerned people. He repeatedly says he has tried everything and the Ministry is actually favouring some other companies. I back off saying I don't know how the Ministry functions and I would not interfere to help anyone but the most I would do, if he fails to get any response from the officials, is to request 'Sahib's office' to pass the word on to treat everyone fairly. The conversation is paraphrased, but anyone reading the transcript or listening to the tapes would not hear anything conspiratorial, corrupt or improper in what I said.

George Fernandes was most worried about the morale of his soldiers who gave their lives defending their country. I was most worried about how dangerous it was for democracy if visitors misused easy access to prominent people and created a feeling of mistrust towards any unknown person who may come close. I was also horrified that the perpetrators of this elaborate hoax, called it investigative journalism. At the height of the uproar, no one at the highest levels in any field asked about the methodology of how the story was developed or about the authenticity of the tapes. (This issue became a part of the mandate of the inquiry commission. Before that, we were left to defend ourselves as rumours had been spread that *Tehelka* had much more material on various important people so everyone may have been scared of when they could be similarly hit.) Instead, the tapes were aired across channels of the Zee TV network, having been reportedly sold to them for somewhere between five and eight million rupees. We all got defamed in the process, even though the screenings were soon taken off the air as nothing was clearly audible or visible, and boredom had set in among the viewers. It was all about TRPs.

~

The media, including women journalists and a host of others, pretending to be fair and over-friendly, held long interviews with me ultimately twisting the stories saying I had promised the visitors an appointment with the Defence Minister and much else. One wrote a fat tome on this episode with a spicy snippet that while I claimed to be a socialist, I was not beyond wearing lacy innerwear of which she got a glimpse as she pinned the microphone to my blouse. She went into discussing George Fernandes's defending me in the Justice Venkataswami and the Justice Phukan Inquiry Commission that followed, expressing envy that I had such a person to defend me, in the style of a literary-romantic trance imitating *Bridget Jones's Diary*, a work of fiction. It was a sad commentary on what the doyens of our media were all about.

The only person who was decent, fair and truly wanting answers to serious questions as a responsible journalist was A. Surya Prakash, who often wrote for the *Pioneer*, and was commissioned by Zee TV to interview me. He took the trouble to first discuss the whole incident with me and after convincing himself that I had some serious things to say, did a lengthy interview which was reproduced faithfully. He is the Chairman of Prasar Bharati today, the head of all government media operations. However, a rigorous and effective Press Council/ Broadcasting Council never emerged as a result of these messy sting operations. The courts have repeatedly, in fact as recently as 2014, asked for laws or regulations to be framed so that stings don't become vigilante-type or hit-operations on behalf of others. So far, nothing effective has emerged here either.

I have my own theories of why all this happened, but they are merely speculative. Connecting the dots and proving anything conclusively is not within my capacity, without documents. The perfect occasion for the government or any of us to get to the bottom of who was behind such a clumsily handled, incompetent 'investigation', carried out without any supporting documents or actions which were a result of corruption, was sadly lost through the undermining of the Inquiry Commission itself.

All I came to know from documents shared by officials, press reports and facts that emerged during questioning in the Justice Venkataswami/ Phukan Inquiry Commission at that time, is that *Tehelka* was heavily funded through the hawala funds from abroad. I know that the Congress Party constantly took an undue interest in the matter and chief honcho of the Enforcement Directorate had a signed confession of a hawala operator in Chennai, who said he received funds from Brussels and had sent them to First Global in Mauritius. This was the company belonging to Shankar Sharma that heavily funded *Tehelka* for Operation West End.

Later, in early March 2001, First Global discovered it was under investigation by SEBI (the Securities and Exchange Board of India) for playing the stock market with hawala funds. This was just a week before the incomplete and factually incorrect *Tehelka* story of defence deals broke. When First Global went to the high court in Mumbai accusing the government of mala fide intent in taking action against them, the court was shown the SEBI orders on the files. They threw out its petition without allowing any further arguments. *Tehelka* claimed, in the media, on their website and at the commission of inquiry, that they had been compelled to break the story, incomplete and with vast inaccuracies, with no documents or evidence because they had been spotted by someone they had been filming.

In the end, Operation West End merely turned out to be a shoddily created tale of how Indian politicians and defence officials could possibly be corrupted if offered money, by pretending it was a genuine business deal, being presented with a fake problem claiming an injustice needing redressal, or call girls forced upon unsuspecting army officers, or plied with enough alcohol to make them boast that they were influential enough to swing any deal in the sin city of Delhi. Just like with their cricket sting, *Tehelka* journalists neither managed to expose genuine corruption in cricket nor did they even touch the surface of the real scams that came tumbling out of the closet later. They obviously targeted the ethical and honest people to destroy them rather than truly go after crooks. I surmised that Congress was an obvious beneficiary of the *Tehelka* defence corruption story, hoping to wipe out public memory of its own Bofors corruption. For example, they had sent a senior law officer of the UPA-I government to unfreeze Ottavio Quattrocchi's London accounts which had the money he had allegedly been paid as commission on the Bofors deal.* P.V. Narasimha Rao's government had earlier reportedly let him flee India overnight to save him from the probes into the scandal. It is hard not to come to the conclusion that big money from unknown persons were behind the Operation West End Project.

*See "Why and how were Q's London accounts defrozen?" in 'The Q files: Acquitted without trial?', Neeraj Mishra and Priya Sahgal, 30 January 2006, *India Today*, http://indiatoday.intoday.in/story/bofors-deal-scandal-under-controversy-upa-government-on-target/1/181913.html

Aditi's wedding was held at Kashmir House on Prithviraj Road in New Delhi. I paid 36,000 rupees for the simple decorations and Aditi's father paid 150,000 rupees for the Kashmiri food made by cooks brought in from Srinagar. I bought Aditi a sari from Nalli's for 8000 rupees. That is all. No jewellery was purchased as we did not need anything except the South Indian *mangalsutra*.*

On the morning of the wedding, it drizzled slightly. Aniruddha Bahal had the gall to send a text message to Aditi saying 'rain on the wedding day is a good omen'! We managed to send invitations to those we could remember at a time when I was distracted with the media storm above my head. More than a thousand people came as guests. The cars were parked from as far a distance as 3 kilometres away. There was no valet parking. Many said the huge response was a show of solidarity by our friends. I had visited Prime Minister Atal Bihari Vajpayee to hand over the formal invitation but gave him a way out in case he was embarrassed to attend the wedding of a person under so many allegations. He not only came, but also stayed for an hour and a half, dining comfortably in the company of George Fernandes and Farooq Abdullah, who acted like hosts all evening. I was very touched by this moral support the prime minister indirectly gave me. Madhuri Dixit, our favourite movie actor, and some of Ajay's cricketer friends came but I refused to let the media enter. After their fierce pursuit of me on the *Tehelka* story, I found it only right that they not be made part of my daughter's wedding. Every guest had to leave their mobile phones outside. One 'friend' brought hers in. She couldn't resist being the journalist she was and took a picture on the sly and posted it alongside a piece in *The Indian Express* describing my clothes and the important hosts of the evening. The only picture we gave to the media ourselves was one taken of the married couple after midnight.

I had so blocked my emotions to withstand the *Tehelka* nightmare that I went through my daughter's wedding like a hospitable robot, with no feelings at all—neither the usual emotions of sadness at giving away a daughter, or happiness and excitement at her marriage. When she asked what I would do after she left home, I joked, 'Oh, it doesn't matter. I will keep five dogs.' She enjoys telling everyone this story to describe how her mother's love for her was equated with her love of dogs.

---

*In traditional Hindu wedding ceremonies, the *mangalsutra* is the sacred necklace the groom ties onto the bride's neck that the latter wears as a symbol of being married.

19

OMISSIONS IN THE COMMISSION

From Operation West End to Operation Abort

IN APRIL 2001, THE NDA government set up the Justice K. Venkataswami Commission of Inquiry to examine the truth behind the allegations made in the *Tehelka* tapes. There were two parts to the inquiry. The first part aimed at examining whether the Defence Ministry had done its job in terms of its fifteen actual procurement decisions that involved aircrafts, missiles, advance jet trainers, rocket launchers, etc. The purpose was to ensure that the purchases had been made without compromising national security. Strangely, these covered negotiations still in progress and even those completed by earlier regimes. The purpose of naming as many as fifteen of these was to seriously call into question all major decisions purportedly being handled by the NDA government.

The second part dealt with the 'documentary' provided by *Tehelka*, one that supposedly showed corruption in action. It was, in essence, a story created with the aim of lending authenticity to allegations of wrongdoing in the actual 'deals'. This set of tapes, accompanied by a vivid, defamatory commentary, prepared the viewer for a ringside seat to seediness, compromise, and illicit back-room conversations soaked in alcohol, call girls, lewd talk, and flashing of currency notes. We were unknowing and hapless actors in this orchestrated drama. The opposition led by the Congress party, of course, thought the government had to fall by the end of the day.

Everyone actually appearing on *Tehelka*'s videotapes speaking about those 'deals', or in any manner engaging in conversation with *Tehelka* journalists posing as arms- and electronics-dealers, however innocently, were issued 8B notices which made them directly answerable to the Commission. George Fernandes was issued only an 8A notice which did not make him an accused but merely afforded him the opportunity to appear before the Commission in case he wished to protect his own interests. From the very beginning, however, he was attacked in Parliament and outside, on a daily basis, as if he was the main accused. That was because I am shown talking to some people who are never visible on screen, from my desk at the office-cum-residence of George Fernandes, the defence minister of India. George Fernandes was never caught on tape as the makers could not get near him. I was attacked on an everyday basis as a rogue, companion, mistress, sleeping partner, conspirator, and a corrupt, greedy, wheeler-dealer engaging with shady characters in the dark back rooms of an official residence to make money through habitually venal methods. *Tehelka*'s website kept up this tirade while the media happily followed suit, except for a few honourable exceptions.

I am deliberately not going into what actually transpired from my point of view, and is part of a vague memory of a wholly insignificant event to no consequence at all because the interminable court case that ultimately followed, is still not over. It is stifling and frustrating for me since I was eager to have the inquiry proceed correctly and quickly, and have my truth heard and assessed. I was certain the sham investigation— full of frame-ups, entrapment and assumed identities—would be revealed for what it was. But it has not happened yet—even after sixteen years. That tortuous journey is another story in itself.

It is another matter that my political adversaries saw to it that George Fernandes and I were thwarted from telling our truth every step of the way. But the bizarre twists and turns that took place during and after the Commission, could go down in the annals of what constitutes dark and convoluted conspiracies or unforgivable ineptitude in legal procedures.

Soli Sorabji, the nation's Attorney General, and the late Kirit Rawal, the Additional Solicitor General, were appointed to the Inquiry Commission on behalf of the NDA government. Gopal Subramanium, an eminent lawyer who was on a retainership by major industrialists, was the Commission's lawyer. He rose to great heights after 2004, when the UPA government came along. He was to play the role of amicus curiae. He chose to take a fee of only one rupee. One of his juniors was a certain Siddharth Agarwal. *Tehelka* was represented by (now prominent) lawyer Siddharth Luthra and Kavin Gulati. Lawyer Prashant Bhushan, represented First Global, the financiers of *Tehelka*'s sting operation. He also assisted *Tehelka*'s team. These dramatis personae are important in the whole story.

My legal team consisting of Niloy Dutta, a senior lawyer from Assam who was living in Delhi because of threats from the militant ULFA (United Liberation Front of Assam), and young Ameet Nayak, lent to me by my son's firm Trilegal, was new to me at that time but have remained dear friends long after their roles ended. George Fernandes had help from Raju Ramachandran, Upamanyu Hazarika, and Abhijat, who some years later was elected as secretary of the Delhi High Court Bar Association. I could barely afford to pay any of them and I had to stay up as an extra hand till the early hours of the morning to help them sieve through the numerous flaws in both facts and recordings found on those hundred and more tapes. I learned to operate a computer only then. I had been planning to go to computer classes for three weeks, but necessity made me learn from our office staff in half an hour flat.

Justice Venkatswami allowed himself to be guided almost entirely by Gopal Subramanium regarding the procedures adopted by the inquiry commission. We accused had no idea what we were being accused of since no formal 'charges' were ever spelled out. We were not allowed to inspect the Commission's records. We had to therefore file affidavits based on flimsy memories. No evidence was shown to us. Any lawyer would say this was not legally correct.

We had to pay five rupees for each sheet of paper of any document emerging out of the judge's orders. If they were to have an official stamp, the cost rose to ten rupees. It was only after I enquired from two commissions being held in the adjoining buildings of the Vigyan Bhavan and found that these are free, that we managed to protest before the judge and have this unnecessary fee waived.

We were not allowed to watch the tapes until a united demand forced the Commission to screen them in a small room for all lawyer-representatives. There would be no rewinds, repeats or pauses. If someone needed to visit the toilet which was in another building, they would have to miss a part of the screening.

There were hundreds of errors in the *Tehelka*'s transcripts. No one heeded our pleas for ensuring accuracy before questioning us. I put together a booklet of pictures, diagrams and images of forensic results pointing out various technical and factual flaws. To defuse my own anger at what had been done to us, I wrote a parody mocking the *Tehelka* story calling it conmen@dhamaka.com, with cartoons prepared by a friend in the media. I distributed them to every MP and all those who attended the Commission's hearings, and the media. There was silence. They must have thought I was crazy but it gave me some relief. It formed part of my instruments of battle.

Today, no taped evidence of any kind and particularly those made during sting operations, are given credence without sending them for forensic examination. However, I had to fight alone every inch of the way from April 2001 till early 2003 to finally have the tapes sent to be verified for authenticity.

A significant part of this battle was when I requested and obtained time from Prime Minister Vajpayee and prominent members of his cabinet and the PMO to view my private forensic expert Milin Kapoor's study and presentation of the many blatant manipulations, in words, sequences and attributions of conversations, visible on many of the tapes. I remember that day clearly: it was the same Sunday morning that the Congress leader Madhavrao Scindia had died in an unfortunate plane accident—30 September 2001. The Prime Minister, Yashwant Sinha, Jaswant Singh, George Fernandes, Arun Shourie—all senior ministers, and Brajesh Mishra, the Principal Adviser to the Prime Minister, were among those who watched and listened to us in silence. In the end, I pleaded that the Attorney General be requested to forcefully argue before the Commission for forensic examination of the tapes at any laboratory, whether in India or abroad, to ensure their authenticity before we are questioned.

Strangely, the stoic silence continued. Finally, Arun Shourie offered a solution in his typically mild manner: 'Why don't you go to court?' I was too surprised and disheartened at this unhelpful comment to stay in the room much longer. I never thought that the highest in the land would reject being my last resort in a public cause concerning the need for credibility of basic evidence in any legal proceedings, especially when the reputation of its own Ministry of Defence was involved.

I did go to the Delhi High Court immediately afterwards. After a few hearings, the judge denied my petition. Shockingly and inexplicably, he referred in his written order to various names and incidents that were not part of my case or pleas at all. This puzzled my legal team. Doggedly, I went to a Division Bench. The single judge's obviously erroneous order was remanded for revision by the Division Bench. The result was an order that expunged all the mistakes but the Bench left it to the Inquiry Commission to take a decision. The long snake you find just before you reach your goal in the board game of Snakes and Ladders had devoured me. I was back to where I started.

Through a reliable diplomat, I obtained the contact of a highly professional private forensic team in the UK. They were regularly used by the UK's Scotland Yard and even had a letter of commendation from the US government for a meticulous enquiry into the FBI tapes of the Waco shootout incident in the US in 1993. I telephoned London and arranged to meet an ex-policeman and forensic expert Chris Mills from this company. I carried our copies of the tapes and hung around London staying with friends while he examined them at his company. He reported that there seemed to be flaws, and the original tapes provided by *Tehelka*, not copies of copies, would need to be examined.

Vasant Pandit, R.V. Pandit's son, had helped Nanaji Deshmukh, the venerable RSS leader and social worker in his rural development projects in Chitrakoot. Vasant gave the Samata Party a cheque of five lakh rupees to cover the costs of Chris Mills's coming to India to depose based on his initial report and opinions, at the Commission. The money covering these expenses were transferred through the RBI. However, Vasant's name came out in *The Indian Express* soon, after which he suddenly started being harassed with court cases on umpteen matters not remotely connected to me. Interestingly, R.V. Pandit has been one of Vajpayee, George Sahib and Advani's closest friends for decades. Yet no one could ever get his son out of a wholly fabricated mess which continues till today concerning supposedly illegal import of health mattresses from Japan.

Meanwhile, Chris Mills appeared at the Commission and was allowed to speak for just twenty minutes on the stand. Gopal Subramanium and his team of lawyers advised the judge to disallow questions by any other lawyers, including all other noticees, *Tehelka* and government lawyers. They simply shut Mills down. Chris Mills was stunned. He told us he felt humiliated and short changed considering the expense we had incurred for him to do his job. I arranged for media interactions and even a television appearance on *India TV* channel. Nothing had any effect, and I was certain the judge was unaware of the ramifications of new digital technologies and their importance.

The proof that the transcripts were incorrect ultimately spilled out inadvertently when a *Tehelka* lawyer's references were not the same as in the transcript held by Soli Sorabji. Sufficiently chastened, the Commission ordered re-transcription of *all* the tapes by the Ministry of Defence—the only ones with available personnel. After several weeks, 700 more pages of transcript emerged, many parts of which contained exculpatory material. We finally got the unedited transcripts.

When we asked for copies of the tapes to view carefully on our own, we were reluctantly given one set and made to copy them at our own expense. Do the accused ever have to pay to receive material provided as evidence of their supposed crimes? Well, the rules seemed to be different in this case.

In 2002, finally, my turn to depose came along. I was excited, eager and confident. The previous evening, when chatting with Niloy Dutta, I had cried for a few moments at the sheer ignominy of being made to convince a complete stranger that I was not a corrupt person. The trigger was an article I had seen in that national Hindi daily about corrupt officers in Uttar Pradesh. It referred to a statement by Mahatma Gandhi I had come across when he was once accused of putting away pounds sterling in London. The gist of the story was that the good always lose out at the hands of the crooked and ruthless. As I said earlier in the context of Gandhiji's influence on my life, this seemed to resonate with me deeply in ways that motivated me to fight more although there was much happening around me that was discouraging.

Niloy was nervous thinking that I would be shaky the next day before the judge. What happened was a comedy of errors. The good old CBI, as a matter of sheer coincidence, had decided to raid the office premises of *Tehelka* on a complaint of causing illegal acts of poaching so as to be able to make a film on poaching in a forest in Uttar Pradesh. It had nothing to do with us. But as expected, there was an uproar against us for manipulating the CBI. I happened to meet the CBI chief at a social function during that period and shared that I had been put in a soup at my deposition because of the CBI raid on *Tehelka*. He replied rather sombrely, 'Ma'am, the CBI does not look all around to see what else is going on the day when it plans its actions.' Fair and plausible enough, I concluded.

The gentler of the *Tehelka* lawyers, Kavin Gulati, was made to cross-examine me. In my chief deposition, I described and displayed the modalities of manipulation indulged in to portray me as a crook. I answered every question without a pause or doubt.

Gopal Subramanium's junior, Dayan Krishnan, thought his next question was going to clinch my guilt. He had a triumphant look of expectation on his face. He asked me, 'You deny that Gopal Pacherwal was present at the scene. Then how have you referred to him by name throughout your deposition?'

I gave the only answer I could: 'You cannot see anyone's face in the tapes except mine throughout the filming. I would have had to refer to everyone as "unidentified person". Instead, I merely followed the names offered by *Tehelka*.' He had nothing more to say.

Niloy, grey haired and usually a bit formal, had a broad smile on his face when I stepped off the stand. 'Can I give you a kiss?' he asked happily.

Incidentally, in the midst of all this, my first grandchild, a boy, was born. I spent my time between Commission hearings every afternoon and helping my daughter with her newborn for the rest of the day and night.

The transcripts of over 10,000 pages piled up as the *Tehelka* journalists answered penetrating questions from the lawyers of so many noticees. They were surprisingly cavalier and blasé about the gaping holes in their allegations. It was as if they were heroes in the eyes of the world and needed to give no credible explanations for inaccuracies, loose ends and statements with no evidence to back them up. After a series of dead ends, when Tarun Tejpal, the chief of *Tehelka* had no credible answer to support presumptions made in the tapes, his answer was he did not have the facts, because in fact 'the Commission was there to find out the facts'. Under rigorous questioning, they admitted to not being necessarily accurate and of actually putting the system rather than individuals in the dock. No one cared to ask why then were those individuals having to have their reputations tarnished and having to spend time answering questions to defend their integrity.

The gem they finally pulled out of their bag of tricks and evasions was 'George is not corrupt'. This, after practically carrying his head on the tip of their swords and doing victory marches.

~

Tehelka's story began interestingly by referring to Joseph Heller's classic anti-war novel *Catch-22*. Everyone had read it at some stage for its dark humour and fierce condemnation of war. I thought it ironic that

Aniruddha Bahal of *Tehelka*, who wrote the ugly commentary, used Heller's writings for his opening mood piece, to go on to condemn the mighty Indian defence establishment itself, whose job, for a start, is to prevent war. The story ends with them saying that the entire brave exercise of the Operation West End documentary ended with them 'getting' a 26-page evaluation letter for a product from the Ministry of Defence as a result of their bribery. But the letter was not really obtained because their 'cover was blown' and the person who was supposed to give it to them was forewarned and became incommunicado. Or so they say. They could produce no record of any sort to confirm any of this, nor of purported demands for call girls or many other conversations, despite several of their stories resting on the strength of telephone calls they never recorded, even when they had the equipment to do so. How could anyone in their right mind have believed them? Sadly, all these questions were never allowed to be analysed.

After one and a half months and over thousands of questions, the best response to questions by various lawyers on why he spread lies among the people they had conversations with in the process of building their story, was given by Matthew Samuel. He was the man who actually went around with hidden cameras, encouraging people to respond according to the lies he had fed them. When asked why he lied for instance about my daughter's non-existent job and my never-happened dinner with a Major-General, he said that he wasn't lying, only boasting. A boast can sometimes be a lie but a lie isn't a boast, but who cared? There were also admissions around the fact that amounts exchanged during the alleged transactions could not be accounted for since they were never filmed.

In another detection exercise, my team set out to demolish *Tehelka*'s claim that the blank tapes were legitimately obtained. They submitted invoices of these purchases. The letterheads and signatures looked fishy so we sent blank letters to all the addresses—in Ghaziabad, Old Delhi and other places by Speed Post. They returned with stamps saying: 'No such address'. Only one turned out to be a modest grocery store. Pinned down, *Tehelka* admitted to acquiring them from the 'grey market' and delivered to the doorstep of an anonymous staffer's home. We took this to the press. The *Tehelka* journalists' comments were printed loud and clear on the front pages of *Mail Today* calling me 'hysterical' and a 'mad woman'. I enjoyed it.

At the Commission, *Tehelka* admitted that a single person accounted for under two names—Anil Malviya and Rajiv Sharma—in their ledgers, who had provided the call girls, was now dead!* The mystery of how this young man died suddenly in Allahabad during the investigation has never been explained. Akshay Mukul, journalist with *The Times of India* followed the story, as did I. *Tehelka* said he died at the Kumbh Mela. I checked with the Uttar Pradesh Chief Minister at the time, Rajnath Singh, who confirmed proudly that not a single person had died at the Mela. Then they clarified that he had died at the railway station during the Mela. I checked with Nitish Kumar, who was railway minister at the time. His office confirmed that there had been no death at the railway station. Finally, *Tehelka* explained that he had felt unwell at the station, had returned home, and died in his bed. We traced the man's family in Mumbai to have this confirmed. There was no conclusive response from there.

George Fernandes thought he would ask the Home Minister L.K. Advani about how to acquire this gentleman's death certificate from Allahabad. When he got him on the phone, it was 11 September 2001. Advani cut him short.

'George, are you watching television?'

'No, why?' asked George Sahib.

'Turn it on immediately.'

I did it for him as he never looked in the direction of a television set.

Images of the twin towers standing in flames in New York were being shown as it was happening. We watched a hugely significant moment in history and left the subject of Anil Malviya/Rajiv Sharma hanging in mid-air forever.

George Fernandes was later reappointed Defence Minister because the situation in our region had destabilized and the country needed a full-time minister to head the crucial department.

~

At the Commission, *Tehelka* finally admitted that they had misrepresented facts about their journalists' educational qualifications, and age. They also admitted to having submitted false bills for purchase of tapes from non-existent shops.** A hawala operator from Chennai named Shamsuddin

---

*All the records of the Commission of Inquiry were handed over to the CBI after the commission was closed down. These are still in its custody.

**All the records of the CoI were handed over to the CBI after the commission was closed down. These are still in its custody.

confirmed in a written confession that six crore rupees had been paid into Shankar Sharma's First Global account in Mauritius, and from there to the same company in Mumbai. It was from this account that Sharma funded *Tehelka*'s Operation West End which they termed in court as 'a leanly funded journalistic operation'. And yet, they calmly denied being able to account for the number of cars and computers they had bought with this money. These records are in some Enforcement Directorate files and full transcripts of all depositions at the Commission are now with the CBI. I have a few trunks full of records too, waiting to be burned in a celebratory bonfire when the whole show is finally over.

Justice Venkataswami may have been partly persuaded by my deposition to send the tapes abroad for questioning, or so we heard through the grapevine. He also announced he would next go into *Tehelka*'s financial matters, as mandated.

In the meantime, Congress's Kapil Sibal mounted an attack on the judge in November 2002 for his appointment as chairman of the Authority on Advance Ruling on Customs and Excise which he had accepted in May at the behest of none other than the then Chief Justice of India. He accused this God-fearing, *tika*-wearing, soft-spoken gentleman of being bought out*. Justice Venkataswami was truly honourable. He quit both assignments on 23 November 2002.

I wrote a private note to Justice Venkataswami regretting that opposition parties had denigrated the judiciary and that he had to face attacks usually faced by us, politicians. I added that despite him often not being sympathetic to my genuine and honest requests, I had always respected his intentions to get to the truth. He wrote back immediately saying,

Dear and respected Ms Jaya Jaitly,

I acknowledge receipt of your kind letter dated 24th November 2002. I thank you sincerely for the sentiments expressed in the said letter.
Wishing you all well.
Please accept my regards and respects.

Yours sincerely,
K. Venkataswami

---

*'Opposition raises storm over new job for Venkataswami', *The Hindu*, 23 November 2002, http://www.thehindu.com/thehindu/2002/11/23/stories/2002112304640100.htm

It was very gracious of him to do that. He need not have replied at all.

But, without a Chairman, the Commission ran aground for four months. Even during this lull, the activist in me did not rest. We had earlier set up a little sting operation of our own called Project Email. This was because during the writ petition hearings in the Delhi High Court, we had begun to suspect the worthy gentlemen on the Commission and *Tehelka*'s legal teams were not just legal buddies. They seemed to be working so closely and in tandem that their statements, responses and questioning of witnesses which were seamless at the Commission's proceedings, were even more convivially and openly carried out in the courtroom. The Commission's counsel would at times be seen whispering relevant information to the *Tehelka* counsel even in the appellate court. Its counsels surprisingly never opposed any plea of the *Tehelka* group. They vigorously supported the view that the videotapes upon which people were to be examined did not need to be forensically scrutinized and certified as genuine although no one knew whether they were the real thing at all. As one of the expert witnesses presented by *Tehelka* said in September 2001, 'For all I know the tapes lying with the Commission could be blank'.

In August 2002, I decided to see whether there was a strong professional connection or only a personal friendship that I was misconstruing. I telephoned the residence of the Commission's junior counsel, Siddharth Agarwal and asked whether it was the office of Luthra & Associates as I was inquiring on behalf of foreign clients. I was directed to telephone a Dr Vijay Agarwal and given his number. A male friend telephoned on my behalf and explained that one Anurag Sharma of May & Co in Dubai was inquiring about a good legal firm to conduct a title search and other basic formalities to set up a cancer hospice in Haryana. He said that as a doctor he would help later but an email should be addressed to his son who was a lawyer. When asked if he was a partner in Luthra & Associates, he said his son and Siddharth Luthra were associated with it but not strictly partners. I sent an email to Agarwal at the address given by his father with a copy to the father, giving all the details of the client's requirements and asking for the profile of their firm, with the names of all the associates and partners. Within two days, on 12 August 2002, I received a lengthy and effusive reply, not from Agarwal but from Siddharth Luthra, the *Tehelka* counsel. He listed the capabilities, achievements and names of all those who worked as part of an 'enthusiastic and capable' team of associates in different areas of specialization in the firm Luthra & Associates. Siddharth Agarwal was listed under various areas of expertise and assistance. He copied Agarwal in the email. This clearly meant that in March 2002 and as on 12 August 2002, the two counsels were very much associated as per their own document. A few more emails passed back and forth including a reminder from Agarwal saying 'we would be happy to meet you', until Anurag Sharma's silence made them suspicious. They then sent three virus-ridden emails to the address I had created. I checked with VSNL to confirm that Luthra's email address was indeed his. It was. I checked with the Delhi High Court records to see whether they appeared as a team out of Luthra's chamber. Court orders of November that year, confirmed it.

My little sting operation was not with the intention of creating a sensation and earning a packet from a television channel; it was done neither to unveil lawyers as being a part of a corrupt system, nor to destabilize the work of the Commission or to put the inquiry under a bad light. However, it was necessary to remind the opposition parties who hounded Justice Venkataswami out of office that if judges have to be credible and therefore not take on two jobs, the lawyers assisting them had equal responsibility to reveal that they too did not have a foot each in both camps. Furthermore, persons in close association with those being inquired into should not have been brought in to assist the fact-finding Commission. After all, there are thousands of other capable lawyers in this country; the government was anyway footing the bill, and 'Caesar's wife' would have been beyond reproach. Following Justice Venkataswami's exit, I exposed the collusion between *Tehelka* lawyers and the Commission counsels and distributed the emails to the media at a press conference.

Since the Commission of Inquiry was in limbo, no one could accuse me of trying to make false accusations. As the news came out, Soli Sorabji. rang me in shock, asking, 'Jaya, what have you done? Poor Gopal!' I replied calmly, 'I am sorry, Soli. If Gopal did not know what was going on, he should have done so.'

Gopal Subramanium and his entire team resigned from their Commission appointments the next day.

From the first ridiculous time frame of four months given to the Commission to finish its task, it seemed as if there would never be a conclusion. This was obviously what the *Tehelka* journalists wanted, because when Justice S.N. Phukan, then heading the Assam State Human Rights

Commission, agreed to simultaneously take up the unwanted hot potato of the *Tehelka* inquiry in January 2003, *Tehelka*, led by its lawyer Prashant Bhushan, who is today a crusader for transparency, let forth a tirade at the resuscitated Commission and announced its boycott. He obviously believed we were corrupt or preferred to assist *Tehelka* since it was attacking a government he did not like. Perhaps his clients or friends were adamant they did not want the tapes, their motives or financing examined. Since Justice Phukan had been appointed to the state commission by the Congress government in Assam, they perhaps could not attack his integrity immediately.

Justice Phukan meant business and did not allow anyone to delay matters. He took calmly the fact that the *Tehelka* team decided to walk out of the Commission's proceedings as soon he announced the tapes were being sent for checking. The Judge also produced a 900-page report on the first part of the Inquiry covering 1400 confidential files of the Ministry of Defence and the depositions in camera of George Fernandes and other officers. He handed this report over to Prime Minister Vajpayee on 4 February 2004. I remember a feeling of relief and expectation upon the fact that at last the report would be made public and the Ministry would hopefully be cleared completely. It had transpired during the examinations that many so-called deals which were supposedly concluded based on commissions and bribes were either matters already concluded by an earlier regime, or not even taken up for discussion, or still in the early stages where no decisions had been taken at all. So *Tehelka*'s unsavoury 'documentary' was more fiction created from meaningless ramblings of people they filmed.

It would have been wonderful to clear the air on this before going in for the early general elections called by the prime minister a month later. Inexplicably, this did not happen. The report lay in cold storage.

By now it was June 2004, and the UPA government had come to power. We did not think it would change things at the Commission since Justice Phukan was powering along at a regular pace.

The tapes had been examined and the expert, Matthew J. Cass, who had done so was brought by the government to depose, as is legally required. When Cass took the stand to speak on 23 June 2004, Justice Phukan announced something we had not expected. It was a communication (of which we were given copies), received from the forensic agency to which Cass belonged in the UK which said:

> [W]e have been contacted by *Tehelka.com* by email requesting an interview with Mr Cass, we have not responded to this. We were also contacted by the India correspondent of the *Guardian* Newspaper yesterday again asking questions[, t]o which we again provided no comment answers. However, from what they said it would appear that a Min[i]ster has pre-empted Mr. Cass' evidence to the Commission and we have found reference to this on at least one news website. Obviously we felt we should inform you of these issues.

Cass's fax implies that the oath of secrecy was violated. Such an astonishing matter was taken lightly by everyone, including our party, and the BJP, which was now in opposition.

On 28 May 2004, Kapil Sibal, a minister in the new government and the champion of *Tehelka* causes, had already announced to the public that the tapes had been found to be genuine. We wondered whether this was telepathy or prescience since no formal document or report had come to the Commission. Tejpal also announced the same news, claiming his source was an army officer, which was highly far-fetched.

This time the new government's counsel tried to cut short the deposition of the British forensic expert by objecting to him being crossed-examined by all of us. Luckily, he was overruled and it tumbled out that in fact, the tapes which were originals *were not untampered* since there were cuts in conversations within them, switches 'on' and 'off' in certain places, sound drops ,and other unresolved areas where the expert could not understand the Hindi dialogue in the tapes.

Justice Phukan was a man in a hurry but the government counsels kept asking for more time since they were unfamiliar with the contents of the mound of documents. They obtained relief from their government when on 1 October 2004, the Ministry of Finance ordered the Commission not to inquire into *Tehelka*'s journalistic motives or the financial aspects of the entire matter. These were precisely the areas in which *Tehelka* would have been caught out because they had already admitted in the Commission that they had sold the tapes to Zee TV for a hefty sum, making it a commercial rather than a journalistic venture. Also, by September, when the Commission was still at work, Sonia Gandhi, as head of the UPA and the National Advisory Council, wrote an official letter to finance minister P. Chidambaram, dated 25/27 September 2004—a copy of which was provided to me by a highly placed source in the Opposition—asking him to ensure that First Global, *Tehelka*'s financiers, are not meted out 'unjust or unfair treatment'. She was, in fact, saying the very same thing I was trying to explain to the *Tehelka* person asking me a favour for the purpose of entrapment. Here again, irony was visiting.

The Commission had by then convened and held 247 hearings. It set the date for the next hearings on 1 November 2004. The date was memorable in that it brought the Commission to an end. Everyone got to know this only through the media. Instead of allowing the government counsels reasonable time to go through documents as they had requested, and fixing a deadline for the Commission to wind up its work, the government, which included the law minister, accused the Commission of delays, not doing any work, not giving any report and 'going nowhere'. The Judge was accused of misusing government facilities and being corrupted. Closing down the Commission became one of the points of self-praise the government put out on its official website celebrating one year in office in 2005.

We could clearly see that the constituents of the UPA had insulted two former judges of the Supreme Court of India, closed down a Commission of Inquiry in the last phase of its work, betrayed oaths of secrecy, blatantly defended unethical and fraudulent journalism and sought to protect its financiers from a simple inquiry. It seemed to me there must have been something very major to hide. *Tehelka* seemed to have powerful guardian angels.

Ultimately, from being noticees in Operation West End we became abandoned victims of what I will call Operation Abort.

Then the government got entangled in its own contradictions. It first said there was no report, then a 'non-report', then a mere 41-page summary*, then an accusation that the Commission had not gone into the issue of corruption. It avoided the fact that Justice Phukan had specifically mentioned he had found nothing irregular in the role of George Fernandes in the fifteen actual procurements. This was crucial to reassure the country that nothing in terms of national security had been compromised. George Fernandes wrote to Prime Minister Manmohan Singh requesting that the report given to Prime Minister Vajpayee in February 2004 be tabled in

---

* 'Government rejects Phukan panel report, terms it incomplete', *Outlook*, 13 May 2005, https://www.outlookindia.com/newswire/story/govt-rejects-phukan-panel-report-terms-it-incomplete/297836

Parliament. Months later, a mere summary was tabled upon the excuse that the whole report would compromise issues of national security. After accusing the Commission of no work, it closed it down before it could complete the last leg and then accused it of not working. With illogical arguments like that, who could win? Sadly, neither the BJP nor other constituents of the opposition NDA raised a hue and cry. It might have been over for them but it was not over for some of us.

All investigations on the fifteen real deals have since led nowhere. All probes specifically concerning George Fernandes have been closed by the CBI. Some cases concerning other victims like retired army officers and civilian officials from the Ministry of Defence, as a result of the UPA government and the CBI working together, are still mired in trial proceedings.

During my court hearings that followed, Tejpal appeared in the witness stand. Vindicating himself of any first-hand knowledge of how the sting operation was conducted, the call girls involved, or any awareness of the apparent misdeeds of individuals whose lives and reputations he had ruined for what for him was high infamy, I recall him leaving the courtroom in his nonchalant manner, heading for Goa.

In the luxury resort atmosphere of Goa, in the company of Hollywood actors, and after a raucous, supposedly intellectual, conclave at a luxurious hotel, Tejpal was arrested in 2013 after being accused by a junior colleague and daughter's friend, of sexual molestation in the elevator. Following that, I wrote an article on Firstpost.com on 4 December 2013, titled 'Truth behind *Tehelka*: Tejpal's Non-journalism and Society's Colluders'*. In that, I reminded everyone of the kind of journalism *Tehelka* had practised.

On 7 September 2017, the Mapusa sessions court in Goa asked that Tejpal be framed of nine charges, five of which are of rape. The court has decided that he needs to go on trial. During *Tehelka*'s operation, I had ironically felt violated by the hidden cameras, the unknown eyes. Perhaps, it is time that one understands how truth is more important than playing 'politics' with the help of 'video-taped ... edited material, sensationalism and hype'**. There, this episode rests.

---

*See http://www.firstpost.com/india/the-truth-behind-tehelka-tejpals-journalism-and-societys-colluders-1266197.html

**See above.

20

ON THE SIDELINES

Provocation and Peace

As THE INQUIRY COMMISSION LUMBERED on, there were many sideshows that occasionally brought sunshine but usually offered more battles to fight, and stingers to swat away.

Even though I was kept fully occupied at the Commission and had stayed clear of party politics, I kept my work with craftspersons on track. I would lose myself in the solace of working with artisans who came to our Dastkari Haat Samiti office in South Delhi. There was a kind of meditational comfort in working with those who neither questioned nor judged me. My world of turmoil did not touch their domain at all. Media circuses and ugly allegations were so unbelievable that our craftspersons ignored them completely. I diverted my mind with constructive work much larger in scope than I had ever done before, and cuddled the dogs for warmth and relief when I got home. I also wrote nearly a dozen articles in various national newspapers on the need for ensuring the credibility and accuracy of taped evidence from a legal standpoint of modern technological changes, justice and fair play. Nothing worked.

My daughter and I visited the Guruvayur Temple in Kerala on 27 January 2003, for the traditional *chorunnu* ceremony (*annaprashanam*) where my six-month-old grandson was to be formally fed rice and given his name, Aiman. I received an urgent call from Delhi saying the *Guardian*, in London wanted me to answer some *Tehelka*-related questions within a week, failing which they were going to publish their story. I asked them to send me a fax. Luke Harding, their South Asia correspondent, wrote that they were planning to publish a detailed story on British attempts to sell sixty-six Hawk advanced jet trainers to India. I was to feature in the report and was being given a formal opportunity to comment beforehand. Hmm, handicrafts and advance jet trainers don't quite go together, I joked to my cousin who was with us. But, thank God, at least they had better journalistic ethics than *Tehelka*, I thought to myself.

Harding wrote that I visited London in late 1999 and held discussions on the Hawk deal with John Weston, the chief executive of British Aerospace; and that I had also discussed the proposed Hawk contract with Chandraswami, a controversial holy man of that period. Harding also asked me to comment on any of the *Tehelka* disclosures. He gave me his numbers in Delhi. It was highly curious that such outrageous accusations were being spread about someone as irrelevant as me across the world. I was convinced of vested interests, of darker forces at play, and I was just a woman to be targeted, a scapegoat to those very interests.

I left our small ceremonial event in the temple to fax a handwritten reply from a small computer service joint in the bazaar. It was by no means as flippant as my initial reactions:

Dear Mr Harding,

I am shocked at the nature of the so-called information gathered by your newspaper. I would like to make it absolutely clear that:

a) I was not in London in late 1999,
b) I have never met or spoken to a certain John Weston whom you say is the chief executive of British Aerospace engineering. In fact I have never met or spoken to anyone from that company.
c) I have never met or spoken to Chandraswami and would avoid meeting such persons even by accident,
d) I have consistently maintained that the Tehelka investigation was fraudulent, stage-managed and concocted. A commission of inquiry is looking into the facts. I firmly believe that everyone should wait for the findings of the quasi-judicial body before giving any credibility to Tehelka.com's kind of journalism,
e) Please note that if The Guardian even insinuates that I am in any way connected with the advanced jet trainer matter I will waste no time in suing it for defamation in the UK.

I would request your reporters to stay clear of vested interests who must be spreading such lies about me. Yours etc.

The *Guardian* story never appeared. However, the correspondent seemed to have some special link with the *Tehelka* group as the newspaper was again mentioned by the forensic expert in the UK as one such entity, along with *Tehelka*, who had sought information from his company about the forensic report at their London office.

Nasty articles and stories appeared in prestigious magazines all over the world. On 13 February 2003, the *New York Times* published a bunch of falsehoods fed to them by *Tehelka* called 'A Web Site in India That Revealed Graft Becomes a Target'*. It was clear that it was almost dictated by *Tehelka*. I sent a rejoinder article titled 'Sensation is not what it seems' in which I sought to demolish all their accusations with the facts as they were, hoping its highly respected editor, James Reston, would publish it, but I never received a response. As luck would have it, he resigned right then amidst some controversy. Thus my contribution died a natural death.

When the *Time* magazine, which I value highly and read regularly, brought out a largely scurrilous story by Alex Perry on 1 December 2003 called 'Teflon Government', I became like our Alsatian dog that wouldn't let go of a dirty old sock. The story referred to another sting called the 'Judeo Tapes' in which it said those 'allegations' 'paled into insignificance when compared to the disclosures' made about Bangaru Laxman and George Fernandes in the *Tehelka* tapes. I was described as the minister's 'friend'. This riled me as words of this nature when put in quotes become like a dirty wink-wink in print. I tried to meet Perry but he could only speak on the telephone. What I thought would be a polite and pleasant conversation allowing me to put the record straight, turned out to be surprisingly contentious. Perry was immediately rude, judgemental and combative. I was shocked that an impartial foreign journalist should behave in this manner. He belligerently asked why I had resigned from my position as president of my Party if I was innocent. I said that that needn't have concerned him. When I remarked that since he had already formed an opinion about our guilt perhaps he should have headed the Inquiry Commission, he sarcastically replied he would have liked to head it. I asked him whether they knew I was no cheap 'friend' of anyone but a woman in her sixties with grandchildren and a thirty-six-year long career working with poor craftspersons without any questions over my integrity ever raised till then. There was no response to that. I wrote to Karl Tarlo

*See http://www.nytimes.com/2003/02/13/world/a-web-site-in-india-that-revealed-graft-becomes-a-target.html?mcubz=1

Greenfeld, Editor-in-Chief, *Time* Asia, Hong Kong, telling him all that had happened, enclosing a rejoinder to the story in a Letter to the Editor. Greenfeld made up for Perry's boorishness by immediately telephoning from Hong Kong and asking me to call him. After that, his Senior Editor, Zoher Abdoolkarim, sent me a fax with a shortened version of my letter which they published in the next issue.

On another occasion, my old college friend, Congress politician Mani Shankar Aiyar wrote an article in the Kolkata *Telegraph* saying I had been caught with my hands in the kitty. I challenged him with a personal letter recalling our friendship and reminding him his daughters still regularly visited my children at my home.

In Lalu Prasad Yadav's regime, cartoon hoardings were put up in Patna with images of my son-in-law and me wearing greedy grins, surrounded by dollar notes, guns and cricket bats. The same happened in Chennai. I could not understand who was up to this in Tamil Nadu. I had to contact the head of police in the city to request him to have them taken down. He did so but traced the source only as far as a small flex hoarding shop. Writers like Arundhati Roy and Madhu Kishwar and various others on the social scene who had been friends for decades, made mocking remarks about *Tehelka*'s brilliance or my crookery. It thrilled their own audiences. Then there was an article in a short-lived newspaper about me by a writer under a pseudonym. It had a whole paragraph on the length of my *choli* (or blouse), which I supposedly wore very short, or long, covering my midriff, depending on the company I kept. It went on to say I was a socialite, not a socialist.

I challenged every piece of rubbish that was published in all but the worst rag mags. It gave me a feeling of engagement. For me this was part of a political fight against false allegations, fake journalists, media manipulations and calumny against women in public life. It wasn't about me alone. I wondered to myself how many women in active politics at my level have had to face such situations where they have been accused of something abominable without a shred of credible evidence. I didn't feel upset or sorry for myself. I only felt very angry most of the time.

Much later, on 4 October 2004, Hans Raj Bharadwaj, the newly appointed Law Minister of India, held a press conference announcing the closure of the Phukan Inquiry Commission and the matter being handed over to the CBI. Later, all newspapers quoted him as saying, 'How could a private person function from the house of the then defence minister and talk about defence deals?*'

I was angry enough to write him on 6 October, saying,

> *You obviously are completely ignorant of facts, law, and what constitutes basic decency in public life.... you are also unaware I was President of an important political party and not a private person ... I have never stayed at the residence of the then Defence Minister.... If the visit and sharing of public work at a party leader's house amounts to 'staying', then how do you describe the presence of your party leader's political secretary at 10, Janpath?.... You also seem to have conveniently forgotten that a truly private person who was also a foreign national stayed at the official residence of the Prime Minister of India and carried out illegal business activities from there, including violation of foreign exchange laws for fifteen years..... By your action of scrapping the Commission of Inquiry and justification given by you, it is clear that your government thinks that the judges of the Supreme Court can be influenced. What was the justification of the Government to scrap the Commission, which had practically finished its work? The Government if it was so keen could have ordered a simultaneous inquiry by the CBI.... Under these circumstances, I suggest that you move to repeal the Commission of Inquiry Act itself so that such institutions do not lend themselves to attack and denigration when they do not work according to the requirements of your government.... the very least you can do is to tender an apology to me for your unworthy and unwarranted comments on me... Yours etc.*

Provocative and pugnacious, but I got my anger off my chest. The law minister went silent.

~

Two memorable moments that helped keep a balance, follow.

One day, I received a packet from a gentleman named Gyanesh Nigam.

---

*'*Tehelka* Commission wound up', *The Hindu*, 5 October 2004, http://www.thehindu.com/2004/10/05/stories/2004100509240100.htm

He had meticulously researched all the documents put out publicly by the government and *Tehelka* on Operation West End, analysing and scrutinizing the facts and logic of everything that happened or was said. His extremely well-written and neatly bound document referred to the McCarthy trials in the USA, and how its targets were hounded. His arguments were incisive and highly logical. It was the best use of the English language I had seen on this issue. I couldn't believe anyone who had never met me would be so interested, and take the trouble to do what no one in India had bothered with. I couldn't use it anywhere but I did contact him by email. He spoke in admiration of George Sahib and even my work in handicrafts. I think he was an analyst with Deutche Bank in Singapore where I have often been but have still not met him.

The next and most memorable ray of light was a five-page beautifully handwritten letter in Hindi I received from a number—yes, the identity of the man was just a number. This happened a short while after the *Tehelka* storm hit us. He wrote that he was a life convict at the Panaji Jail in Goa. I have no idea what crime he committed or what his former status in society had been. All I could see was he was well-educated and knowledgeable about the history of the Lohia socialists in India. He expressed his deep admiration for George Sahib's valour and integrity, and my lifetime of work in rural areas. He expressed deep sympathy for what had happened to us. I read the letter many times over, just for the beauty of the sentiments and handwriting. I carried it in my pocket diary all the time. Sadly, on a trip to South Africa in 2003, the diary fell out of our vehicle and it was gone. I have tried to search for this nameless 'prisoner for life' through the Governor of Goa so that I could visit him some day. No one has been of help yet, but I haven't given up hope of thanking this nameless individual personally for his kindness, if he is still alive and in jail. A convicted criminal with intellect, education and compassion is worth pursuing.

21

A SMALL MOMENT OF GLORY IN MANIPUR

This Is Politics

WHEN WOMEN IN POLITICS SAY or do something, their words and actions are viewed differently from those of men. Or at least, the attacks on women in public life, are either harsher or more underhand.

Within the trade union and the Party, I always knew that the men felt they could not attack me openly since I was 'obviously under the umbrella' of the big boss George Fernandes, whose support, benevolence and leadership they could not risk losing. Was I the protégée? Protectee? Undeserving confidante? Keeper of the purse strings? Puppet? Slave? Or something worse? All those with self-serving ambitions that overrode the Party's collective interests certainly put me in one or the other of these slots. Some honourable exceptions were always decent and supportive, but in a slightly condescending or patronizing way. There was no doubt that even they were perfectly prepared to dump a woman at the drop of a hat if their own interests were affected within the Party.

A small example of how a woman can be treated can be seen in what happened to me once. I was fast asleep a little after midnight at my Khirki home when the phone rang. A loud male voice in heavy Bihari accented-Hindi filled my ears. I kept asking the caller to slow down and speak softly. He finally did only to ask, in carefully chosen words: 'What kind of a *randikhana* (whorehouse) do you think you are running in Delhi instead of a political party? Do you know what's going on in Bihar? So and so is attending a meeting called by Shakuni Choudhury (at that time a dissenter who later joined Lalu Yadav). What have you done to stop it?'

Stunned, I couldn't answer but concluded he must have been drunk even though his words hadn't slurred. I asked who he was. He gave me a typical north Indian name—Ram something or the other—Prasad. It's hard to recollect now. I put the phone down but it took a while to get back to sleep. When I told George Fernandes about it at office the next morning, he was shocked and called up a few colleagues. They all unanimously agreed that the real person of the same name was a soft-spoken, decent veteran politico who would not have spoken like that. They concluded it must have been an impersonator.

There is a more significant story to share since little is remembered about a very interesting, short-lived saga in the recent history of Manipur, which was always a state close to my heart. For certain concerned people, it is a time best forgotten. The story here may be longwinding, but it helps demonstrate the following:

1) common occurrences in the Northeastern states which lie ignored by the Centre,
2) how governments can, at times, be formed without any exchange of money,
3) how good men are not allowed to govern for long if it clashes with other interests,
4) how political allies at the Centre can become rivals in a state,
5) how a Party leader can abort a decision to be taken in the Party's and state's interest for the sake of personal interest, and
6) how all this set me up as a target of ire of such Party leaders.

It was late into the year 2000. Manipur was at a standstill. Earlier in 1997, Wahengbam Nipamacha Singh, the Speaker of the Assembly, had quit the Congress, formed the Manipur State Congress Party (MSCP) and become the chief minister. Later, he became an ally of the NDA under Vajpayee in 1998. By late 2000, many MLAs revolted against Nipamacha Singh and collected together in a 'camp' at Speaker Dhananjay Singh's residence to pull the chief minister down. While most MLAs were from the Congress; there were six from the BJP, one from Manipur People's Party, and one (Basanta Kumar Singh) from the Samata Party.

The chief minister's supporters huddled in his home. This ridiculous situation continued for more than three months. Government operations came to a standstill. At such times, local militant groups have a heyday and the common people are put through immense discomfort. Basanta contacted his friend Radhabinod Koijam, MLA and former chief minister from the Congress, and suggested he join the Samata Party and the NDA since George Fernandes, its Convenor, was considered a popular and trusted national leader in the Northeast. They came to Delhi to meet George Sahib and me. Koijam agreed and led nineteen MLAs, excluding the veteran Rishang Keishing, out of the Congress, and into the Samata Party. The BJP lost the opportunity to stake its claim. Some Congress MLAs were still at Dhananjay's camp. They were invited by Samata Party General Secretary Shambhu Sharan Srivastava to breakfast at Koijam's home the next morning and agreed to pledge their allegiance to this side.

Hemachandra Singh, son of an old socialist colleague of Fernandes, and collegemate of my son Akshay, assisted Srivastava to go undercover to Nipamacha Singh's residence at 2.30 am to persuade those who were there to leave his government since it had no hope of survival. Some gentle arm-twisting later, Nipamacha agreed to let his people go, provided Koijam's group had the numbers. Typical of local friendships overriding political rivalries, the two remained friends till Nipamacha passed away in 2012. Interestingly, the entire exercise was carried out in close coordination between Shambhu, who had stationed himself in Imphal through all this, and me. With great difficulty, I managed to track down Nitish Kumar in Bihar to apprise him of the developing situation. He said, 'go ahead'. I do not recall where exactly George Fernandes was but he was on tour and was not in contact on telephone. He got to know a short while later. The Samata Party then created a historic majority—it got fifty-eight members on its side in a house of sixty!

The BJP was astonished. Its senior representatives in Imphal met Srivastava and requested he speak to L.K. Advani before taking any further steps. We all did not feel it was necessary to seek the permission of another Party when our Party's interests were at stake. No Party does that, not even the BJP. It is an understandable political stance to take in a democratic polity. Advani was the home minister then and the point person for all federal issues. His office called me late in the evening and requested me to meet him at his North Block office. He looked very displeased and asked me what had happened. I recounted the events faithfully and argued that Koijam had all the credentials to be a good chief minister and that we, as NDA, after months of instability, now had a good majority government in place in which we were all partners. Salaries to civil and police officials had not been paid for months and the militants were on an extortion spree at the time. He did not argue but was clearly most unhappy. I could not understand why. I met Jana Krishnamurthi, President of the BJP, to apprise him of Koijam's credentials and felt I also had the tacit support of Khushabhau Thakre whom I met several times during this period. They gave in to my submissions, and expressions of solidarity and goodwill, as ally to the NDA without much objection.

The BJP and others wanted to be sworn in as ministers in the first round along with the chief minister, but there was already the predictable tussle for ministerships between all parties which took place in the presence of George Fernandes in Delhi. So, Koijam was sworn in alone at first. George Fernandes and I went for the next round of oath-taking when those nominated by all partner parties were inducted. We were quite pleased at having been able to install the very first Samata Party state government in the country. We thought we had pulled Manipur out of a stalemate. Not a penny was exchanged or anybody lured through extraneous promises. The BJP was still unhappy.

Koijam and his team came to Delhi for funds to tide over the financial crisis. Finance Minister Yashwant Sinha promised to do the needful and set the ball rolling among officials. Koijam announced salaries would be paid by Holi. Sadly, half the money was held up for various reasons under instructions from the Home Ministry.

There was a serious issue hovering in the horizon at that time. Manipur's people were against the extension of ceasefire outside the territory of Nagaland into Manipur and other states. It was a major emotional matter in Manipur which had seen unanimous resolutions in the Assembly and mass demonstrations on the streets. However, a mere courtesy call on Prime Minister Atal Bihari Vajpayee by Koijam on the same trip to Delhi was announced by the Home Ministry as a meeting in which Manipur had agreed to the extension of ceasefire. The chief ministers of other affected states in the Northeast including Koijam made contradicting statements. They said they were not in agreement as the Centre could not decide an issue which encroached upon their federal rights and territories. Koijam also held a meeting in which all security forces, including the army, were on board announcing a temporary ceasefire within the state for Holi, unitedly appealing to all insurgent groups within Manipur to reciprocate. This infuriated the home minister who questioned Koijam's move. Koijam argued it was his right to do so as the head of government in charge of law and order in the state. Koijam also made a bold move in cutting the direct external telephone lines of all officers within the Secretariat to prevent militant groups from harassing them directly to extort a part of their salaries as they regularly did.

The Centre insisted that the proposal to extend the Nagaland ceasefire to other states would remain. The people were incensed and lost faith in the Samata Party-led government. The end result of this was that Koijam's residence was attacked while his family was inside. They managed to escape unharmed. He was the target of rumours that he was close to drug traders. The Assembly building was burned down. Eight people died in the unrest.

The Home Ministry was forced to withdraw the proposal for the extension of the ceasefire. The chief minister called for a show of strength in the Assembly to demonstrate that he had support for his actions. I did another round of visits to the BJP headquarters in Delhi to seek their issuance of a whip to their members to be present and vote. Though they promised to do so and said they had, their MLAs in Manipur denied receiving any instructions. The three-month-old government fell.

The Centre then had no option but to impose President's Rule in June 2001. I say this now with no rancour towards the BJP. This is all a part of what is known as 'politics'. There is nothing dishonest or illegal about it. The BJP did some similar fleet-footed activity to its advantage in Goa and Manipur in 2017, after the results of the Assembly elections were announced. Radhabinod Koijam is now with the BJP, which currently governs the state. So who can blame the other in the game of Round Robin? I have known this quaint phrase for years, but in the age of technology I find the Google description amusingly apt:

> Round-robin (RR) is one of the algorithms employed by process and network schedulers in computing. As the term is generally used, time slices (also known as time quanta) are assigned to each process in equal portions and in circular order, handling all processes without priority (also known as cyclic executive).

The reaction of the Samata Party leaders from Bihar to the Manipur events was revealing. The Samata Party held a National Executive at Vishwa Yuvak Kendra, Delhi, soon after President's Rule was announced, to assess the situation of our own senior ally toppling our state government, of which it was also a part. I described the broad picture. Shambhu gave the step-by-step details. There was great indignant oratory and disapproval of the central government's actions. Shambhu proposed the ministers in the

NDA from the Samata Party sign a collective letter resigning from their ministries and hand it over to George Sahib. It was mostly a symbolic gesture but some of us were serious about it and George Fernandes did not object to this line. After all, we were not withdrawing support from the government; we were just refusing to being ministers in it.

After everyone left the meeting, Nitish Kumar turned on Shambhu and said, '*Ek chhote mote rajya ke liye aap ne yeh kya kar diya?*' (For the sake of one small inconsequential state, what have you done?) He seemed to refrain from expressing his anger towards me. But we could see that he did not perhaps appreciate the fact that it was another state that had held up the Samata flag first, before he could do so in Bihar. Moreover, some other Bihar leaders had hoped for ministerial births in an expected expansion of the cabinet in the wake of the formation of Samata Party in Manipur. They couldn't have cared less for Manipur though. Nitish Kumar was maybe voicing the collective concerns of this group as well. In the end, Shambhu and I made some enemies. George Fernandes was ultimately a practical politician who could swallow his emotions and indignation, so the letter of resignation of our ministers never saw the light of day. In the following elections, the Congress won a comfortable majority and the NDA lost its opportunity to demonstrate honest and sane governance in a crucial state. Here was a lesson in one facet of coalition politics.

22

THE POLITICS OF COALITIONS

George Fernandes, the Leader and Firefighter

COALITIONS ARE TRICKY. EACH CONSTITUENT looks for extra leverage, and the tensions between the leading party and its allies are always below the surface. Anyone rocking the boat is condemned by all.

Post the 1980s, many fell away because George Fernandes gave the fight against injustice greater priority than acquiring power. An example of this was his decision to resign from the Janata government in 1979, despite having personally suffered the excesses of the Emergency. Essentially, the Janata government of 1977 was a coalition government in which parties had technically submerged their identities for what turned out to be a very short period. He had then defended the government powerfully in Parliament in 1979 upon the request of Prime Minister Morarji Desai. Overnight, he changed his stance, shocking and deeply disappointing his socialist colleagues and the rest of the country. During the night, having tried his utmost to persuade the Left parties headed by Jyoti Basu, and other senior colleagues in government, not to contribute to the imminent collapse of the government, he was subjected to a long political and finally emotional argument by Madhu Limaye. Limaye failed to convince George Fernandes with his ideological arguments to resign on the issue of the Jan Sangh's dual membership in the RSS. Finally, he lobbed him a big sentimental ball: 'Do all our years of friendship mean nothing to you?' he asked. At that point George Fernandes stood up and said, 'Madhu, if it all comes down to just that, I will submit my resignation tomorrow morning.' And that is what happened.

George Fernandes's action had many unpleasant repercussions. The ones that dogged him as an individual lasted almost a decade. He was well aware of the negative impact his political reputation suffered because of his old comrade-in-arms Madhu Limaye; however, although he visited the latter less often after that, he never said anything to blame him.

George Fernandes fought his way out of an almost isolated political existence by leading the battle against the Rajiv Gandhi government's reported corruption in the Bofors and HDW submarine deals. He constantly hurtled through the length and breadth of the country for trade union gatherings. During this time, he also played midwife in the delivery of V.P. Singh as an alternative 'clean' leader. It was during this entire period that I believe he decided that he would never again be responsible for the fall of a government which he helped create and thus became a disciplined soldier in other coalition periods.

∽

In late 1989, as the National Front government set itself up, the walls of power came up alongside. V.P. Singh, with his typical caginess, kept even his closest colleagues on tenterhooks, informing them that they would become ministers only half an hour before they were expected to be sworn in. Some eager ones were said to have already got their *bandhgala* suits, ones with tight necks, stitched in anticipation. Everyone seemed to be waiting anxiously for an advance indication from the prime minister, but that did not happen. George Sahib nonchalantly went upstairs for an afternoon nap and had no time to change into a fresh kurta when he was woken up and told to reach Rashtrapati Bhavan in twenty minutes. His colleagues and I sat in the office downstairs in his tiny apartment at Hauz Khas, amazed at the lack of dignity in the way this was done. Everyone felt ridiculous.

A day or so after the swearing in of the council of ministers, the portfolios were announced. George Fernandes was astounded that he had been allocated the Ministry of Railways. He said he had led the biggest railway strike in Asia and headed railway unions. How could he be sitting across them at the table now? For three days he refused to go to Rail Bhavan to attend office. Finally, V.P. Singh assured him he would change his portfolio after three months. That never happened. George Fernandes went to office in his old diesel Premier Padmini car driven by his Mumbai colleague Freddie D'Sa. The guard at the Ministry's entrance wouldn't let him in and told him to get an entrance slip made at the reception first. He hadn't recognized the new boss who had arrived with no prior information or pomp and splendour.

During George Fernandes's time in the Ministry of Railways, we tried to introduce handloom cloth for railway uniforms, sheets and towels, and earthen *kulladhs* (clay cups) for tea in trains. We formed potters' co-operatives to organize supply systematically. The trade unions, under George Fernandes, printed thousands of leaflets I had created, that if passengers and unions demanded to use handlooms and earthen pots the livelihoods of many thousands of weavers and potters could be supported. It just meant ordering material from a different source. The money allocations would not increase but only be redirected to the more needy suppliers. I worked on these aspects as a trade union and Party activist while George Fernandes implemented very long-standing demands like the construction of the Chhitauni-Bagaha bridge between Uttar Pradesh and Bihar, the Konkan Railway along the western coast, and initiated work on the Delhi Metro Rail project.

∽

In 1998, the NDA government chose George Fernandes as the convener of the alliance. He had helped draft the Common Agenda for Governance and was considered by the BJP to have given it the legitimacy required to reassure all the dithering 'are we secular/are we not?' allies to come on board to give it a clear majority. This alienated many of his socialist colleagues like Madhu Dandavate and Surendra Mohan but even they were divided between the younger and more ambitious ones who stayed because they wanted to pursue an active political life and felt George Fernandes was the best bet to help them achieve it in alliance with the BJP. He always felt happier being among colleagues with a fighting spirit who had a strong nose for electoral politics. Thus he ignored those who were alienated unless they too came occasionally to ask for small personal favours like school and hospital admissions, which he happily facilitated. As mentioned earlier, party workers and even coalition partners constantly asked for favours, from cash to free travel passes to positions on committees that would give their acolytes some clout; there were requests for even getting children who had failed their examinations to be cleared and accepted at interviews. He was always angered or saddened by this, wondering where the fervour to serve without asking for anything in return was disappearing. Most such people nursed grouses against him thereafter, grumbling that if other parties and politicians helped their people, why he could not. It was just not his style to distribute patronage and largesse, since he had never demanded such things for himself. A lot of the time antagonisms built up against me because of my role as messenger of negative news to these favour-seekers but it did not seem to bother George Sahib in the least that I was the 'fall guy'. I grumbled, but did it anyway.

The role as convener of the NDA was sometimes a disappointment for George Fernandes. He thought that there should be a proper mechanism for consultation and coordination between allies so that any political or policy matters could be smoothened out before being made to look like ideological disagreements which were strictly to be kept out of the common agenda. When in the first year of the NDA, something like the singing of 'Vande Mataram' in schools in Uttar Pradesh came up, the media chased different coalition partners for their comments, hoping disparate responses would emerge to show dissonance among them. Some nudging must have come from the Congress behind the scenes since the media loved to create headlines like 'Mamata and Samata cause headaches for the BJP' or words to that effect. I didn't hear any defence on the 'Vande Mataram' issue coming from the BJP. Thus when the media rushed to me expecting a negative reaction, I stated what George Fernandes had said to me earlier in the day: 'It has been sung in Parliament for quite some time and the practice was introduced by a Congressman. Hindus and Muslims have sung it together during the freedom movement so why should it be considered objectionable now?' But this was all very ad hoc and uncoordinated. Now that the BJP has a majority in Parliament, playing one off the other doesn't get anyone anywhere.

As convener, George Fernandes was expected to be the prime minister's firefighter and political headache remover—termed Sankat Mochan (saviour from troubles). He readily agreed to visit trouble-spots like Orissa when Australian missionary Graham Staines and his two sons were murdered, or when nuns were allegedly raped. He went to West Bengal in a delegation with Mamata Banerjee to visit victims who were raped supposedly by party workers of the Left government in power at that time. Even then, 'communal rapes', i.e. rapes happening in states under BJP rule, were highlighted by the media and the opposition, while similar incidents under 'secular' rule were underplayed. They hated the fact that George Fernandes was content playing the role of the secular face of the 'Right-wing Hindu Nationalist' government as the western press described the NDA and took the flak stolidly when he came back to tell the truth about any of these incidents. He would often comment that telling the truth was what made him controversial, as no one liked to hear it if it did not suit their agenda. I often felt the same way. It would rankle them that both of us, despite being staunch socialists, were comfortable with the policies of the government, fought against corrupt industrialists from within (if individuals in the government seemed to be favouring any), and saw no benefit in state control over defunct public-sector institutions (that swallowed money and produced no output). He did not believe that the words 'Hindu' or 'Nationalist' needed to be treated like abuse, as if being either was a crime. He did not go to churches or temples, and accepted the humanity of Christianity, equating it with socialism, while believing in the teachings of the Gita as a tome on the values of life. We would laugh when he heaved a sigh out of exhaustion and sank into a chair after some strenuous activity, saying, '*Hey Ram*!', and I would jokingly say to him that he had better not let the secularists hear that.

∽

One important event and its endless ramifications on our polity needs recording as experienced by me personally. I have done this before, elsewhere, but it is too important to leave out of my life's engagement in public activities. A little déjà vu offering on my part should not be faulted since the Gujarat 2002 riot incidents and accusations have been repeated ad nauseam anyway.

It was my dear friend, colleague and Samata Party MP Dr Betty D'Souza who came rushing to my office space at 3, Krishna Menon Marg, when Parliament stalled immediately upon hearing of the burning of *kar sevaks** in a train in Godhra, Gujarat. She said that a furore was created by the members of the NDA while the Opposition refused to be part of a unanimous resolution to condemn the gruesome incident. Some muttered that the *kar sevak*s deserved it. Others said the ruling members were making enough noise on their own, and thus doubted the need for the Opposition to add their voice to it. It was callous and short sighted, as it may have led to a calmer reaction to the events in Gujarat if national voices had condemned it. This was the tone adopted

---

**Kar sevaks* refer to those who voluntarily provide support and service for religious purposes

by most editorials in the national papers as well, apart from Vir Sanghvi's editorial which said nothing could justify such barbarity. This resulted in a bandh the next day called by the Bajrang Dal in Gujarat. Late that afternoon, violence ensued.

I remember clearly that George Fernandes rushed in as the evening light was fading. He had been at the prime minister's residence when they had received a fax from Narendra Modi, chief minister of Gujarat, asking for the army to be sent urgently to Ahmedabad to quell the violence.

George Fernandes came away to his residential office, shared this news with me and his personal staff. He ordered for his senior officers to reach Raksha Bhavan immediately. The troops were at that time deployed on a special exercise called Operation Parakram on the Rajasthan border. They were called back hastily and redeployed so that they could reach Gujarat in the early hours of the morning.

This is what I wrote in an article titled 'George Fernandes and Gujarat riots' on thenewsminute.com website, on 1 January 2007*:

> George Fernandes stayed at Raksha Bhavan for most of the night and himself left for Ahmedabad on the early morning flight. He was soon on the streets of Ahmedabad standing in a truck among the troops. The army helped families escape violent crowds, of which photographs appeared in *The Economic Times* and others. Harsh Sethi, a well-known Left intellectual wrote in a centre piece in *The Hindu* sometime later that the army coming out under George Fernandes saved thousands of lives. I know for a fact that Narendra Modi was in constant touch with the Defence Minister and even supported and co-operated when he later organised a citizen's peace march of 7000 people, including Muslims, through the city. I too was present. Modi addressed the marchers at the end of its journey, thanking everyone for working towards peace. Interestingly, some newspapers reported this totally peaceful and uneventful march the next day with the headline 'Fernandes'[s] peace march walks over dead bodies'. There was not a moment's tension or frustration in the relationship between Modi and Fernandes, whether before or after, and this is a fact even

*'George Fernandes and Gujarat riots: Jaya Jaitly recounts the events after Godhra', 1 January 2007, http://www.thenewsminute.com/article/george-fernandes-and-gujarat-riots-jaya-jaitly-recounts-events-after-godhra-55075

> if this has annoyed many Modi-haters and some of Fernandes'[s] socialist compatriots....
>
> ...On a later visit to Gujarat in an all-party delegation in which Sonia Gandhi was also a member, I was confronted by a belligerent youth activist of the Bajrang Dal who asked me to tell George Fernandes to stay away from interfering. I answered that he was no one to speak to me and that George Sahib was asked by the Chief Minister to assist in quelling the riots, and he had responded as was his national duty.

~

The all-Party delegation referred above was an interesting experience in contrasts. I had written an article in *The Indian Express* chiding the Congress for accusing the Gujarat government for causing the riots, reminding it of 1984 where its role in the pogrom against Sikhs was well documented. I also explained reasons for the riots in Gujarat from my intimate knowledge of its rural and urban people over years of travel and interactions. I was fiercely attacked in various articles written at the time for having taken this position. The late Pramod Mahajan also noticed my article and put my name as one of those on the delegation to visit Gujarat. I found myself on the flight with various MPs including Sonia Gandhi and S.S. Ahluwalia. We visited Godhra and spoke with the very articulate woman district magistrate, saw the burnt bogies, and heard how the perpetrators were the remnants of the gangs belonging to a famous Mumbai don.

From Godhra we came to Ahmedabad where Ashok Bhatt, the state health minister and an old socialist, took us to meet the victims. The Godhra burn victims were unrecognizable, burned black to such an extent you could only see their white eyeballs and the pink of the insides of their mouths. In the other wards, were the victims of gunshot wounds, knife attacks, broken bones and other injuries. They all said it was terrible for the first few days but they were being looked after now. Sonia Gandhi did not say a word.

We then went to the local municipal hospital which was under a Congress municipal administration. Here, incongruously, two rows of white cap- and kurta-clad youth hailed Sonia Gandhi. She cheered up and spoke to many of the patients. We had meetings with the police chief and other senior officials of the administration. I was a little disappointed at the slightly lax body language of the police officers. It seemed as if they were out of shape and had not been alert enough to prevent a lot of the incidents. Many officials were transferred after that.

At the house of Pravinsinh Jadeja, Samata Party president in Gujarat, I met all our Party workers from different localities. Many of them were Muslims. They all said things had been pretty bad but the ministers and administration had responded to every call for help made by them. We also visited some makeshift camps for the victims which were nowhere near as teeming or organized as ours were in 1984.

In later tours to villages where my craftspersons and Party workers resided, many old hands among the Muslim community came with their Hindu neighbours and pleaded, 'Please, Jaya-*ben*, ask these NGOs and others to stay away from Gujarat. We are at peace with each other and do not eat our meals unless we are sitting together. Some radical mullahs are being sent to spread trouble. We have bundled some into our cars and sent them away.' I repeated these words at a *Telegraph* newspaper debate on secularism in Bengal a couple of years later, when these attacks on Narendra Modi would not die down. Interestingly, the whole audience applauded.

I have been unwelcome among many of the intellectual and political elite for defending Narendra Modi, the chief minister of Gujarat, on many occasions post the 2002 riots. But it was simply because I saw the truth as it was and not as people wished it to be.

Here, it is worthwhile remembering the Bhagalpur riots of October 1989. I became involved in relief work by compelling Sharad Yadav (after he took over in 1990) to find a way for us to donate bundles of dhotis and saris to the victims. I visited scores of powerloom establishments, and weavers' and tailors' homes with a team of Party workers from Bihar and tried at least to calm my conscience. It was clear to me that it was the large Muslim population that had been attacked and many of those who joined in doing so were part of Lalu Prasad Yadav's caste. It was because of his interest in protecting the attackers (as was widely believed because of his failure to take any action) that even though some eye-wash commissions were set up later to get to the truth of these riots, they never got off the ground. When Nitish Kumar took over from Lalu Prasad Yadav as Bihar chief minister, the results of the Justice N.N. Singh inquiry were finally tabled in 2015, indicting the Congress government in Bihar at that time and recording that over a thousand people were killed.

Lalu Prasad Yadav, the subsequent 'secular' darling of Delhi's intelligentsia, came to power on the Mandal wave (burying this ugly riot away from those who point to Gujarat 2002 and Delhi 1984). He has kept his clansmen in check by rushing to Yadav localities when troubles occurred later, to reassure the Muslims that he alone could provide them protection. Lalu further cemented his secular credentials by prevailing upon V.P. Singh to allow him to arrest L.K. Advani during the latter's *rath yatra*.

Even while George Fernandes took a lot of flak for his personal insight on Nawaz Sharif, China or even statements in Parliament, and on behalf of the perceived ills of the BJP during NDA-I government, he knew he was still often being used by his colleagues in the BJP without any advantage accruing to him or his Party. As a coalition partner, it was impossible for us to negotiate even one extra seat prior to elections. Even if the Samata Party candidate was stronger and more likely to win, the larger Party in the combine would rather fight and lose than give up the seat to another Party, losing its hold in the future. Coalitions are good for a point of time, but otherwise stifling for individual partners and eventually become a contentious mess if too many small parties are involved, too many disparate agendas and ideologies clash. Ultimately, all they have is the ability to threaten to withdraw support as a bargaining chip.

The close rapport between Atal Bihari Vajpayee, L.K. Advani, Jaswant Singh and George Fernandes worked extremely well in matters of handling the Kargil War, or keeping allies on the same page on important policies especially if George Fernandes was sent as a persuasive emissary to bring them on board. They knew he was totally committed to opposing the Congress, and the Samata Party had remained a comfortable ally in Bihar. They respected his political stands on most things. He was always ready to do this as he was determined not to be the cause of a non-Congress government falling this time no matter what he or his colleagues lost as a result. His efforts to keep chief minister and head of the AIADMK, Jayalalithaa, for the short period that she supported the NDA, was hilarious. She threatened to pull out at the slightest pretext and he found himself rushing to Chennai all too often. None was supposed to know of many of these trips as we were all sworn to secrecy. The most crucial one was when it seemed likely she would pull the plug on Prime Minister Vajpayee's first opportunity to speak from the ramparts of the Red Fort. On the overnight dash to save the day, Sasikala, close aide of the Tamil Nadu chief minister, served Jayalalithaa and George Fernandes an elaborate many-coursed lunch with expensive Baskin Robbin's ice cream at the end. George Fernandes meekly ate that in the larger interests of government stability much against his 'swadeshi' preference for Amul ice cream.

Interestingly, his troubles were more within the Samata Party, with many political leaders from Bihar working at cross purposes, and fighting or making up with Nitish Kumar, while George Fernandes had the miserable task of keeping everyone placated and in place. He always said Nitish Kumar was one person whose mind he could never fathom. A democrat before all else, it would be frustrating for him when Nitish Kumar refused to agree upon a date to hold a meeting of the National Executive, or overturned a consensus arrived during such meetings by visiting him alone later at night with *his* view which he insisted on being implemented. Often, this made the Party lose good people to the BJP; these people who would often spend time having tea with me and sharing their woes about Nitish Kumar. I thought it my duty to convey such matters to George Fernandes, but I knew too that it would inadvertently add to his anxieties. He would always give in to him rationalizing the irrational for the sake of a larger goal.

I am sure the tensions he suffered throughout his entire tenure in the Ministry of Defence in matters concerning security, politics of coalitions, the Party, lack of Party funds, and disappointment with issues like Bofors which were not taken to its logical end, added to the neurological ailment building up silently in his brain. The final nail in the coffin could perhaps have been the humiliation George Fernandes suffered by being rejected as the rightful candidate for his own beloved constituency of Muzaffarpur in a rude and cursory manner by the Party colleagues. By the end, I saw his many frustrations being translated into far too many extended silences.

23

WHY JAYA DIDN'T MAKE IT TO THE RAJYA SABHA LIST

Negatives Make News

THE TITLE OF THIS CHAPTER draws from the headline of a four-column news item in the *Hindustan Times* of 28 August 2003 (see photo section). It is funny that something that did *not* happen should become news rather than the opposite; I suppose, I have to now tell the tale which has a 'pre' and 'post' part.

Most people, who get a nomination to Parliament, a major national award, or an important position in government, are presumed to have clawed everyone aside, massaged the egos of important people, fought furiously or lobbied shamelessly among the powers that be. Our elite are so cynical that very few recipients are considered truly deserving and even less are believed if they say they had never asked for it. With some honourable exceptions, they are not speaking the truth because public life isn't that simple. Yet they blush and pretend the honour was totally unexpected. Many friends and acquaintances have lobbied through me hoping to reach George Fernandes and other influential leaders. It would be a shame to mention names and I have no intention of shaming anyone. But, I have seen it all.

In my case, it is easy to tell the absolute truth of why I did not make it to the Rajya Sabha, and no, I truly never asked for it. Again, since I never had any expectations, I have no bitterness, no fact to hide, no regret to offer. I have enough self-respect to admit that had I been in the Upper House, or the House of the Elders as it's supposed to be, I believe I would have been a deserving elder for the years of work I have done in my field and the extent to which I have contributed towards the well-being of India's arts and crafts communities. Not being there hasn't deterred my work at all, but hopefully an honest disclosure clears the air for another convoluted story in my life among the scorpions.

In 2003, the leaders of the Party decided that the Samata Party would merge with the JD(U) to become a bigger force against Lalu Prasad Yadav's Rashtriya Janata Dal (RJD) in Bihar. The JD(U) had only recently split from the RJD. Samata was a bigger Party and had fought against Lalu Prasad Yadav for a longer time. This had given the Party headed by Sharad Yadav psychological supremacy. Top leaders of both parties met in George Fernandes's drawing room. The decision was taken and a press conference slotted to announce this momentous event had already been organized at the back verandah. Digvijay Singh, who passed away suddenly some years later in London, came to me in the side room after the press conference was over and told me the news. The Parties had merged, the new formation was now the Janata Dal (U), George Fernandes was its head, and Sharad Yadav was the chairman of the Parliamentary Board. The most remarkable and significant aspect of the decision was that I was no part of it. I felt like I had been knocked off my feet. When did this happen and why is it not named after the Samata? Why was I not in the picture? In fact, why was I kept clueless by everyone, including him and George Sahib? To my load of questions Digvijay Singh's only answer was, '*Khair, Jayaji, ab to ho gaya.*' (Well, Jayaji, now it's done.)

Just because I was deeply hurt and humiliated, did not mean I should have tried and do the same to those who took the decision. Instead, silently, with no noise, drama or public recriminations, I quit Party politics.

The small advantage George Fernandes seems to have seen in this act of mine was that he thought I could now be nominated for the Rajya Sabha under the Arts & Culture/Public Service, Social Work category. He did not speak to me about this, but discussed it with his colleagues, Prime Minister Vajpayee, L.K. Advani, Jaswant Singh and Venkaiah Naidu, who was by then president of the BJP. They apparently had a long discussion on whether the *Tehelka* allegations might come in the way. The Law Ministry was said to have given its view on file that no crime had been committed. The group of big wigs decided I was perfectly capable of defending myself on the floor of the House if an attack from the Opposition came my way. George Fernandes told me all this only after they had finalized their decision.

The only thing I said was, 'Wait and see, it won't happen!' I don't think he liked my negative attitude but he remained silent as usual.

One Sunday morning in August 2003, Venkaiah Naidu called and asked for my biodata to be sent to L.K. Advani's residence. When I asked why, he just laughed. Subsequently, eight files for eight nominees were prepared and one was mine. Later that month, the prime minister went to meet the President of India, Dr A.P.J. Abdul Kalam, for his signature on the files. According to the *Hindustan Times* news item, when the list was later released, there was one vacancy. I was in Ahmedabad working on a crafts map with a traditional artist and a graphic designer. Digvijay Singh called to say there was a picture of me in the *Hindustan Times* looking '*khoobsurat*' (beautiful), and that my name was off because of the *Tehelka* controversy, but that I had been on the list that included actor Hema Malini, former RBI Governor Bimal Jalan, journalist Chandan Mitra, former wrestler Dara Singh and others. I wasn't surprised, just very curious.

When I returned to Delhi, I nudged George Sahib to ask the prime minister, although he was hesitant and uncomfortable about it. I couldn't help my curiosity although my original prophecy was correct. He asked him about three weeks later and was told the President had hesitated because of the allegations against me. Some weeks later, he was meeting the President on some defence matters as he was also the Commander-in-Chief of the Armed Forces. I awkwardly asked whether he could enquire about what happened, as the President and he had a very good personal equation. George Sahib returned to convey that the President described how the prime minister had requested him not to sign my file as a senior BJP colleague had expressed reservations about attacks on me in Parliament. Apparently, the President had responded by saying his duty was to sign on the dotted line so he would do whatever the prime minister asked. It was hard to believe it was this colleague, a woman, who had dissuaded the prime minister at the eleventh hour. I felt someone else was behind it. Since it was only a guess and the person is no more, I will not venture a name. It was one of the strangest situations, knowing the top two people in the land were telling contradictory stories about me. It was hard to make sense of it, but I was glad the issue was over.

Unfortunately, George Sahib did not let things rest.

Sardar Tarlochan Singh is a well-preserved Sikh with a personality that makes you notice him in a crowd. He is pleasant, well-mannered and extremely effective at what he sets his mind at. I met him in 1990 when I first walked into the office of the Managing Director of Delhi Tourism to propose the idea of Dilli Haat. He was receptive and supported me in all the follow-through as a good deputy to the Chairman, S. Regunathan, of whom I wrote in my story of Dilli Haat. He served in many positions of the Punjab government and later became Press Secretary to the President of India, Giani Zail Singh. That time was such that he became politically oriented and moved to networking between the leadership opposed to the Congress party in Punjab and Haryana. We became something between acquaintances and good friends over a decade. He often accompanied Akali Dal leaders or Om Prakash Chautala's group visiting George Fernandes. I would nearly always join the political discussions.

During the elections to the Haryana Assembly, the Election Commission of India (ECI) had asked Chautala, as chief minister, to keep away from his own constituency and the state itself on polling day because of some earlier history of violence. I spoke up as an ally at our Party's daily press conference protesting that the ECI had denied a citizen his right to vote, and a chief minister from fulfilling his responsibility to maintain law and order in his state. Chautala later went to court and won the case. Sometime later, Tarlochan Singh accompanied an Indian National Lok Dal (INLD) group with Chautala to thank me for my support among other things. He often conveyed the appreciation of the Badals and Sikhs in general for the work I had done to support the victims of 1984. Sometimes he just came over to chat with me to share political views about what was going on in the NDA government and outside. Whenever we would be on our own or in the presence of George Sahib, he would repeatedly say that I should be in the Rajya Sabha for the work I had done for crafts, democratic politics and the Sikhs. I would brush the suggestion off brusquely and George Sahib would remain silent as he did about most things concerning me.

One day, in 2004, George Sahib was at his desk when I walked in. He looked up with an odd expression on his face.

'What's the matter?' I asked.

He answered at a slow pace. 'I spoke to Chautala today about giving you a Rajya Sabha seat from Haryana. You remember Tarlochan has been repeatedly suggesting this.'

'I don't like the sound of this. Why did you do it?' I burst out.

'Wait and listen,' he cautioned. 'Listen to what Chautala said.'

'It's silly. Anyway…what?' I was impatient because it was an awkward subject.

'Chautala said he wished I had told him earlier. He would have happily obliged. He says now he has given his word to Tarlochan Singh who has been after him for a Rajya Sabha seat for a long time.'

I closed the conversation once and for all with 'good', thoroughly embarrassed by now and feeling quite foolish that this subject had come up again.

Anyway, Tarlochan Singh did a good job in Parliament on behalf of Sikhs worldwide, and I am happy for that.

With all the *Tehelka* flak I had to bear, and the ongoing inquiry, I believe George Sahib thought I deserved some kind of public compensation in the form of a position of value that the society at large and the political world recognized. He had always expressed faith in my activism, my work among craftspersons, and had mentored me for thirty years by then, putting me into every difficult situation he could think of, to hone my understanding of political matters. He was probably the only man who has ever made me feel without any hesitation or condescension, that I had an intellect and capacity worth respecting. He also had the patience to teach me when I was being foolish or ignorant. And so, he would not give up on the Rajya Sabha issue. He never discussed it with me, knowing my prickly responses.

After the NDA was defeated in March 2004, the Bihar elections of late 2004 put Nitish Kumar firmly on the seat of the chief minister. George Sahib asked me to request Nitish Kumar to drop by at AIIMS where he was recovering from a neurosurgery to treat the collection of fluid in his brain. He said he wanted to talk to him about governance and development issues in Bihar. Later I learned that he had spoken to him about finally acknowledging my contributions to the Party by sending me to the Rajya Sabha as an elected candidate from Bihar. Apparently he had readily agreed, saying it was long overdue.

In March 2005, Nitish Kumar asked me to give him a plan for the development of handicrafts in the state since it was a subject I had been constantly involved in for so long. I took a month to compile fourteen pages of detailed plans for different crafts across Bihar, including those where sources of funds could be accessed. It was sent to him by hand with a covering letter offering to be involved further, if required. I never received an acknowledgement. The chief minister apparently dropped in briefly once on Holi to greet his leader, where he reassured him I would get the nomination. I cringed when George Sahib told me; I did not believe it.

Instead, I was told to prepare the documents required to be filed, including details of my assets and bank account. No one would believe the pathetic state of my finances. There were no assets worth anything, so it may have surprised those used to seeing Rajya Sabha aspirants having crores. This part was ironic since I was accused of bribery and corruption by *Tehelka*.

The Rajya Sabha nominations were to be filed in April 2005. I was told to await a call from Bihar telling me when to arrive there. Nothing happened. On the morning of the very last day for filing nominations, just after the last flight had left Delhi for Patna, George Sahib received a call from the chief minister saying he could not give me the seat as he had decided to give it to 'King Mahendra' (Mahendra Prasad), a businessman who had moved from Congress to RJD to Congress and now JD(U). He said he had helped the Party in the elections. George Sahib tried to argue that I too had done a lot for the Party over the years and that they all owed it to me. I watched him speak from across the room. His face became stiff and after a few moments of silence, he put the receiver down.

'He says he has done a lot for women by keeping 50 per cent of seats reserved for them at the *panchayat* level in Bihar. He disconnected the phone after that,' George Sahib recounted the entire conversation, in complete disbelief.

Ironically, a few minutes later, King Mahendra walked in unannounced, to touch George Sahib's feet and seek his blessings. With a grim face, George Sahib said, 'But you already have them,' and ended the conversation. I left the room to save us both from further embarrassment.

24

COURTS IN INDIA
A Slow Halal

IS IT TOO MUCH OF a cliché to say that the wheels of justice move slowly in India? Except for those stuck in the octopus-like grip of our legal system, people consider it as a given, and look away since it is not their concern. After all, surveys at the end of 2016 show around 61,000 cases pending in the Supreme Court, around four million in the high courts and approximately 28 million in the lower courts. If an average of three persons are involved in the case, it has been calculated that 84 million people are waiting for justice. Just as a statistic, I am one of those nearly 28 million stuck in the legal system of our country since 2006. It has been eleven years so far.

Ninety-four per cent of the cases have been pending from five to fifteen years. The average is three years and nine months in the Delhi High Court which is considered one of the better ones, but my own appeal, the one filed in the same high court against a lower court decision to send me to trial, has not been fully heard for four years so far. Lawyers ask why the high court should stay the trial now, when it is reaching its end. I ask what the point of the recourse of an appeal is if it is never heard. Instead, both are seemingly stuck in a block of concrete.

Sometimes verdicts take over two years to be pronounced although the rules say they should be taken within thirty days. There is a chronic shortage of judges, but apart from that, the delays are mostly because lawyers seek numerous adjournments both for the sake of a criminal client who prefers to evade progress towards judgement day or because lawyers have to keep juggling too many balls in the air to earn a living. In either case, they end up with no available dates for early hearings. Then there are gazetted holidays, long vacations, 'the judge is leave today' days, and lawyers' strikes to add to the frustrated client's woes. Lawyers blame it on the 'system' that prevents them from offering solutions to expedite a case.

Delays of all kinds—from the judge's habitually slow pace, lack of a sense of urgency, or a heavy workload—emanate from the fact that in India we have only 17 judges per million cases, while France has 124, USA 108, Australia 40, Canada 33, and even a small country like the UK, 22 judges.

Preoccupations of state-prosecuting agencies are taken as a given. For lawyers, it is par for the course. Most lawyers look at a case as just one more case to be handled with the rusty tools and creaking systems available to them. They see nothing unusual in my situation where, the prosecution has taken 468 weeks to produce forty-seven witnesses with the final witness, who is their main one, playing hide and seek for three years.

India's current Finance Minister Arun Jaitley hit the nail on its head in his address to the CBI in his D.P. Kohli memorial lecture in 2016:

> The investigator follows the golden rule that if he gives a report that the accused is prima facie not guilty, then, questions are going to be raised about him. Therefore, his golden rule is he must somehow make the case and it is the accused's good luck whether he gets a fair trial...

With such clarity of perception in the new government, I imagined our pace of trials would find ways of picking up. But take my case filed by the CBI, for instance. I presumed that a certain official serving in an important capacity in the Venkataswami/Phukan Inquiry Commission was to serve it without prejudice or forming any opinions of his own. Therefore, I found it significant that when the Commission was disbanded, although that official returned to his Ministry as an ordinary official, he saw it fit to lodge a complaint with the police that the noticees, including me, had committed a crime. The obedient law enforcement agencies took note and an FIR was filed against me in December 2004. I was informed of this when the media came rushing to me at Dilli Haat where I was conducting a workshop. When the media came disrupting my craft work, I gave them short shrift. They were so surprised at my vehemence that they backed off and left, but it caused much excitement in the media. My answer to reporters' breathless queries about my reactions to the FIR was simply, 'Let them. I don't care.'

The CBI finally filed a charge sheet much later in April 2006. My daughter, and a friend, Sunita Sachdeva, came to court with me. Sunita posted fifty thousand rupees as bail. My son wanted to replace her bail surety deposit with his, but that too required him and her to appear in court, file affidavits giving reasons why, applying for withdrawal by one and replacement by the other. It sounded so tedious and painful that they both dropped the idea.

Hearings at Patiala House courts near India Gate in 2007 took place in two different rooms before two different judges within a short time. But then the case abruptly shifted to the district courts in Rohini in far-off north-west Delhi in the middle of a court hearing which had simply been adjourned for lunch.

Till 2010, I went to the Rohini courts by changing two metro lines and then going the last stretch by cycle rickshaw. Finally, it was so wearisome that I went by car since my children had gifted me one for my birthday that year. Three judges changed during my case at Rohini. At 8 am on the day of a hearing, my lovely golden retriever Honcho, afflicted with non-Hodgkin's lymphoma, dropped dead at my feet. I could not go to cremate him as I had to reach court by 10 am. My daughter-in-law, Isabelle, came across to handle it for me while I went to court compelling myself to push down the sadness inside. I remembered an incident when the late J. Jayalalithaa, former chief minister of Tamil Nadu at that time, had abruptly discontinued a meeting with seniors of the NDA in a rare visit to Delhi because her pet dog had fallen ill in Chennai.

The ridiculous things that happen in Indian courts, by one of which I was rather affected, is reflected in a formal letter I felt compelled to write to then law minister of the UPA government, Veerappa Moily in 2010:

> *My reason for writing this letter is to bring to your kind attention the status of a charge sheet filed against me by the CBI in December 2006, under the Prevention of Corruption Act, almost four years ago. It is connected with a completely hyped, motivated and fraudulent set of allegations made initially by a journalist's website called Tehelka.com. in March 2001, that is, nine years ago.*
>
> *The Enquiry Commission functioned from April 2001 till October 2004 when it was aborted just before the honourable retired Supreme Court judge was to give the second and final part of his report. The enquiry could not be concluded although we co-operated with it fully for four long years.*
>
> *The UPA government handed the matter over to the CBI which took two years to file a charge sheet, and that too only when it managed to*

twist the tail of a petty businessman and made him change his original story, given under oath in the inquiry Commission. Even today, the witness statements provided by the CBI with the charge sheet do not tally in facts. However, that is for the honourable judge to take note.

The proceedings started in the Patiala Courts in 2007 and later shifted to the Rohini Courts (for speedier processing). The appointed judges have changed four times already without any meaningful hearings beginning till date. Even persons with good memories of events that were significant would forget what happened leave alone trying to recall a meaningless event. Each new judge means starting from the beginning.

I am also happy to have been one of the victims of highly inefficient court systems since it gives me the opportunity to bring it to your notice, hopefully, for correction.

The judges on my case have now changed for the fifth time. The honourable Delhi High Court does the transfer of judges, but the judge gets his powers from the Lt. Governor of Delhi. The gap between the two processes leaves the judge 'powerless' for 20 days to a month, wasting his and everyone else's time. A parallel judge can rule in his case if he is absent but not when he is present even if he cannot do anything.

A court clerk's mistake about the next date of hearing (which all the accused, their lawyers and even the CBI's public prosecutor noted correctly) resulted in our bail's being cancelled and bonds forfeited by the parallel judge. We had to rush to get a stay, but the parallel judge who ordered the cancellation would not do it since the main judge was present. But, the main judge was 'powerless' so we had to rush to Tees Hazari courts to get the District Judge to order the parallel judge for the stay. What a perfectly ridiculous situation for all concerned. It took four trips to courts to rectify the situation. What is the point of a 'powerless' judge...

Sir, can you not ensure that transfer of a judge and according of powers for the judge to function happen simultaneously?

The law minister had no objections to the tone of my letter. He was kind enough to reply promptly with some kind of positive assurance that the situation would be rectified. That was more than I expected, but I have no idea whether things have improved on this front.

Then the case got transferred to the Dwarka district court in another far-off area of Delhi. It seemed to me as if the presiding judge had pre-determined intentions. In 2012, when he allowed me to travel to Singapore to attend a reunion of the Smith College alumnae from Asia, he arbitrarily raised my deposit fee from 25,000 rupees to 3,00,000 rupees. It was a big jump; I did not possess this amount. I told him so when he passed the order but he simply shrugged and smiled smugly with his arms crossed in triumph.

I had to appeal to the high court quickly with passbooks and demonstrations of my meagre resources. Fortunately, we got this order reversed so that I could travel to be amongst some of the highest Asian achievers among my alma mater. When I shared my political experiences, including the struggle to get to Singapore, the audience burst out into applause.

Since the same judge had convicted the unfortunate former president of the BJP, Bangaru Laxman, a heart patient in his late seventies, to four years in jail, I was apprehensive that I was next in line irrespective of our arguments. His orders to frame charges in my case were based entirely on speculative and far-fetched conjectures. In fact, he blatantly made up for the lapses in the poor CBI's public prosecutor's inept arguments in open court to send my case for trial. I appealed to the Delhi high court the next day but while the appeal was admitted and notices issued, it has not been heard yet. Four years have gone by.

Providence intervened and took us out of this judge's hands. We found the case shifted to the district courts at Saket in South Delhi in the court of Special CBI Judge Manoj Jain. He seemed eager to move the case forward quickly by often mentioning the need for daily hearings which never came about due to the dilly-dallying by the CBI team. He was, however, patient with the CBI. We did manage to get through a few more witnesses.

Judge Manoj Jain completed his roster and was shifted. By then he was already irritated about the fact that Matthew Samuel of *Tehelka*, the final and most relevant of the CBI witnesses who kept pleading ill health and not appearing on appointed dates, was delaying matters.

Interestingly, on the last day of his hearing our case, the honourable judge called me back from the exit door when the proceedings were over. He addressed me in front of the CBI team and others who happened to be in court. 'Madam, I want to thank you for your patient and calm demeanour and your co-operation in court. If you are innocent you have nothing to worry,' he said. This was one of the pleasant surprises in all my experiences with courts. It reminded me of Justice Venkataswami's kind response to my letter to him.

Judge Rakesh Kumar I (so named because there happened to be two of the same name) replaced him. He was followed a couple of years later by Judge Dr Ramesh Kumar.

During this period covering three judges so far, Mathew Samuel has avoided deposing in about twenty-one out of twenty-eight hearings. His excuses range from diabetes, constipation, piles, fistula surgeries, feeling unwell, lengthy bed rest, stuck in traffic, busy in the Kolkata High Court in the Narada Sting Operation case and going for training to the USA for eight weeks. The latest was that his mother was in hospital. Even his own opening 'chief' deposition is only half done.

One day in court on yet another fruitless trip, I took out my calculator and did some 'back of the envelope' mathematical calculations. At an average of attending hearings ten times a year for ten years, I would have made approximately a hundred trips to court. Add to that, another thirty sundry trips for applications for travel and extending validation of my passport which initially got curtailed to only a year's validity. Add the notional costs of lawyers for all accused persons at the aborted Inquiry Commission and then at various district courts. Add to that expenses on paper, photocopying, stationery, petrol and transportation for all concerned and other consultations and extraneous expenditures. It would have cost a minimum of 400,000 rupees a year for ten years.

The costs to the Government of India for this entire exercise would be many, many times that amount—forty million rupees spent over this case over the whole period, in the very least, on bringing all the accused to justice. My head whirled at trying to arrive at a grand total when a lawyer reported that a judge had revealed that while in court it cost the government 3500 rupees each time a case file had to be taken from the registry and brought to the courtroom. This did not include what was spent and aborted on the Commission of Inquiry for four years before this.

All this has been for the 'state' to use all the legalities and instruments at its command to find out whether I (and others) actually, knowingly, met arms dealers, asked for and took 200,000 rupees in corrupt circumstances from a man—a private poseur—on a pretend deal, and subsequently assisted them through the Minister/Ministry of Defence in advancing their interests.

My answer always remains: 'Prove it quickly and lock me up, or finish with it and let me go.'

I am often asked, perhaps rather foolishly, whether some evil figure behind the scenes is orchestrating such a slow halal. I believe that it's just that the pernicious Indian legal 'system' doesn't care if an innocent person who is entitled to speedy justice, dies an agonizingly slow death after getting entangled in its clutches.

25

LIMBO AS A STATE OF BEING
Alzheimer's Disease and the Under Toad*

BOOKS ARE GREAT FOR A reason. They help create a new order, a clearer design, in which to fit your own experiences and beliefs. When they are written in evocative language, words, sentences, ideas, even nuances—they stay with you forever. I came across some of my list of favourite novels while studying English, French, American and Latin Literature in the USA. Some I read later. I often refer to these special ones: Marcel Proust's *Remembrance of Things Past*, George Orwell's *1984*, Simone de Beauvoir's *The Second Sex*, Günter Grass's *The Tin Drum*, Kiran Nagarkar's *Cuckold*, Joseph Heller's *Catch-22*, Frank McCourt's *Angela's Ashes* and John Steinbeck's *The Grapes of Wrath*.

Of the books I have read, admired, kept, remembered, revisited often, John Irving's *The World According to Garp* stands out, as I write this chapter of my memoir. Published in 1978, Irving's *Garp* is a powerful, humorous and tragic story of the family of T.S. Garp—about the love of writing and literature, and of radical feminism with its repercussions on society at that time. In it, I came across the use of effective symbolism for dreaded events to come. I found myself recalling this book when inner instincts compelled me to write of looking at the first imperceptible signs of Alzheimer's Disease in the life of George Sahib. Moreover, like everyone else, I feel a certain solace in sharing emotions that are both personal and universal.

~

In Irving's book, the Garp family recalls visits to the New Hampshire seaside every summer. Their familiar beach is known for its strong undertow. 'Watch out for the undertow!' and 'The undertow is strong

*Names of a few individuals have been changed in this chapter.

today', become frequently used warning phrases if the roads are icy or some other danger anticipated. Garp's four-year-old son Walt, however, begins to form his own ideas. One day, the family finds him with his little feet in the swirling surf, with him staring intently into the waves. When his mother and elder brother ask him what he is doing, he replies: 'I'm trying to see the Under Toad…How big is it?'

Little Walt asks if it's slimy or green or brown. It is only then that his family realizes that for all that time he had imagined the 'undertow' to be a giant, loathsome, toad-like monster waiting to leap out of the water to swallow him. It becomes an allegory for the presence of death or at least the unavoidable, in everyone's lives. Walt is later run over and killed by his father in a freak car accident in their own driveway. The parable seeps ominously into our uneasy consciousness telling us that misfortune and death, the grim reaper, will eventually come. There is no avoiding it by fighting endless battles against it. One just has to live life to the full until that time arrives.

~

The 'undertow' that changed the nature of my work routine began at 9 am one morning in 2004 with the discovery that George Sahib suddenly could not remember the code to open the combination lock to his bedroom. Turn clockwise to twelve, anti-clockwise to twenty-eight, then clockwise back to ten. He had returned from somewhere at midnight and spent the night on the sofa in the adjoining study with the bedroom door still locked. He had refused to let Durga, the household help, call me earlier. I felt a slight tug at the pit of my stomach, but brushed it aside. I thought he may have been tired from hectic travel. After all, in 1978 his travel schedule had been so frantic that he, for a few moments, had forgotten his own name. Only he, Aditi and I knew the sequence of numbers to open the lock. We, because he would sometimes call from office or out of town asking urgently for papers lying locked in his room to be found and sent to him. It was the only room in the house that was locked in his absence. Papers and books always covered the entire twin bed next to where he slept. Sometimes, the dogs would occupy the empty space of his own bed. He would leave them undisturbed and sleep on the floor instead. Lord Snowden photographed him on this bed, fast asleep, amongst his books, when he came to photo-document famous political personalities of India for a coffee table book.

This is available as archival material now.

As signs of forgetfulness and confusion increased in number, he was examined by his friend and neurosurgeon Dr V.S. Mehta of AIIMS. They found he had water accumulating in the brain; it was probably a long-term effect of his brain injury and surgery in 1995. Surgery was performed to permanently drain the fluid away through a tube. He also underwent tests for cognitive abilities but no note of adverse effects was put in his file.

He recovered and was active again but had recurrent headaches. He was so stubborn that he continued to bury himself in Parliament work, meeting visitors, exercising, reading and writing. He refused to dwell on any signs of discomfort. He was keen to refresh himself with a spell of treatment in Kerala, so I arranged to take him to my Kollengode family home, now formally called Kalari Kovilakom*. It was now a well-appointed Ayurvedic health establishment run by a sophisticated hotel group with a team of highly competent doctors, cooks, yoga teachers and sundry programmes to rejuvenate the body and mind. I had not seen its transformation from an empty palace to an internationally acclaimed luxury spa. We were treated as guests of the proprietors since they saw me as the granddaughter of the late Rajah of Kollengode, and therefore not allowed to pay for any of the services availed of. This was June 2006.

Politician Margaret Alva, and her husband, a poet from Australia, and two frazzled corporate ladies from the UK who wanted to detoxify their systems were also there with us for eleven days. It was almost exactly the same as in the days of my childhood except now there was electricity, modern plumbing, Internet and high-end contemporary fittings in the bathrooms. No one was allowed to leave the premises, wear leather, eat non-vegetarian food or drink anything intoxicating. There was no television either. George Sahib was delighted and missed nothing of what was disallowed since he did not care for them anyway. I was amused at the amount people paid to *not* have luxury but the message was that true luxury lay in a calm mind and good health. The initial medical inquiry took four hours. Special medicated oils were brewed, and a diet created for each kind of body-system was cooked and served accordingly. An eggless cake was baked for his birthday. There were newspapers and evening talks or

---

*Kalari Kovilakom has a website containing its cultural history. Those interested could visit http://www.cghearth.com/kalari-kovilakom

cultural performances for information and entertainment. In my honour, they staged a Kathakali performance of *Kuchelavritham*, the very same story I had learned and enacted with my cousin in our teens. I was also asked to give a lecture on the history of our family and take the occupants on a tour of the establishment. For once, the media left us alone.

George Sahib felt refreshed and re-energized but a couple of minor surgeries followed some months later to clean the blocked pipe that drained the fluids from his skull into his peritoneum; the series also included the removal of a gall stone, and cataract surgeries. George Sahib continued his walks in the garden, his many public engagements, and markedly blossomed when visitors from all over the country came calling. He enjoyed nothing more than company and music. He even insisted on travelling to Japan and Taiwan for political visits although I was completely against the idea. He simply avoided listening to me and got his staff to make the arrangements anyway.

The undertow in my innermost gut was getting stronger, more insistent, demanding attention and instilling dread. I silently went through the typical and well-documented symptoms (or so I discovered later on the Internet, reassuring me that my range of feelings were common) of a person finding a loved one increasingly afflicted by something unfamiliar, terrifying, unmentionable and incurable.

It isn't easy looking back into the past, but while it was happening it was like being at the darkest edge of a constant nightmare. Denial, rejection, isolation, helplessness, anger, despair, are all listed in hundreds of studies about Alzheimer's and the traumatic emotions their caregivers have to confront. I had no one strong or mature enough to whom I could confide my worries and sadness. George Sahib was a famous public figure. One could not announce such things publicly. It would have been intrusive and too heart-rending. I was, perforce, the only close and committed caregiver since George Sahib's brothers lived far away, and his wife and son had distanced themselves decades ago. His political colleagues kept a safe distance on matters of incomprehensible sickness. Old colleagues who cared, lived in other parts of the country and could not give up their work and families to look after him on a daily basis. His non-political friends only made awkward enquiries. Political opponents like Mani Shankar Aiyar either mocked or ignored him until they discovered the truth of his jumbled responses, and graciously apologized. I felt alone and isolated in this new, unexpected maze that was becoming part of the quotidian.

I tried very hard to explain to George Sahib what was happening to him—that he may indeed forget everything and everyone, including me. I told him not to be alarmed and that, as we had fought every battle together for so many years, this would be the same. I had to reassure him constantly that I was there. He wanted me by his side all the time, but he could not grasp what was happening. He would make Durga telephone both morning and evening to ask when I was reaching 3, Krishna Menon Marg. I had my own work as well, so I struggled to divide my time between his establishment, my handicraft programmes for the hundreds of craftspersons associated with us, and my travels outside of Delhi for them. These had to be worked around keeping George Sahib company morning and evening and dealing with any important papers and visitors. There were meals, exercise, conversation, medication, and any emergency to be handled as well.

The sorrow that wells up while watching a person undergo the many cruel and undignified manifestations of Alzheimer's Disease is undeniably one of the most crushing emotions anyone can feel. Today, when people who are occasionally forgetful, joke that they must be getting Alzheimer's disease, I react with unexpected seriousness that surprises them, warning them never, ever, to speak of such matters lightly.

To watch the personality of a person, his very element, essence, mind and soul disappear gradually and cruelly is heartbreaking enough. George Sahib would clutch a dog-eared biography of himself written in Kannada that had a picture of him on the cover. This was a manifestation of Alzheimer's where a person losing their memory holds on to straws to remind them of who they are. It is quite another tragedy to see that person, transforming gradually from being chief mentor, political guru, who had been father, mother, brother, best friend, caretaker, well-wisher and confidante over a period of thirty years, to something like an incurably ailing child. I would always hope that relationships between any two people, anywhere in the world, irrespective of gender, age or status, based purely on mutual respect, honesty and unselfishness, could be like the one we shared. Equally, I now knew, that no one, no one at all, should be afflicted by this disappearance of the self into a black hole of unknowingness while the body remained healthy.

~

On 3 June 2009, unusually, Leila Fernandes dropped in at 3, Krishna Menon Marg, to be present at George Sahib's birthday. This had happened after decades of her absence. Birthday celebrations were always low-key. Some cake, simple snacks, tea, the Burmese students singing and Tibetan friends honouring him. The only people present always were the office staff, some political colleagues and persons from Muzaffarpur, his Parliamentary constituency, old friends like Swaraj Kaushal, and my children and grandchildren. Leila was greeted and photographed amongst Burmese students singing to him. Then she left abruptly just as the cake was brought out. Later in the evening, George Sahib, puzzled, asked me who had invited her. I had no idea.

In mid-December that year, I was told by the office and household staff that Mrs Fernandes and her son with his family had visited in the afternoon. They, I was told, had shut the door and forcibly had his thumb marks imprinted on some papers. When I visited him in the evening he was staring at his thumb, purple from the stamp pad. He was muttering and shaking wildly in agitation. He could not express what had happened. A week later, I received a formal letter with his thumb impression, referring to me as 'Mrs Jaitly', informing me that the Power of Attorney accorded to me had been revoked. Frederick aka Freddy D'Sa in Mumbai received a similar letter. So far we had jointly handled his cheque payments, including annual taxes, salaries or household expenditures all of which had been impeccably recorded.

At the inception of this sudden turn of events were three people, ones with strange minds and obviously dangerous agendas. The association with them goes back years but especially to events in 2008 and onwards. I should have sensed the undertow but I was already preoccupied with the myriad little manifestations of George Sahib's illness, his deeply troubling insistence on fighting the elections in Bihar, and the number of people who arrived like flies to demand money on occasions like these.

The first was Ananth Hari, long-time political and household errand boy, and an eternally aspiring Party functionary who had attached himself to George Fernandes from 1992. He had been living for many years at the Krishna Menon Marg residence with no serious contribution to political, trade union or publication work. In 2008, George Sahib lost his temper and pulled him up sharply, asking him to engage in meaningful work instead of household errands. He had often been found missing from the residence in the middle of the night in times of crisis during George Sahib's recuperation from surgery. Ananth took umbrage and left, telling friends in the media that I had turned him out at 3 am. I was nowhere on the scene when these incidents took place. Subsequently, he began spreading the word among Fernandes's brothers, JD(U) leaders, and the media, that I had a complete grip on 'Sahib's' finances. He joined the JD(U) office in Patna as campaign secretary and worked actively against him in the 2009 Lok Sabha elections.

Next was Nitin Kumar, Section Officer, National Commission for Scheduled Castes/Scheduled Tribes, charge sheeted by the CBI for giving information to *Tehelka*, later turning approver. He would regularly visit George Sahib in the evenings after work, to discuss various political ideologies. He fancied himself as an intellectual but soon began to imagine God was speaking to him and giving him strength to pass on to George Sahib. He would rush to join any occasion where religious heads like the Dalai Lama would visit George Sahib. He would get himself photographed and pose as a part of the family.

Nitin began to involve himself in the Lok Sabha campaign of George Fernandes in April 2009 and went to Muzaffarpur where he began to complain bitterly that the campaign was being run badly. He was asked by George Sahib's local colleagues to stay away from all this activity since he was a government servant. He was 'deeply affected' by George Sahib's defeat. He blamed me, in George Sahib's presence, of deliberately sabotaging the elections by attempting to physically do away with him and taking money from Nitish Kumar to defeat him. He even claimed he had a text message from me offering him money to sabotage the elections but could not produce it. It was even more ironic since political leaders like Sharad Yadav were accusing me publicly of having compelled George Sahib to fight the elections. He accused me of medicating him wrongly and not taking him to New York for treatment. George Sahib was utterly befuddled, and brusquely asked him to stay away and not enter the house anymore.

This made Nitin rush to Mrs Fernandes. He told her that Freddy D'Sa and I had made George Sahib sign away all his money to us. In truth, a General Power of Attorney had been prepared in the presence of a notary public since banks were refusing to honour cheques with George Sahib's illegible signature. Nitin began telling friends that he was his adopted son and professed great love and concern for him while spinning conspiracy theories about those who had been close to him for nearly thirty years. He was found present at Leila Fernandes's house when she held a tea party to celebrate her grandson's visit to India in December 2009. On 18 December 2009, he accompanied them to revoke our Power of Attorney. He was party to and 'official' witness to get George Sahib's thumb impression under duress. All this, as a government servant.

The third in this list of dramatis personae was Ramesh Vinayak, later discovered to be a part-time informant for the Intelligence Bureau, and neighbour and friend to Nitin. He was not known to us until April 2009. Nitin had brought him as a volunteer to assist George Sahib's front office in coordinating the election campaign. He met him for the first time briefly as George Sahib was leaving to file his nomination papers in the first week of April that year. It was subsequently discovered by the old staff that he had prepared a bogus appointment letter from George Sahib to himself, as his political secretary and biographer. The letterhead was of a Lok Sabha member which George Sahib was not. It was dated 28 March 2009, at a time when he had not even spoken to George Sahib. In truth, George Sahib had never signed an appointment letter for any of his personal office staff at any time and had never had a private 'political secretary' in his life. George Sahib vociferously denied that he had made any appointment, speaking to D'Sa about it when he went to Mumbai. D'Sa came to Delhi and politely terminated Ramesh's 'appointment'.

In the meanwhile, Ramesh had started playing off various visitors against each other, interfering in political activity without knowing his boss's friends, interests or principles. As soon as George Sahib was made a member of the Rajya Sabha, Ramesh took undue interest in his MPLADS (or Members of Parliament Local Area Development Scheme) funds, offering constituency colleagues projects, bullying school principals for admissions, etc. Post August 2009, he wrote a letter to the Rajya Sabha secretariat asking for his salary to be forwarded to his account, which was formally revoked by a letter from George Sahib. Many visiting colleagues from across the country complained about Ramesh's behaviour to me. On being asked to leave, he deleted many entries from his office computer and entered the house without permission early the next day to take away papers from the cupboards. He conducted a campaign saying he was a victim of injustice at my hands. Mrs Fernandes began meeting him and taking his advice.

At the very end of December, Ashok Subramaniam, George Sahib's erstwhile official personal assistant, came for a brief visit. As he was leaving, he stopped on the outer verandah and whispered in my ear,

'Ma'am, there is a massive conspiracy brewing against you.'

The Garp undertow pulled inside me strongly, but I was mentally exhausted and disheartened. It had deeply troubled me that the chief minister of Bihar, Nitish Kumar, had sent recently nominated Rajya Sabha MP 'King Mahendra' to wheedle George Sahib into accepting the Rajya Sabha nomination when he was clearly unfit. He tried weakly to refuse but failed. I sat and watched helplessly, too powerless to intervene. I felt they were making a mockery of him. After all, if he had been incapable of participating in the Lok Sabha elections, how could he cope with the Rajya Sabha now? I sensed the purpose was not respect for George Sahib but a mocking gesture merely to assuage their guilty consciences.

My short answer to Ashok's grim warning was my usual one on such tiresome occasions, 'Let them. I don't care.'

After all, what could I imagine was brewing, and what would I do in any case?

I had already emailed George Sahib's brothers asking them to come to Delhi urgently and take care of their eldest brother's future, since the money for his household expenses and medication was no longer available to me. With my assistance on an earlier visit, and advised by Fali S. Nariman, the premier constitutional lawyer of the country and a good friend, they agreed to persuade him to dictate his will, and formally have it managed by a competent fund management company; this last, also recommended by Nariman. Paul Fernandes, George Sahib's brother, consulted Leila Fernandes and shared with her details like George Sahib wanting to leave his money from the sale of the Bangalore land to various labour institutions, an old age home, a Tibetan hospital, and some other public causes that had always been close to his heart. George Sahib had indicated he wanted to leave his books to me. He knew the only things I treasured were books.

Obviously, alarm bells rang for Leila Fernandes, although Paul states she had agreed on all these points quite cheerfully at the time she was consulted.

There is no place here for another long and complicated story of public attack and personal misery so I would rather keep it as short as possible by putting some facts in place.

On the last day of December 2009, I had left George Sahib after seeing to his dinner at 9.15 pm. He asked, as he did without fail, when I would come the next day. I assured him I would come in the morning and stay all day as it was a Sunday. The Fernandes brothers were to arrive in Delhi at midnight from Bangalore. They were to go from the airport to 3, Krishna Menon Marg. Instead, Leila Fernandes and family drove in to the residence an hour earlier, and padlocked the gates giving instructions for no one to enter. The entire operation was obviously guided from someone on the premises. The brothers were compelled to come to my home in Sujan Singh Park. We spent the rest of the night talking, stunned by the developments.

Sushanto, whom I had lovingly cared for when he was a young kid, declared me persona non grata, telling the media he had written to the home minister of India for 'additional protection from Jaya Jaitly' as he feared for the father's safety. Ananth, with some riff-raff crowd, led slogans against me at the gates of the Krishna Menon Marg residence the next day, although I had made no attempt to go there. Leila Fernandes accused me in the media of keeping George Sahib in a dark unventilated room smelling of urine. In a long feature as a cover story titled, 'Caught in a Squalid Saga of Love, Money and Greed' in *Society* magazine (March 2010), she accused George Sahib of having been a liar, spoke about his womanizing, and hit out at everyone.

Fortunately, earlier I had taken all my *Tehelka*-related files for convenience of working on the court case to our lawyer Abhijat's office, so I have them with me today. Otherwise I would have been royally stuck. Every other possession of mine—whether books, documents, paintings, political work files, pens and pencils, personal photographs that were part of my office space, and my late mother's furniture which I had lent to 3, Krishna Menon Marg, were no longer available to me.

I waited six months to ask for permission to visit 3, Krishna Menon Marg to collect my own modest possessions. By then, only the dogs and goods were left. George Sahib had been relocated to a rented house near Leila Fernandes's. I was refused permission and questioned about the ownership of the goods I claimed as mine. After some amount of persisting, I was told to coordinate with the personal assistant Bernard and take what I could identify.

On the designated day, 30 June 2010, Bernard chose to stay away. George Sahib's brothers, Michael and Richard Fernandes, were in town and accompanied me to collect some family photographs that had hung on the wall. We were met by the police and a hostile group on the other side of a firmly closed gate. They shouted ugly accusations at us and refused us entry. The brothers, both senior citizens, squatted on the pavement in protest in the sweltering June heat. I was accompanied by a volunteer friend and a young colleague from my craft office, both women. Much shouting and threatening later, another friend, Amina, wife of my forensic expert friend Milin Kapoor, arrived. She persuaded the Party thugs to let her in. Inside the house they told her they wanted to strip me naked and parade me on the streets. One man, claiming to be from the trade union wing of the JD(U), showed her a country-made pistol sticking out of his pocket in silent warning.

The whole episode outside the gates was filmed by the media gathered around us. I don't know who called them, and the police. All this is documented by various television channels and in national newspapers for the world to see forever, and on YouTube. All you have to do now is Google my name to see how I am painted on the one hand as a villain and another as a serious, erudite handicraft expert and writer of many books.

The day following this incident, I wrote an email to Leila Fernandes expressing disappointment at the 'warm welcome' but I made a final try and asked her to at least let me have this very old, metal folding table tray that I had lent George Sahib after my mother passed away. The art work on it had been fading away over the last sixty years. My mother used it to have her tea and evening soup till the end. George Sahib had his tea and biscuits kept on it every evening. It was worth nothing, but now carried a double sentimental value for me. She brushed me off, writing, 'I thought you had given it to George.'

I gave up on retrieving anything, telling myself that once loved ones are gone, there is perhaps no point in clinging on to their 'things'.

But I did not give up on George Sahib. In 2014, senior human rights lawyer Colin Gonsalves managed to fight for me all the way up to the Supreme Court to get permission to visit George Sahib at Leila Fernandes's house for fifteen minutes every fifteen days. I do so faithfully, allowed by Leila to visit at strictly 11.05 am every time. We communicate the request and acceptance through brief polite text messages.

I am instructed not to go near George Sahib, not to speak too much, not to touch him, to take off my shoes, and to wear a mask. It is as if he is in ICU, or preserved in a museum, not allowed any socializing, although he is very much alive. Music is never playing and I understand that the rare visitor is not encouraged to engage him. Who knows if that is the doctor's orders? He is conscious, but there is neither any sign of cognizance of anything nor any communication. I have watched more sadly through each visit as his mumbles have gradually dwindled to silence, and his facial expressions are turning blank.

George Fernandes was once a man no one could ignore, he exuded so much energy. His personality was such that he could never disappear into a crowd. I recall an incident when we were once rushing down a railway platform somewhere in Maharashtra to catch a train, and someone had shouted out to him in Marathi, 'Hey, sir, you look like George Fernandes!' He had stopped only for a fraction of a second to answer in Marathi, 'Yes, many people have told me so.'

His speeches, whether in public gatherings or in Parliament, were mesmerizing. He was not satisfied until he could go on for at least an hour. At times I would wish he would conclude soon as we would usually be perilously close to missing a flight or train after the program. I would tease him about starting at the slow speed of a car in first gear with a low and sober pitch, moving slowly through second and third gears to the high pitched fourth-gear punch lines before we could expect him to wind down and end. Fortunately, he never seemed to mind my irreverence. He knew that it was my way of admiring his eloquence.

George Sahib had the ability to work at multiple levels, thinking, speaking and writing of different things at the same time. He seemed to be a man in a hurry to do all that he possibly could in as many hours as he could stay awake. This made him incapable of holidaying, or even watching films or television; the latter were mere imitations of what was real, he believed. He had seen and experienced too much in life to need to see depictions of sorrow, violence, politics or poverty on a screen. He feared nothing and no one, and never had a possession or position he did not mind giving up in a moment. Precisely for this reason, he was both loved and hated since he did not allow himself to be vulnerable, and remained unfazed in the face of all the attacks that came his way.

The care and concern he showed towards human beings formed the singular attributes which George Sahib could be identified with. He never made anyone feel irrelevant or unwanted. He would carry airline toffees in his pockets to his next destination in case there was a little child, or a dog he met when he arrived. He loved crowds and people, struggle and combat, never giving up a fight for justice till the very end. He didn't believe in court cases, and instead preferred public struggles or political fora. But he was equally happy alone, retreating into books and western classical music, not needing another soul for conversation or companionship.

George Sahib never owned a comb. He was, in fact, presumed to be a rabble-rouser who never combed his hair or wore clean clothes. However, he was most sophisticated and meticulous about his personal appearance, bathing twice a day, and washing his own clothes every day till he was over 70 years old. He consciously chose to wear simple khadi and cotton pyjamas so that he was like an ordinary person and not one of those stiff, self-conscious leaders whose badge is to wear highly starched and bleached white khadi kurtas. He had a gruff exterior which did not invite small talk or superficial conversation. And despite that, I was often surprised at his grasp of some fact or subtlety that was far beyond his usual scope of interests. He read the first lot of the Harry Potter books alongside biographies of world figures, the writings of Dr Ambedkar, Mahatma Gandhi, Winston Churchill, philosophical tomes or legal histories involving complicated international human rights cases. He particularly loved to devour economic surveys and carried them wherever he went, but occasionally bought the latest popular novel at an airport. He had a huge library in which there was no book he had not read at some time, including ones in Kannada and Hindi.

Today, I find it bizarre to describe George Sahib in the present tense since he is medically lost to us and the world at large. It is, therefore, with an underlying feeling of discomfort that my verbs, with reference to him, are formulated in the past tense. He used to say: 'politics is life and politics is for people'. I feel honoured that George Sahib shared that life wholeheartedly with me for thirty years.

I can proudly say I never spoke negatively of him, betrayed him, asked him for anything for myself, or ever told him anything but the complete truth for all of the thirty years I was his colleague and friend. There was something about him that demanded complete unselfishness. My providing him with a quiet logistical support in his political activity and loyalty during a difficult period of time when he lacked importance, position or ability to do much for anyone, perhaps made him believe I was a steadfast and reliable partner in times of struggle. He had no car and no one to pick him up at airports. I would drive him, sometimes waiting on the pavement at times when there was no overhead roofing, no seating and no digital signboards outside the airport. I did it because I was convinced he was a person born to lead and do many things, and no one should be expected to function without a support system. I also felt sorry that he was abandoned by all his younger acolytes and erstwhile activist colleagues, and therefore needed help. This may have built his confidence in me which never ended even in those last moments when his mind was fading rapidly and he was often suspicious of those around him as happens to many at a particular stage of the neurological disease that was to overpower him later. He would only let down his guard with me at times like this. This is what made it particularly poignant when later, I was unable to give him the familiarity and reassurance he needed at the most vulnerable of situations because of restrictions imposed on me by his family.

Among the obscenest words in a medical dictionary, at least for me, are 'amyloid beta protein plaque deposits', 'neurofibrillary tangle' and 'presenilin mutations'. These monsters have all but closed the communication lines in George Sahib's brain. In other words, as someone in a beautiful documentary on Alzheimer's once said, 'It is as if, slowly, the electrical circuits in a house go off, one by one, till the entire house is dark.'

~

Many must be considering it odd that the legal heirs of George Fernandes should go to such crude and demeaning lengths to gain control of him and his material assets, and go to the extent of such drama, stealth and intrigue to capture him from his officially allotted residence. No one seems to have sought an answer from them as to why they could not come in broad daylight, conduct a civilized reconciliation with him, his colleagues, family and friends, in sheer goodwill, and seek everyone's assistance while they took charge of his care. The only reason I can think of was that people not worthy of him convinced Leila Fernandes that I was the terrible villain who had to be removed from the scene.

Anyway, for me now, my interminable CBI court case and George Sahib himself, are both in a state of limbo.

~

I have, in more introspective and weaker moments throughout life, during every struggle, indulged in wondering whether I had not just been good enough to deal with political life, or not smart or intellectual enough to gain acceptance in circles dominated by men. I remember the flush of triumph when the *Economic & Political Weekly* first published a long article of mine about the lives, financial troubles and suicides of women mat weavers in Kodungallur in Kerala. I often thought, why so? What was I trying to prove and to whom? It was directed towards everyone who had made me feel intellectually small.

I have also wondered whether my role in politics harmed my interests in the handicrafts world. I have come to the conclusion that being in politics has actually widened my understanding and perception of the socio-economic issues in the lives of our artisans. I realize that aesthetic creativity and political activism can coexist even if our elite cannot always accept it. I have decided that the most important struggle for all women in public life is to firmly reject those signals in society that tell us that it is a crime to be born a woman, and a punishment to be in politics.

After the many undertows, some Under Toads have revealed their presence. But, as in Garp's world, life, with all its joys, sorrows, energies and challenges, still gives us something new and interesting every day.

26

BEING HUMAN
The Sadness of Caring in Public Life

THE STORY OF HOW A woman feels about public issues cannot be complete without sharing two incidents, the memories of which have never left me. One was fleeting and did not actually involve me. The other drew me in as much as a woman and a mother as it did as an activist. Both are unforgettable.

It was a chilly morning in a winter month in Delhi in the year 2000. I was returning alone by train from somewhere. The skies were still a flat grey, one that precedes sunrise, with just a slight hint of gold in the eastern sky trying to break through it, at a distance. At the station, everyone scurried about loaded with luggage, looking ahead at the exit without distraction. I was walking along the over-bridge, dawdling a bit as I was not in a hurry to get to 3, Krishna Menon Marg to pick up the car and Pepper, the dog. She always went home with me after work but was deposited at George Sahib's residence while I was away, for the company of the other dogs there and to enjoy the big garden instead of being alone at my home. I happened to glance down to the edge of the walkway near the stairs. A fairly young man, covered in an aura of dustiness, with grey-brown hair, a tattered grey-brown shawl, dry grey-brown skin—the typical colours of poverty—and flashing wild red eyes was sitting on his haunches pleasuring himself unknowingly in full public view, if one could call those rapid, desperate and tragic gestures 'pleasuring'. His pleasure was probably less than that felt by an animal, his obliviousness to the world around him a blessing. The basic desire of any living being for some warmth, comfort, reassurance and human touch—in any measure at all—seemed to have taken control. I was stunned at the depths to which a person could descend, losing his sense of power and control, dignity and privacy, when poverty is all-engulfing, and a complete disconnect from reality takes over. I felt as if I was either going to cry, or vomit.

I reached 3, Krishna Menon Marg in an auto-rickshaw. (Yes, I was the Party president at that time but it had not changed my usual ways of travelling when someone could not come to pick me up.) The sky was brighter now. The usual batch of seven newspapers had not yet been delivered. The dogs and Durga, the cook, were just waking up when I rang the bell. George Sahib was still asleep. I could not go home just yet. The experience of watching that man at the station had been too much for me. I know I was being emotional, irrational, and there are many theories one could present at seminars or speeches one could deliver from political platforms as to the reason for such conditions of poverty, and maybe even whom to blame. But what would be the use of that? I wondered whether all the meaningless attack, defence, fighting, counter-fighting, strategizing and manipulating, smooth talking and aggressive abusing that goes on in India's daily political life could provide any solution to prevent the circumstances that created the utter misery of the human condition I saw at the station.

All I could do in my helplessness was to stare out at the dogs half-heartedly chasing five peacocks that regularly strutted around the vast garden space.

~

One morning, quite soon after I became Party president, *The Statesman* had a story about how a very young girl-child who turned out to be an emaciated four-year-old was found dumped in garbage and had been taken to a nearby hospital in West Delhi by the police. Sadly, the name of the hospital doesn't come to mind and the newspaper clippings of that time were in Samata Party files which became unavailable to me from early 2010. I decided to enquire about her condition and ensure she was properly treated for the injuries from dog bites and whatever else was described in the news report. I went to the hospital and met the superintendent. A representative from the office of Kiran Choudhury, Congress politician and MLA from that area, was already in the room. I introduced myself as the president of the Samata Party and explained that I had come to reassure the public and myself that this abandoned child would be cared for properly till someone else took responsibility for her future well-being. The head doctor said she was not seriously harmed and that her injuries were being treated. I went up to the children's ward to see her. There lay a skinny little girl in a dirty dress, looking ahead blankly. I asked the doctor what kind of support she needed to recover completely. He said their routine medicines were enough.

'I want to help. How can I do that?' I asked.

'You could provide a full-time attendant if you wish. Then she would have proper attention,' he replied. Kiran Choudhury telephoned me to say she was glad I was handling it and expressed her concern and solidarity. I hired a female attendant from a nursing agency at nine thousand rupees for the month, and gave everyone at the hospital strict instructions to note that I was taking responsibility for the child's care and should therefore be informed if the little girl needed anything. I wanted them to know that they could not be neglectful because the child was not wanted. Everyone agreed.

Every week that I visited her, the child improved. She began smiling. Her skin became cleaner, lighter, and less shrivelled. Her hair was brushed, and her eyes developed a shine.

'*Aap ka naam kya hai*, baby?' (What is your name, baby?)

'Munni,' she said. She was finally well enough to speak. We were thrilled.

I decided to visit her for Diwali with a set of new clothes and some sweets for the children of the ward. Aditi and I went shopping at the Malviya Nagar market for girls' vests, cotton panties, slips and simple dresses. We kept being shown useless velvety, sequinned, synthetic, pink-net things which were only fit for partying. When I finally explained to the shopkeeper the situation of the child for whom I was shopping, he took out a pile giving them to me free of cost, adding, that if I was doing something so kind, he too wanted to contribute his share. A fancy 'branded' shop would never have done that.

When I announced to George Sahib that I was going to visit Munni in hospital for Diwali, he decided to come along. The Party workers were encouraged since the big boss was going. They had not bothered earlier because it was only about a sick child and the woman Party president.

At the hospital, we distributed sweets to the elder children in the ward and dressed Munni in fresh new clothes. She responded to these gestures and even carried on a hesitant conversation. The attendant had grown fond of her and looked on proudly. George Sahib noticed that the hospital was filthy. Banana peels on staircase landings, rubbish all along the outer corridors, with a rat or two in the midst of garbage heaps nearby. He was furious, and ordered the Party workers to get some brooms and buckets. As we all started cleaning up the litter, the cleaning staff, embarrassed and penitent, came rushing to take over the task from us. All this was duly reported in the newspapers, with the male Party workers hastily arranging for a photographer and posing for pictures of the social work they had indulged in.

After almost a month following this incident had gone by, I spoke to Amod Kant, the police officer who had established an NGO called Prayaas which took in orphaned and abandoned children. He agreed to take Munni in and said he would send a social worker with me on my next visit to complete the formalities and take her to their establishment. I had decided, that, if necessary, I would take Munni home with me for an interim two weeks to give her good food and the warmth of a snug bed to ensure she was really strong enough to face the world again.

I reached 3, Krishna Menon Marg and telephoned the superintendent to tell him to prepare the discharge papers as we would be at the hospital to collect Munni by 11.30 am.

'Oh, didn't you know? Munni died five days ago,' he informed me in a flat, even tone.

I was completely stunned. A stream of questions came tumbling out: How could they have let this happen, why did they not inform me, was she ill, what exactly happened to her, did they not take care of her, had I not told them to keep me informed of everything at all times, etc.

The same bland voice responded, 'We thought the woman attendant you had employed would have told you.'

But what happened to Munni when she was improving so rapidly?

'We don't know. She got fever in the morning and died the same evening,' he replied, in a flat tone again, and disconnected the phone without waiting for me to say anything further.

I wanted to scream and very loudly into a huge void space. Instead, I telephoned Aditi and gave her the news. She came over to keep me company. We sat in the late November morning sun, in the same back verandah at 3, Krishna Menon Marg, crying over each other's shoulders. I wrote to the then Chief Minister of Delhi, Sheila Dikshit, recounting the entire story, asking her to look into the episode as the hospital came under her government's charge, to institute an inquiry and ensure an end to such callousness. I sent a copy of the letter to Kiran Choudhury.

The chief minister never replied. And little Munni became one more girl child treated like the garbage in which she was found.

It is only in sharing these stories that I can hope to exorcise the pain of remembering.

EPILOGUE
I Don't Believe in Sad Endings

I was wondering what a suitable Epilogue should contain. After all, whatever needed to be written has already been written. I surfed on Google for inspiration and found something that suited me exactly.

Suggestion: *Unless you're already dead, you probably don't want an epilogue to memoirs.*

Response: *In which case someone else will write it for you, silly.*

Also, recently, I saw a cartoon of a small kid sitting at his desk, writing. His older friend asks him what he is doing: 'I am writing my autobiography.'

'But you only have one sheet of paper.'

'Yeah, coz' I'm only six years old.'

Unlike the little boy, I am 75 years old, so my reader will forgive me for filling up a few more pages.

If asked why I chose to be in public life, I refer to the opening pages of this memoir, where the woman in Malaysia chose to sit for a month in a glass cage with scorpions. Like her, it was a 'choice' I made. It has not been a bed of roses. I have learnt and unlearnt in the process of engaging with the many scorpions and those that weren't. In the end, it has remained just that—a choice. I do not know why I made it; I just did.

ACKNOWLEDGEMENTS

It would have been beyond my imagination to think of writing a book around my life. After having written over eight books on crafts and textiles, hundreds of articles published in newspapers and journals, and some children's stories, I thought I had gone well beyond my target of writing five books by the time I was sixty-five years old. This was part of a small personal pact with myself. I believe that books last on some shelf or the other forever, even if people make it a point to destroy any other visible contributions made during one's lifetime. Institutions could die in spirit, policies could get overturned, development programs could be terminated, flourishing kingdoms can decay, and victorious battles could always be forgotten. But it is seldom that anyone would go through the trouble of destroying a person's contributions to knowledge and ideas as embodied in writings in books. Some library or family member may dust them off occasionally, and their thoughts can live on.

When a newly-born online media house conducted two wholly unacceptable sting operations on my loved ones and me in the years 2000 and 2001, the stories went into labyrinthine coils of intrigue and complications. The daily occurrences around me were adding up to making two fine detective stories. Ranjana Sengupta, a long-time friend, editor and wife of an Indian diplomat urged me to write about them as part of my life. I was hesitant to make it about myself, but she insisted people would be interested to know how a woman from the southern part of India and an aristocratic background got mixed up in the caste politics of Bihar and in conversations with arms dealers. I began hesitantly, and soon, far too many circumstances overtook me.

Along came my old friend Kapish Mehra of Rupa Publications some years later. Many persuasive meetings later, he managed to get me to seriously resume my efforts. If it had not been for him breathing down my neck in the most polite, encouraging and gentlemanly manner you can imagine, the few early chapters I had written would never have progressed. Without the sweet natures and hours of dogged diligence of editors Shambhu Sahu and Rinita Banerjee, I would have been in serious doubt about wrapping it up.

I was never worried of writing what came from my heart and mind or of the outcomes of all my books on crafts and textiles, but this one makes me nervous. It is not easy to put one's own life out there. I thank Rupa Publications entirely for having so much faith in me.

Jaya Jaitly
New Delhi, 2 October 2017

INDEX